Kant and Job's Comforters

A. L. Loades

AVERO

©1985 A. L. Loades

First published in Great Britain in 1985 by
Avero Publications Ltd.

All rights reserved. No part of this publication may be
reproduced, stored in a retrieval system, or transmitted, in any form
or by any means, electronic, mechanical, photocopying, recording
or otherwise without the permission of
Avero Publications Ltd.
20 Great North Road,
Newcastle upon Tyne, England

British Library Cataloguing in Publication Data

Loades, A.L.
 Kant and Job's comforters.
 1. Kant, Immanuel—Theology
 2. Theodicy
 I. Title
 231'.8   B2799.T4

ISBN 0-907977-12-X

Printed in Great Britain by
Unwin Brothers Limited
The Gresham Press
Old Woking, Surrey
A member of the Martins Printing Group

CONTENTS

Acknowledgments	iv
Note	iv
Introduction	v

Part I

Kant's context : i	1
Kant's context : ii	29

Part II

Bayle and Leibniz : 1	55
Some controversy about Leibniz : 2	83

Part III

Kant's optimism before 1781	101

Part IV

After 1781 : moral sentiment and authentic theodicy	133
Bibliography	159

ACKNOWLEDGEMENTS

Permission is gratefully acknowledged for the use of quotations from the following:
Routledge & Kegan Paul, London, E. M. Huggard's translation of Leibniz' *Theodicy* (1951).
O.U.P., J.C. Meredith's translation of Kant's *Critique of Judgement* (1952).
The Open Court Publishing Company, La Salle, Illinois, T.M. Greene and H.H. Hudson's translation of Kant's *Religion within the limits of reason alone* (1934), (1960).
Bobbs-Merrill Publishing, Indianapolis, for the translations in *Kant, On History* (1979).
Experimental versions of some of the material used in the book have appeared in various journals and books, and are re-worked and used by kind permission of the editors of the following publications:
'Kant's concern with theodicy', *Journal of Theological Studies*, 27, 1975, 361-376.
'Kant as optimist', *British Journal for Eighteenth Century Studies*, 1, 1978, 149-168.
'Kant and Job's comforters', *New Studies in Theology*, 1, 1980, 119-138.
'Moral sentiment and belief in God', *Studia Theologica*, 35, 1981, 73-83.
'Immanuel Kant's humanism', *Studies in Church History*, 17, 1982, 297-310.
'No consoling vision: Coleridge's discovery of Kant's authentic theodicy', in ed. J.R. Watson, *An Infinite Complexity. Essays in Romanticism*, Edinburgh U.P., 1983, 95-124.

NOTE

The references to the German text of Kant's works are to *Kants Gesammelte Schriften*, 32 vols. (Berlin 1910-) some of which are now available in paperback as *Kants Werke*, Walter de Gruyter & Co., Berlin, 1968. These are indicated in the footnotes as KW, with volume, and page number; and there are occasional references to the 'Reflections', indicated by number. All the translations are from the standard ones available, as indicated in the footnotes.

INTRODUCTION

This study expounds a neglected element in Kant's theological reflections. In order to appreciate what he had to say, the study first tries to put him in historical and literary context, with the theme of theodicy in mind. The second section focusses on the major source of stimulus to the debate about theodicy during his lifetime, the great *Théodicée* of Leibniz, provoked by Pierre Bayle. Further controversy comes to the surface in the work of a spectrum of British and Continental writers, to which Kant was alert. The rest of the study returns to his writing.

Before his so-called critical revolution, Kant on the whole wrote about theodicy in the manner of a Leibnizian. Without some knowledge of that theological writing before 1781, much of his post-1781 theological comment is hardly noticed as being a *self* - critical exercise, critical of his contemplative optimism centered primarly though not exclusively on the phenomenon of natural evil. After 1781, with rare exceptions such as the first part of the *Religion* and the 1791 essay on the failure of all attempted philosophical theodicies, Kant did not devote whole sections of his writings to the problem. Nevertheless, his underlying preoccupation with it is evident if one pays careful attention to his texts, and does not read simply in terms of what neatly coheres with his strictly critical philosophy. Indeed, the 1791 essay is so succinct it seems to require a certain familiarity with his position as he had developed it. So far as theodicy is concerned, his attention came increasingly to be given to the phenomenon of human evil. The work of the very last phase of his writing career especially illuminates the 1791 essay, that is, parts of the second and third *Critiques*, the *Religion*, and the 1794 essay on eschatology.

In the two chapters on Kant's different styles of theodicy, the treatment is somewhat different. In 'Kant's optimism before 1781', the topic is traced out following the chronological order of his writing. In the chapter, 'After 1781: moral and authentic theodicy', the treatment of the topic requires a reconstruction of Kant's position. This chapter relies on identifying in his writing the remarks which illuminate his view, but deliberately tries to avoid the technicalities of his philosophy and its linguistic peculiarities.

Overall, the study has drawn on the work of a wide range of modern authors, writing in English, French and German. The available commentary on some of the contributors to the eighteenth century debate on theodicy is vast, and no pretence is made of being exhaustive. Nevertheless, it is hoped that the extensive footnotes and bibliography will be found useful in helping interested readers to find their way through some of Kant's texts and some of the livelier sources of comment on his work. Among these, it will be specially evident that no student of Kant can fail to be illuminated by the work of Professor D.M. MacKinnon, F.B.A.

The writer owes a particular debt of gratitude to Professor W.R. Ward of Durham University department of modern history, from whom she has learned a good deal about eighteenth century European religion, though it is unmistakeable that the present study is not the work of a professional historian! Professor Ward saved the writer from many errors - those that remain are her own. Finally, Professor W.A. Whitehouse of the universities of Durham and Kent, is in a sense the author of the study, since he introduced the writer to Kant's theology in the first place, as well as providing invaluable comment as the work progressed. And whatever the writer understands of theology she has learned largely from him.

PART I
KANT's CONTEXT: i

Prussia[1] was colonised and 'Christianised' largely by the activities of the order of Teutonic knights, 'the Servants of St. Mary', in the thirteenth century. Military techniques learned in Palestine enabled the knights to build a succession of fortresses firmly to hold on to their new territories. Königsberg (Kaliningrad), Kant's home town on the river Pregel, was founded as a fortress in 1255 in honour of Otakar, king of Bohemia, who had joined the knights, and it was later to enjoy the privileges of a Hanseatic city. The knights were followed by German traders, farmers and town dwellers. In time new immigrants were able to buy land which earlier would have belonged to the order:
> like all frontier existence, that in Prussia imposed sobriety, duty, precision and clarity of purpose, for only these qualities could ensure survival. Indeed, to the lack of them may be attributed the downfall of the order. It was, and remained, a hard environment. Little wonder, therefore, that this territory failed to produce even the palest imitation of the Renaissance; little wonder, also, that it produced Immanuel Kant.[2]

By 1466 and the Peace of Thorn (Torun) the order had to concede Poland access to the Baltic, with eastern Prussia becoming a fief of the Polish crown. The fief included Königsberg, the territory that stretched up to Tilsit (Sovetsk) and Memel (Klaypeda) the southern lake district and a sweep round to the Vistula. The wedge of royal Poland into the fief of Prussia was the bishopric of Ermland (Warmia) founded with the other three bishoprics of Prussia in 1245. The Polish king nominated four candidates for this bishopric for the chapter's choice.[3] Johannes Dantisticus, a humanist who added Latin to his Polish and German, was bishop from 1536, and saw the publication of the work of Copernicus, perhaps the greatest scholar of Renaissance Poland. Copernicus had been born at Thorn, one of the earliest of the order's strongholds, and spent the years 1516-1519 and 1520-1521 as administrator of the chapter's castle at Allenstein (Olsztyn) in the lake district, strengthening the defence capacity of the castle there against the knights. Frauenberg (Frombork) on the Vistula Bay was his main place of work between 1510-1543 (the year of his death) where in a tower in the cathedral fortifications he worked at his 'De revolutionibus orbium coelestium'.[4]

1

Kant himself was later to appeal to Copernicus' achievement as having provided a model for his own intellectual revolution. The work was finally published in Nuremberg in 1543, Copernicus receiving the first printed copy on his death bed.[5] It had an anonymous letter to the reader by Andreas Osiander, a controversial reformation theologian later to be a teacher in the university of Königsberg.[6] As a result of Osiander's 'letter', Copernicus could be read as presenting his elaboration of an earlier Pythagorean theory as an hypothesis, the justification of which was to be found in the greater accuracy of the conclusions which could be arrived at by deploying it, yet it could readily be seen that he was claiming more than hypothetical status for some features of his scheme:

> But in the centre of all reigns the sun. For who might, in this most beautiful of all temples, set such light in another or better place than whence the whole can be illuminated at once? Since some aptly call it the light of the world, others its soul, and still others its master. Trismegistus terms it the visible God, and Sophocles in his 'Electra' the all-perceiving eye. So in fact the sun is seated on the royal throne and guides the family of planets revolving around it. And yet in no way is the earth robbed thereby of the service of the moon, for as Aristotle says (in the book on life), the moon has the closest relationship with the earth. But the earth conceives from the sun and annually becomes pregnant with life. Thus we find in such order of things a wonderful harmony and dependable harmonious relations between the motions and paths of the planets, which otherwise cannot be found.[7]

The last grand master of the order of Teutonic knights (and the first to come from Brandenburg) was Albrecht of Brandenburg-Ansbach. He became first Duke of Prussia by negotiation with the Polish king Sigismund I at Cracow in 1525. Seizing his chance to salvage what was left of the order's standing and possessions for himself, he acted on Luther's proposals for the secularization of religious orders with the Catholic king's support, securing his seat as a Polish duke in the Polish senate, and bringing East Prussia into the Hohenzollern orbit. Albrecht himself became a Lutheran, and on returning to Königsberg, announced on 6th July 1525, 'that the Holy Gospel, the word of Christ, pure and simple be preached in his possessions',[8] with exile as the penalty for non-compliance. Albrecht's strength lay in the tradition of efficient administration which he had inherited from the Teutonic order, and in the great stretches of territory, including good wheatlands, which were in his personal possession. His weakness lay in the tendency of such nobles as there were to appeal against him to the Polish crown, and in the increasing isolation of Prussia from the western and southern 'German' territories. However, on Luther's advice, Albrecht married first a Danish princess,[9] thus establishing the first political connection between Prussian and Scandinavian Lutheranism. His second marriage was useful in re-establishing a link with the west, for his wife was a lady of the ducal house of Brunswick-Kalenberg. Prompted by Luther and Melanchthon, and with an eye on the conversion of his dukedom in 1540 Albrecht set about the foundation of the Albertina university in Königsberg. The fourteenth century cathedral and its school was to be closely associated with the new university. By 1544 the university had its three original faculties of theology, law and medicine, and Georg Sabinus, a philologist and Melanchthon's son-in-law as its first Rector and professor of rhetoric. The privilege of a printing press given to the university made it one of the most important centres for the production of Lutheran propaganda in northern Europe. Much of the output of this press was directed towards Poland and Lithuania (the Polish-Lithuanian Commonwealth). Prussia became a refuge for adherents of the reformation as well as a centre for the training of Protestant pastors. On the other hand, in Ermland, Stanislaus Hosius, bishop from 1551, became an important Counter-Reformation theologian.[10] In 1564 he brought the Jesuits to Braunsberg, his diocesan capital, to take charge of the college there, so that as well as educating the laity it would produce well-trained priests to rival the Protestants from Königsberg.

In 1618, after the death of the second duke of Prussia, Albrecht Frederick, the dukedom fell to his son-in-law, the Elector of Brandenburg, whose house inclined to Calvinism. By the time of the accession of Frederick William in 1640, Prussia was of the greatest economic importance to Brandenburg, ravaged by the Thirty Years War. Apart from the duke's ability to raise funds directly from his own vast estates, he gained from the success of Königsberg in exporting the produce of Prussia and Lithuania and importing both necessities and luxuries. Königsberg was in fact three towns, not to be united till 1724, the year of Kant's birth: Altstadt, Kneiphof and Löbernicht. Each had its colleges of aldermen, its courts and guilds, crafts and commons, and was capable of opposing both duke and nobility. For example, on 8th February 1634, the burghers of Königsberg declined to accept the King's edict for the return of runaway serfs.[11] The complete destruction of serfdom was not to come about until the post-Napoleonic period, though it might have helped some areas to recover from the devastations of the 1655-1660 war between Poland and Sweden, and the terrible plague of 1709-1710. So far as religion was concerned, Frederick William's Calvinism was less a source of dissension than his encouragement of religious toleration. And in this he had the support of Georg Calixt, a Lutheran professor of theology from Helmstedt. Calixt developed an approach to the systematic organisation of theology by focussing it on the topic of man's salvation, and thus commended theology as a means by which Lutherans and Calvanists could recognise their brotherhood in Christ.[12] Calixt's approach received a welcome from Christian Dreier, professor of theology at Königsberg who had studied at Helmstedt, earned the praise of both Leibniz and Thomasius, and was not without importance for the ideals of the new University of Göttingen to be founded in 1734.[13]

By 1657 Frederick William had emancipated Prussia from its feudal dependance on Poland. Between 1662 and 1672[14] he forced first the Königsbergers and then the Prussian nobility to accept his authority and to abandon appeals to Poland as futile. Taxation uniformly administered paid for his standing army, in which the nobles found positions as they did in the developing state service. The army found its billets amongst the townspeople, turning Königsberg (as other towns) into a garrison. After the defeat of the Swedes at Fehrbellin and the success of the whole campaign against the Swedes Frederick William's army established itself as a formidable force and he himself was to be known and remembered as the Great Elector.

One achievement of his rule was to be particularly significant for the development of religious life in the next century. Having secured the duchy of Magdeburg in 1660 Frederick William had developed Halle, its main town, as an increasingly important commerical centre. He improved the navigability of the river, expanded the mining industry, and developed textile and other manufactures. Brandenburg-Prussia thus had a town which came to rival Leipzig in Saxony. The edict of Potsdam was the Great Elector's response to the revocation of the edict of Nantes, and Huguenot immigrants fully justified his confidence in attracting them to his territories for the part they played in the development of Halle alone. He could soon afford to develop the existing academy at Halle into a university, the Fridericiana, in 1649. Christian Thomasius,[15] philosopher of law, was already present at the academy before its transformation. He had had to leave the university of Leipzig partly because of his objections to the treatment of the pietists by Orthodox theologians there. Having taken himself to Berlin (Brandenburg-Prussia's capital) in 1690, he had gone thence to the academy at Halle, and was appointed to the faculty of law. Ironically, by 1702 he too had fallen out with the pietists who were to be present in strength at the new university.

Philipp Jakob Spener also a contemporary of Leibniz had made his contribution to the pietist movement within Lutheranism from 1670 onwards, when he was principal Lutheran pastor in Frankfurt.[16] He endeavoured to revitalise parish life by holding meetings of his *collegia pietatis* in his own home. When eventually he lost his post as senior court chaplin in the Saxon court at Dresden he took himself to Berlin. Frederick William's successor, Frederick III, was enthusiastic about the ability of the pietists to get behind the inherited divisions of Lutheran and Reformed Christians as well as about their practical efficiency, and his government engaged Spener to appoint members of the faculty of theology at Halle.[17] He looked for people both devout and energetic, who would promote in their students the capacity to cope with problems such as settling immigrants and the dispossessed of the wars. Located as it was, Königsberg could never have a monopoly in the production of language specialists, doctors, pastors and civil servants.

Frederick III had secured enough support for the elevation of his duchy into a kingdom. Taking 'Suum cuique', the motto of the new order of the Black Eagle as his own, he crowned himself as Frederick I king *in* Prussia on 18th January 1701, in the church in the castle at Königsberg.[18] Another pietist August Herman Francke was to be the chief representative of the movement for Frederick and for his successor, Frederick William I. Francke too had had to leave Saxony where at Leipzig university, as a member of the faculty of theology, he had joined a 'college' for bible study. He was turned out of his living at Erfurt, to be summoned by Spener, and appointed to a post in the newly founded Fridericiana as a specialist in languages and theology. Halle became the greatest centre in Europe for the publication of vernacular Bibles, and religious literature in many languages, especially slavonic, in many of which there had been nothing of the kind before. It was under Frederick William I that the mathematician and Cartesian philosopher Christian Wolff was actually expelled from Halle in 1723, not to return until 1740 and the accession of Frederick II.[19] Frederick I sucessfully harnessed pioneers of the early enlightenment with pietists in various enterprises. For example, his wife Sophia Charlotte urged him to act on Leibniz' plan to form a society of sciences in Berlin. Founded in 1711 with Leibniz as first president, the society was to concentrate on the development of technology, extensive trade and communications beyond the confines of Europe, and the encouragement of German as a language of education and culture.[20] It was regenerated by Frederick II as the *Académie des sciences et belles-lettres* with Maupertuis presiding.

One of Francke's pupils had helped to found in Königsberg a small school which was to develop into one of the town's most outstanding institutions,[21] known as King Frederick's College after 1701. Pupils could study Greek, Latin and Hebrew, French, poetry and philosophy, philosophy and mathematics, history and geography. Where possible, work was related to Biblical material. One of the most outstanding men associated with the school was Franz Albert Schultz, a pupil of both Francke and Wolff. Schultz had established himself as a man after Frederick William's heart by his work as an army chaplain.[22] By 1730 he was in charge of the Altstadt church and a university teacher of theology. So when in 1733 he took up his appointment to direct the Collegium Fridericianum he was well placed to contribute to the school reforms of 1736. His work with the army had alerted him to the religious ignorance of the soldiers, and he fostered initiatives to found six hundred new village schools.[23] Also, to Schultz was entrusted the task of settling the Salzburgers of the 1731-32 emigration.[24] Königsberg was the centre from which was launched the re-settlement of those areas depopulated by the earlier plague. Leopold von Firmian, archbishop of Salzburg since 1727, had precipitated the crisis when he found recalcitrant Protestant peasants in the remote districts of his archbishopric. Served only by wandering preachers, they had maintained their religion by reading Luther's Bible and other religious works. They did not convert to catholicism despite the zeal of von Firmian's missionaries. He employed Habsburg troops to expel the Protestants from Salzburg and wherever they could be reached, at between a week and a fortnight's notice. Many left his territory almost destitute. Detachments of the Prussian army met those who took up Frederick William's invitation to settle in Prussia, and got them to Berlin, and thence to their destinations. Some sixteen thousand of them were to find themselves in east Prussia. Königsberg Lutheranism and pietism also were united in their interest in the evangelisation of Lithuania and Poland. For example, the university had a Lithuanian seminar established in 1718, and in 1724 a friend of Schultz, Georg Friederick Rogall, returned to his birthplace and by 1728 had established a Polish seminar. They combined to keep the activities of the Herrnhuters within limits so that even by the end of the century there were not more than two hundred and fifty of them within Königsberg.[25]

Pietism survived in Königsberg longer than elsewhere in Brandenburg-Prussia because of the very considerable abilities of men like Schultz who contrived to be disciples of both Wolff and Francke. Even Frederick II had to tolerate Schultz as Rector of the Albertina, in view of the latter's outstanding record. Pietists were not necessarily hostile to intellectual sophistication as Schultz and his pupil Martin Knutzen showed.[26] Pietists and rationalists alike valued individual appropriation of convictions above reverence for authority, and morality above doctrine. Lively interest in new knowledge could be characteristic of those whose religion rested primarily on their confidence of salvation, a confidence warranted by a conversion experience.

Frederick's preference for Rector on more than one occasion was a fine linguist, Johann Jacob Quandt.[27] He was the chief Lutheran minister at the castle church as well as being responsible for the training of ministers at the Albertina. He produced an edition of the 'Preussische Hausbibel', and his elegant German commended him to Frederick as the first president of the Royal German Society. As the German Society, it had been founded in 1740-41 by Coelestin Christian Flottwell, on the model of the French Academy in Paris, and it received royal patronage in 1743. A similar society had been fostered in Leipzig by Quandt's follower, Johann Christoph Gottsched. A candidate in theology, Gottsched had preached for ten Chancellors of the Albertina, and produced a distinguished work on the method of preaching, using philosophical and logical principles culled from Wolff.[28] He had suffered from Frederick William's insistence on compulsory military service, from which candidates for the Lutheran ministry were not exempt until 1737. He had therefore left Königsberg and in 1724 established himself in Leipzig, almost simultaneously with J.S. Bach. Following the prompting of Leibniz and the lead given by Thomasius in 1687 he made it his business to promote the development of German as a literary language in what was one of the most important centres for intellectual and cultural life throughout the century. His friendship with Flottwell had kept him in touch with developments in Königsberg to which he was able to return from time to time. Enthusiasm for Leibniz had been communicated to him by his own teachers at Königsberg,[29] and he was well placed to play his part in maintaining Leibniz' reputation. The credibility and value of Leibniz' theology and philosophy were to be put to the test throughout the eighteenth century since Leibniz' writings were to help to characterise developing German culture. In 1734 Gottsched added to his professorship of poetry the professorship of logic and metaphysics. He edited a German translation of the Des Maiseaux edition of Bayle's *Dictionary* and followed it up with a new German translation of the *Theodicy* (1744). He lost no opportunity to praise Leibniz' presentation of the goodness and wisdom of the divine being as the answer to the mischief wrought by Bayle. Further support was to come from Brucker, the great historian of philosophy, and such men as Christian Kortholt, whose nephew was to become one of the first teachers of theology at the new University at Göttingen.[30]

In 1724 the year of Kant's birth, Königsberg had some forty thousand inhabitants including Dutch, English, French, Swiss, Swedes, Danes, Lithuanians and Russians, as well as Poles.[31] There were also up to five thousand soldiers quartered in and around the town. As Kant himself was to comment:

> A city such as Königsberg on the river Pregel - a large city, the center of a state, the seat of the government's provincial councils, the site of a university (for the cultivation of the sciences), a seaport connected by rivers with the interior of the country, so that its location favors traffic with the rest of the country as well as with neighbouring or remote countries having different languages and customs - is a suitable place for broadening one's knowledge of man and of the

world. In such a city, this knowledge can be acquired even without travelling.[32]

The presence of British traders and travellers in Prussia was enough to give credence to belief that Kant's family had come from Scotland, a belief which probably originated with his great-grandfather, an innkeeper, and his grandfather, a leatherworker in Memel. In fact, Kant seems to have been of German stock, with the family having intermarried with people from Kurland and Lithuania.[33] Kant's father, Johann Georg, also a leatherworker, had travelled to Königsberg and settled to work with one Caspar Reuter. He married Anna Regina, one of his employer's daughters, and their son Immanuel was born on 22nd April, the fourth child of a family of nine. The family were devout pietists, with Rogall as their mentor. Kant never lost his respect for the sense of inner security and serenity which characterised pietism at its best. A younger brother, Johann Heinrich, was to return to Alt-Rhaden in Kurland as pastor. Kant was educated for eight years at the Collegium Fridericianum during the period of Schultz's directorship of the school. Transferring to the Albertina at the age of sixteen be became devoted to the young and brilliant Knutzen, currently teaching logic and metaphysics as well as theology. Kant may well have become increasingly aware of the diversity of Christian religious life represented in Prussia during his period at the Albertina. Outside Ermland, Catholicism continued to have little status, but there were to be found in Königsberg groups of Quakers, Mennonites, Socinians, Herrnhuters, German Swiss Calvinists and Huguenots, though none of these groups increased very much at the expense of organised Lutheranism. Frederick II himself firmly followed the tradition of his house and recommended religious toleration.

In 1744,[34] when the Albertina celebrated its two hundredth anniversary there were one thousand and thirty-two students, about half from east and west Prussia, and including Germans from Livland and Kurland, Poles, Lithuanians and a few Scandinavians, Russians, French and a selection of others from all over Europe. Five hundred and ninety-one of the students were enrolled in the faculty of theology, and four hundred and twenty-eight in the faculty of law. Only thirteen were enrolled as students of medicine. Kant was enrolled in the faculty of theology, and studied mathematics and sciences, geography and philosophy. His mother had died in 1737, and the death of his father in 1746 meant that he had to earn his living as a tutor in a private family. The village of Judtschen where he spent four years was one of those being re-established with French Swiss families, though with a German pastor, Daniel Andersch. From there he went to Gross Arnsdorf, and possibly to Schloss Rautenberg. He may thus have been in the service of the Keyserling family, important for the way in which they prompted the culture and music of East Prussia and who certainly later became his friends.[35]   L.W. Beck writes:

> We do not know what benefits the children gained from Kant's lessons; we can be more sure that Kant learned much from the social intercourse he had with the noble families with which he lived. Kant had been brought up in very straitened financial circumstances and an inelegant social milieu; when he returned to Königsberg about 1755 he was apparently fluent in French, polished in the artificiality of aristocratic conversation, something of a dandy in dress and comportment, and the 'galant master' as he was known in the University. How good a tutor to the children Kant was I do not know, but he was an apt pupil of their parents.[36]

It is arguable that had the opportunity been open to him at the time Kant might have become a great ornament to the newly founded Georg-August university at Göttingen, though certainly he was able to share in its work by correspondence, and the exchange of papers, books, and even pupils. The new university was to be of increasing importance for the development of German intellectual and scientific achievement,[37] and become a successful rival to Halle, as Halle had rivalled Leipzig. The Elector of Hanover (George II of Britain) was persuaded to found a new university to help develop this corner of his territory, and to rival the Berlin academy. For the claim of the founders of the new institution was that it would fulfil the aims of Leibniz, a claim that may well have provided some of the impetus for Frederick II to reconstitute the Berlin academy. Leibniz had not wanted to separate the European cause from that of the future of European Christianity. To discover and encourage theologians like Georg Calixt at Helmstedt had been as important as his own projects, though some of these had come to grief with the revocation of the edict of Nantes. However, Leibniz' own efforts to achieve encyclopedic knowledge represented an ideal that not even a Leibniz could fulfil, and he had written to Ernest August of Hanover in 1680 about establishing an academy at Göttingen where there was already an outstandingly good school.[38]   When the university came into being, (founded Michaelmas 1734, inaugurated September 1737) the school was closed and its students became members of the new establishment. Leibniz' ideal was of a 'Societas Theophilorum vel Amoris Divini-ad gloriam Dei', a cosmopolitan network of informed and enlightened scholars who would foster goodwill through their shared concerns. Philosophy and theology were to crown the encyclopedic construction of human knowledge, but were to be studied in such a way as to express the vitality of the human spirit, rather than crush it by misplaced and indefensible dogmatism.

It was Gerlach Adolph von Münchhaussen, one of two brothers in the service of the Hanoverian monarch who implemented Leibniz' proposals so far as he could by the initial appointments for which he was responsible. He had himself studied in Halle, Jena and Utrecht by the time he became librarian and historiographer in Hanover, to carry on with Leibniz' work on the history of the Guelphs. He wanted an institution in which both theology and philosophy were to be taught, but were not to become grist to the mills of polemicists, no more than were politics, science and law, medicine and the natural sciences. Another notable addition was Johann Lorenz Mosheim, who from 1747 until his death in 1755 was chancellor of the university.[39] The irenical tradition of Georg Calixt and Molanus of Loccum found further expression in Mosheim's work. Whilst at Helmstedt, he had produced a Latin translation of Ralph Cudworth's *True intellectual system of the universe*[40] as a work for theologians and philosophers to share, and had become president of the German society in Leipzig. At the outset of his chancellorship he tackled the question of the standing of theology in the new university via a discussion of 'theological rabies',[41] a subject he pursued through the writing of his substantial history of the church from its beginnings until the turn of the eighteenth century, begun at Helmstedt and completed shortly before his death.[42] One instance of his approach (freely paraphrased by his nineteenth century English translator) concludes a summary of the value of church history:

> It was by the lamp of history that those councils, whose decrees had so long been regarded as infallible and sacred, and revered as the dictates of celestial wisdom, were exhibited to the attentive observer as assemblies, where an odious mixture of ignorance and knavery very frequently presided. Our happy experience, in these later times, furnishes daily instances of the salutary effects of these important discoveries on the state of the Christian church, and on the condition of all its members. Hence flow that lenity and moderation which are mutually exercised by those who differ in their religious sentiments; the prudence and caution that are used in estimating opinions and deciding controversies; the protection and support that are granted to men of worth, when attacked by the malice of bigotry; and the visible diminution of the errors, frauds, crimes and cruelties, with which superstition formerly embittered the pleasures of human life and the enjoyments of social intercourse.[43]

Not surprisingly, he had much to say about the sentiments and trials of Calixtus, 'to whose charge many other things were laid, beside the *crime* of endeavouring to unite the disciples of the same master in the amiable bonds of charity, concord, and mutual forbearance'.[44] Anyone reading his account of Calixtus would have been reminded of the tradition of toleration fostered by the Prussian ruling house, at least from the time when Frederick William had chosen Calixtus 'as colleague and assistant to the divines sent from Königsberg' to the conferences at

Thorn in 1645. The Saxon deputies 'were greatly incensed to see a Lutheran ecclesiastic in the character of an assistant to a deputation of reformed doctors'.[45] Only the rise of 'pietism' seemed to have put an end to the controversy over syncretism.

Göttingen was also the place where Albrecht von Haller from Bern, perhaps Kant's favourite poet, came between 1736 until 1735 to foster an outstanding career. Haller was responsible for the teaching of medicine, especially physiology; and for establishing the university botanical gardens.[46] The *Göttinger Journals* published from 1747 became in 1753 the *Gottingische Gelehrte Anzeigen*, edited from 1753-1770 by Michaelis. From 1751 Haller also promoted the 'Sozietät der Wissenschaften', the first of its kind in a German university. According to Haller, by 1748 when there were thirty other universities to choose from, Göttingen already had seven hundred students, so it was clearly likely to be as successful as older universities such as the Albertina.[47]

As well as his pleasure in Haller's poetry, Kant was also to be keenly interested in the work of J.D. Michaelis, a product of Halle, who went to Göttingen in 1745, became a friend of Mosheim and Haller,[48] was professor of philosophy and then of oriental languages. Amongst his works an interesting one from Kant's point of view was Michaelis' *Compendium Theologiae Dogmaticae*, 1760, with a German translation in 1787.[49] Michaelis wanted to find a way out of writing stultifying catechetics, and although almost all his references were to biblical texts, the substance of his writing drew on existing traditions of writing philosophical theology. For instance, he began with 'revelation' and the characteristics of the deity, such as eternity, omnipotence, omniscience, etc. plus the doctrines of the unity and trinity of deity. Then he moved to the doctrine of creation, and treated the topics of why the world was created, and not eternal; he then discussed the best world and the presence of evil in it,[50] employing the same kinds of arguments as had Leibniz' *Theodicy*.

In the same year as the publication of this compendium, the eighteen year old G.C. Lichtenberg, arrived in Göttingen which had already superseded Jena and Halle as the pre-eminent place in which to study mathematics and physics.[51] Having learned his love of the sciences and of astronomy from his father, he worked his way through the university to a chair for physics, chemistry and natural history. He became a Fellow of the Royal Society in Göttingen in 1776, of the English Royal Society in 1793, and in the following year of the Petersburg academy, together with Kant. Enlightenment for him came with the realisation that Leibnizian-Wolffian philosophy was a fraud that did not square with experience.[52] He moved on to read Locke, Bacon and Hume, and from James Beattie's replies to Hume a respect for philosophy for men, not for professional sceptics,[53] and thence to an exploration of 'Kantian' idealism.[54] His interest in Kant proper led him in two directions. One was towards the application of Kant's epistemology to the applied sciences, but the other was peculiar to him, and connected his understanding of the second and third *Critiques* to his love of certain aspects of English culture. His excellent grasp of the English language, polished up on journeys to England in 1770, and 1774-75 (apart from befriending English-speaking visitors to Göttingen he was in 1785 tutor in mathematics to the youngest three sons of George III) enabled him to appreciate the moral importance of the writings of Sterne, Defoe and Fielding. For him, these writers in particular exhibited the tragic and pessimistic elements of life brilliantly illustrated for him by Hogarth,[55] and on stage by Garrick. Lichtenberg made his own contribution to psychology as an aspect of the development of the 'enlightened' study of man, especially of the face as the outer expression of emotional conditions.[56]

It is tempting to think of what Kant might have produced in the context of the Georg-August, but since he consistently refused all offers to leave his beloved Königsberg, he may have decided to try to translate some of the ideals of Göttingen to his own university, once he had established himself there as a teacher. It may be worth bearing in mind the Göttingen stimulus to the study of Christian theology and history when one comes to read Kant's own work on religion.[57]

In 1755, the city of Königsberg was celebrating its five hundredth anniversary, just before the outbreak of the Seven Years War.[58] Frederick had begun to be known as 'the Great', and, with his sister married to the Swedish Crown Prince and his uncle on the British throne, he could hope to exploit Prussian influence when it suited him, though Prussia's interests were hardly likely to coincide with those of Hanover.[59] Having gained Silesia, Frederick had incurred responsibility for a substantial Roman Catholic population and a province which was one of the sources of the wealth he needed for success in his other schemes.[60] He and his ministers had begun the long process of reforming Prussia's administration and judiciary (work completed in 1794, eight years after his death) as well as improving land and communications.[61] So Kant was establishing himself professionally at a time of growing Prussian self-confidence and justifiable self-esteem, despite some staggering reversals and setbacks. On 12th June 1755 Kant was admitted to his degree of 'master' for a treatise on fire, and on 27th September, authorised to work as a 'privat dozent', a teacher of natural philosophy at university level working from his own lodgings. This he achieved by defending his *New exposition of the first principles of metaphysical knowledge*. A third essay of that year was the first he had felt bold enough to dedicate (though he published it anonymously) to Frederick, as a small tribute to the encouragement the latter had already given to learning in 1755, the year of the Berlin academy competition for an essay on optimism. Kant's *Universal natural history and theory of the heavens, or an essay on the constitution and mechanical origin of the whole universe according to Newton's principles* enabled him to give an exposition of some of his fundamental interests which he never entirely repudiated, however much he qualified the expression of his theology or re-assessed the status of the knowledge of nature he explored with such sureness and excitement.[62] To these he added some short papers containing his reflections on the Lisbon earthquake, published in the spring of 1756. Certainly one problem was the significance of the life and death of rational beings in a world of such staggering immensity and complexity,[63] though he mitigated his sense of the fleeting and threatened character of human life by urging people to work for the human future.

He competed unsuccessfully for Knutzen's vacant post in 1756, so continued his teaching career from his lodgings. He had begun with some eighteen pupils, giving them classes in a very wide range of subjects, and a number of young men who were later to distinguish themselves came to him for tuition. The Lutheran tradition was mediated to him afresh not simply by colleagues, but by some of his most gifted pupils, such as J.G. Herder and L.E. Borowski. Herder worked for a period as a teacher at the Collegium Fridericianum whilst he was a student at the Albertina, and attended Kant's classes between 1762-1764.[64] Despite their later disagreements,[65] he wrote a most sympathetic tribute to Kant as a teacher, as a man of cheerfulness and joy, who could be tempted neither by prejudice nor desire for fame. 'He incited and gently forced others to think for themselves - despotism was foreign to his mind'.[66] L.E. Borowski (from a Polish family settled in Königsberg, one of many who had thrown their lot in with Prussia) had done well in his course on rhetoric and had been able to join the Royal German Society and help other students with their German style. After three years at the Albertina, at the age of eighteen he worked as tutor to the families of army officers, and gained experience as a field preacher. Aged twenty-two he was ordained in July 1762 by Provost Süssmilch and served as a chaplain in a prestigious regiment as the first step in his long career. Next he became a parish minister and from 1782 was back in Königsberg in charge of the Neurossgärter church. After wide experience in church and school government he was able to find himself the choice of Frederick William III as leader of the reconstituted church after the struggle with Napoleon. Certainly Kant's position could result in hostility between himself and the Lutheran state and ecclesiastical establishment, as he was to find out to his bitter cost in the last decade of his life, but anyone who supposes that he was regarded as being hostile to religious belief as such might amend their opinion on reading Borowski's affectionate account of him. It was put together in 1792 with the substance of it approved by Kant himself, and published on Kant's death.[67] Borowski would have liked Kant to hold to Christian belief as he himself understood it, but at least he recognised that Kant's life work was completed in homage to the deity, a fundamental characteristic of his life and thinking that so exasperated devotees of non-theistic enlightenment. Kant's pupils learned that he would have no pretence of belief, that is, belief without the support of reason and conscience, and young theologians studying with Kant learned to be wary of those fruits of enlightenment which did not foster religious and moral sensitivity, as well as to think for themselves. Another characteristic commended by Borowski was Kant's intense interest in humanity (reflected in his lectures on geography and anthropology). This interest Kant was later to express as on the one hand *'the universal feeling of sympathy'* and on the other, 'the faculty of being able to *communicate* universally one's inmost self-properties constituting in conjunction the befitting *social spirit* of mankind...'[68]

Kant's early major projects were initiated in wartime conditions. It has been said that the fear that dominated Frederick was 'his belief that his territories would soon be invaded by tens of thousands of Russian troops in the pay of Great Britain',[69] and major diplomatic efforts went into the achievement of the convention and then the Treaty of Westminster. Prussia was temporarily allied to Britain (with Prussia in theory functioning as protector of Hanover), and Frederick ordered the invasion of Saxony, rather that wait to be slaughtered. So began the Seven Years War, with all its attendant horrors, Poland and Lithuania being one of its most miserable battle areas. By Frederick's own account, one in every nine persons was to perish during the course of the war, and by the end of 1761 it looked as if Prussia would collapse. The war was over quickly for East Prussia, however, for the Russians invaded for the second time in six months in January 1758. Königsberg fared well, in being able to capitulate to von Fermor from Kurland, which was nominally Polish although in effect under the control of Russia. The young Russian officers livened up Königsberg society and came to Kant's classes in mathematics and allied subjects. (Moscow university had been founded in 1755, the year before the war began). Even under von Korff who replaced von Fermor, there were but minor troubles such as when Prussian state insignia were removed from public places or Alexander Nevski day was celebrated. The greatest hardship was caused by the levies the citizens had to contribute to the Russian war effort. It may be added here that Frederick was never to forget that some of his landed nobility were distinctly Russian in their sympathies in this war. Elizabeth of Russia had wanted the collapse of Prussia, but she died in January 1762 and her nephew, Peter, who came to the throne held Frederick to be a hero. Peter had come from

Holstein, and was without enthusiasm a Lutheran turned Orthodox. Peace between Russia and Prussia was quickly concluded in March 1762, and when Peter was murdered in June, his widow Catherine (formerly Sophie Frederike from Anhalt-Zerbst) confirmed peace the next month although she hated Frederick; and by August Königsberg was clear of Russian troops. Her agreement to the peace made it possible to conclude peace with Austria also in February 1763, and Frederick found himself still in possession of Silesia, but without other gains.

The period of war had been a productive one for Kant. As well as teaching, he was writing philosophy, theology and natural philosophy. In 1759 (the year of the publication of *Candide*) Kant still thought the world the best possible despite the war. 'I am happy to see myself a citizen in a world which could not be better. Having been selected as an insignificant member, unworthy in itself, to serve in the most perfect of all possible schemes, I appreciate my existence so much the more. I call out to all creatures who do not render themselves unworthy of being so described: Hail to us - we are! And the Creator is well pleased'.[70] One substantial production re-stated and developed his theological position. *The one possible basis for a demonstration of the existence of God* attempted to state Kant's understanding of the concept of the all-sufficient deity though marking the point beyond which one could not ascend past that concept - there could be no absolute proof that this is a world than which no better could be made by a deity than which no better could be thought. Kant was developing his own perspective on theology, however, for he was not only exceptional in the Albertina in the 1760s for his interest in Hume's philosophy, but especially for his admiration for Rousseau since the publication of *Emile* in 1762. He had an engraving of Rousseau hung on his walls at a time when Rousseau's works were not to be found on the shelves of the Albertina's library. Keeping track of Rousseau's work was of central importance from the 1760s through to the posthumous collection of Rousseau's writings in 1782.[71] Rousseau's achievement was comparable to that of Newton, and his effect on Kant was to help him secure a basis for his theology in his analysis of morality rather than in the realms of natural philosophy or theoretical metaphysics. Kant grasped what it is to have a moral and not simply an intellectual ideal, and he did so in part by lecturing on the business of being a member of the human moral community. The study of geography[72] had been introduced at Göttingen in 1754. Kant introduced it to Königsberg in 1756, giving his course forty-eight times, and added anthropology as the study of what man can and should make of himself as a branch of study into the German university curriculum. His *Anthropology* was his handbook of thirty years of lecturing on the subject, alongside a programme of publication in this subject area that began with *Observations on the feeling of the beautiful and sublime.*

If Rousseau denounced the follies and vices of man, it was largely that he might justify the ways of God. To paraphrase the opening words of *Emile* on 'Tout est bien', - everything is good as it comes from the hand of the Creator, but things become evil in the hands of men.[73] The law of reason means a common sense of justice which has gradually formed itself in the minds of men during long periods of moral self-discipline and the practice of positive law. The closing words of the 1762 work on the social contract related a person's ethics to his politics. 'To the gains conferred by the civil state must be added that of his moral freedom. And it is this alone which makes him master of himself. For the promptings of mere appetite are slavery; and obedience to the law which we impose on ourselves is what constitutes freedom'.[74] However, Rousseau is properly vulnerable to criticism for arguing that the coercive authority of the state should be brought to bear on those who did not subscribe to 'civil religion', and on this matter Kant most firmly differed from him. Kant would not tolerate any form of religion which fostered hypocrisy, and understood as well as anyone that a faith which integrated intellect, feeling and action with one another was almost certainly likely to be injured by coercion.

Kant wanted to find a basis for theology which could be commended to anyone who took seriously the moral problems of human interaction. Mistaken intellectual exercises could be as distracting as reports of extraordinary religious experiences, such as those of Swedenborg.[75] Kant did not want to deny that Swedenborg had some abnormal powers. For instance, the reports of his 1759 vision of the burning of Stockholm whilst he was in Göteborg seemed reliable. It was a different matter, however, when Swedenborg, by all accounts a distinguished and competent figure in Swedish public life, and a member of the Stockholm Royal Academy, claimed commerce with the spirit-world. (Swedenborg had a 'revelation' in 1745, and the *Arcana Coelestia* was published between 1749-1756, and a series of other works in Latin until 1771, the year before his death.) Kant chose to make his points about Swedenborg in conjunction with explaining his objections to much contemporary speculation - sometimes oversystematised, cataloguing subject-matter without regard to epistemological considerations, transgressing the limits of experience and evidence, and delightfully distracting. He may have taken Voltaire's point that metaphysicians are the sort of people who dream with their eyes open.[76] Kant detected 'hope for the future' as a fundamental motivating interest for rational beings conscious that the same death that comes to all organic creatures prompts those of virtuous life to hope that there may be a future for them beyond death.[77] Without this concern prompted by ethics, there is no justification for eschatology. Purity of morals does not issue from speculation about such a future, but from paying scrupulous attention to what purity of morals requires. The closing words of Voltaire's *Candide* were for Kant wholly appropriate in response to Swedenborg, - that we should look to what serves our happiness, get into the garden, and work.

Kant's life became easier financially. His already distinguished work helped him towards a recommendation to an appointment in 1765 as an under-librarian at the castle library, April 1766 - May 1772, a library which functioned as a useful supplement to that of the Albertina. Professionally, he was becoming very well known. He was invited to take up a post at Erlangen in 1769 and at Jena in 1770, but Frederick confirmed his appointment to a permanent university professorship at the Albertina in March 1770 (hence the dedication of Kant's inaugural dissertation). The appointment was ratified by the university senate the next month, and on the twenty-first of August Kant presented himself in the Albertina's Auditorium Maximum to defend his philosophy of the forms and principles of the sensible and intelligible world. Marcus Herz, a former pupil from Kurland/Livland, now a medical practitioner, was the co-defender of the dissertation. One important point made by the dissertation was the rejection of mathematics as the sole norm for all forms of knowledge - 'sense' was not obscured intellect. By 1774 Kant was well enough off to take himself to live in a house belonging to Johann Jacob Kanter, a great entrepreneur of the book trade, and by 1783 to a house of his own.

In the meantime, the Georg-August at Göttingen had helped to promote the publication of a new and important collection of work. Rudolph Eric Raspe was a doubtful character who eventually lost his membership of the British Royal Society when it was discovered that he financed his work as a mineralogist by selling purloined items.[78] Earlier in his career, however, beginning from the time when he was secretary to the Georg-August Library, he had gone on to search the royal library at Hanover, and produced in 1765 Leibniz' *Oeuvres philosophiques, Latines et Françoises*.[79] Raspe persuaded A.G. Kaestner, professor of mathematics and philosophy at Göttingen, to write the foreword, and dedicated it to von Münchhausen. The plum of the collection was Leibniz' *Nouveaux Essais sur l'entendement humain*[80] originally written in reply to Locke's work which had dominated epistemological theory in Britain since its appearance. The combination of reading a re-discovered Leibniz, together with the first part of Hume's *Treatise* to add to Kant's earlier familiarity with the *Enquiry*, and Kant's own creative genius at work, were to help precipitate the writing of the first *Critique* and its publication in its first version in 1781.

Raspe's collection was followed in 1768 by an enterprising French Protestant, Louis Dutens.[81] Duten's work constituted an impressive broadside on Leibniz' behalf, although not containing a major new work comparable to the *Nouveaux Essais*. The 1768 *Opera Omnia* (dedicated to George III) was published in Geneva and Tournes as the major achievement of Dutens' literary work. Dutens had launched himself as an able tutor in English families, and embarked on a minor diplomatic career as chaplain and secretary to Lord Bute's brother, working for long enough as George III's envoy in Turin to give him time to search for his Leibniz material. In a justifiable mood of self-congratulation he made his readers aware of the difficulty of the task he set himself. 'During the fifty years, that had elapsed since his death, five or six learned Germans had undertaken to collect his works, and all had been vanquished by the difficulty of the task. The fragments were dispersed throughout all the periodical journals of the time; or incorporated with those of contemporary writers, or manuscripts in the dust of public libraries'. He wrote to everyone he could discover who might help him, and 'At the commencement of my undertaking, Voltaire wrote to me thus: 'The writings of Leibniz are scattered like the leaves of the Sybil, and are as obscure as the writings of that old woman.' But when I sent him a complete copy of that author, elegantly bound, he said to me, 'You are like Isis, who collected the scattered members of Osiris, and caused them to be worshipped.''[82] %Y

The first of the large volumes was a collection of theological work, beginning with the *Theodicy*, familiar though it would be to anyone interested in Leibniz. Both in his memoirs and in his preface Dutens paid tribute to Brucker, whom he had been fortunate to be able to meet in Augsburg about six months before he died.[83] Brucker had given him help with the compilation, and permission to reprint the section on Leibniz from the *Historia Critica Philosophiae*. Dutens related that on his visit to Leipzig all the learned Germans he met came to visit him 'to come and make heavy compliment to the restorer of the glory of Leibniz, the sun of the university of Leipzik'.[84] Dutens sandwiched Brucker's chapter between a reprint of Fontenelle's *Eloge* and his own account of how the *Theodicy* came to be written, plus a summary of Leibniz' supporters and antagonists as far as Voltaire and his own day. The conclusion of the first volume was a reprint of work by Leibniz' friend, Christian Kortholt, the *Disputatio de philosophia Leibnittii: Christianae religioni haud perniciosa*. This tried to deal with the problem of Leibniz' view of the authority of scripture and his understanding of the doctrine of salvation, inevitable problems for a philosophical theodicy, uncomfortable with the question of the relevance of historical data for argument. Kortholt tried to make out a case for saying that Leibniz had defended the doctrine of the incarnation, and that his philosophy was an elaboration of the doctrine of the holy spirit. An elaborate Leibnizian *confessio fidei* made detailed reference to Leibniz' works, attempting to support Leibniz' claim in the preliminary discourse of the *Theodicy*, that faith and reason were in conformity with one another, a position for which in his own manner Kant was to plead.

Copernicus was the notable intellectual hero who was to provide Kant with a model for his own revolutionary epistemology in the first *Critique*, a hero who by a twist of events was so to speak now appropriated by Prussia. As soon as she had concluded peace with Prussia at the end of the Seven Years War, Catherine had exploited the political chaos in Poland and Poniatowski was elected king. Poniatowski and the Czartoryski opted for political reform before making a bid for Polish independence, though internal strife made both unlikely. Russia's success in her war with the Turks was limited, and she was ready for compensation by acquiring a limited area of Poland. Frederick had his eye on Ermland, though as recently as 1768 had denied that he wanted the dismemberment of Poland.[85] He changed his mind partly because he was persuaded by his brother Henry engaged in diplomacy at the Russian court, and partly because Austria seized 11.8% of Polish land and 18.6% of her population, gaining the richest saltmines in east central Europe and good agricultural land. Russia took 12.7% of the land, and 11.5% of the population, providing her with the western boundaries she wanted. This first partition of Poland in 1772 ended the isolation of eastern Prussia by linking it up with the main mass of Frederick's territories, and he became King of Prussia by acquiring the lands of ancient Prussia, much of which had been evangelised by the knights who had founded Königsberg.[86]

As it happened, in the autumn of 1771, Rousseau in Paris had helped a French political theorist with advice on a Polish constitution, finished four months before the August 1772 agreement in Petersburg that began the process of destruction. Rousseau's 'Considérations sur le gouvernement de Pologne' appeared in the first volume of the 1782 collection of his works, volume twelve of which contained Rousseau's 1761 synthesis and criticism of L'Abbé de Saint Pierre's project for perpetual peace.[87] It is clear from one of the pair of important political essays in 1784 that Kant had taken Rousseau to heart, as well as from one of his 1786 essays published in the year of Frederick's death. Kant wanted men 'to step from the lawless condition of savages into a league of nations' and to exercise their reason to that end rather than succumb to 'devastations, revolutions, and even complete exhaustion'. In such a league, 'even the smallest state could expect security and justice'. Wars are attempts 'to establish new relations among states, and through the destruction or at least the dismemberment of all of them to create new political bodies...'[88] He referred to the problem Rousseau had tried to solve, the problem of 'how culture was to move forward, in order to bring about such a development of the dispositions of mankind, considered as a *moral* species, as to end the conflict between the natural and the moral species. Now here it must be seen that all evils which express human life, and all vices which dishonour it, spring from this unresolved conflict'. He wrote of how 'the never-ceasing and indeed ever-increasing preparation for a future war' uses up all the resources of the state and the fruits of its culture, curtailing freedom. With respect to war, then, we are surely ourselves the cause of all the evils we lament so bitterly.[89] Further fruits of his reading of Rousseau's political reflections were to be born in a piece of political philosophy of the period of the French revolution and its aftermath.

In the meantime, with the acquisition of Ermland, the Prussian church consistories had fresh scope for evangelisation and education. 'Between 1772 and 1775, 750 schools were built; by 1778 there were 177 Protestant and 58 Catholic teachers employed in the Bromberg region (the present-day Bydgoszcz), with strong preference being given to those who could speak Polish in addition to their native German. Frederick's instruction to his successor to acquire a knowledge of Polish also dates from this period. This instruction was followed for almost a century'.[90] Königsberg did not immediately benefit from the partitions, since territories which had previously supplied her with goods for export became Russian. However, by 1777 Wraxall could report that Königsberg possessed many points of superiority as compared with Berlin or Potsdam.

> The river Pregel, upon which Königsberg is built, exceeds in magnitude the Havel and the Spree, as much as the surrounding country exceeds in beauty and fertility the barren sands of Brandenburg. By the Pregel, Königsberg communicates, at a few miles below the city, with the Baltic: and its vicinity to the Russian provinces, particularly Livonia, enables it to maintain the closest relations, either hostile or amicable, with Petersburgh. Behind it lie the northern provinces of Poland, many of whose most valuable productions are exported from Königsberg.[91]

Kant was by now distinguished, established in his university, itself located in a principal city in a prosperous part of a vigorous state, but not even he may have supposed that he was within a decade of an achievement comparable to those he himself admired as his own models.

Notes

1. S. Haffner, *The rise and fall of Prussia*, trans. E. Osers, Weidenfeld & Nicolson, 1980, reminds his readers that 'Prussia' was the name of a Baltic people colonized by Teutonic Knights who strangely adopted the name of the conquered territory.
2. H.W. Koch, *A History of Prussia*, Longman, 1978, p.21.
3. *The Cambridge history of Poland to 1696*, C.U.P., 1950, p.256. Cf. W. Hubatsch, 'Das Westliche Preussen und das Ermland zur Zeit des Copernicus', pp.138-154 of F. Kaulbach and U.W. Bargenda eds., *Nicolaus Copernicus zum 500 Geburtstag*, Bohlau, 1973.
4. A.M. Duncan trans., *Copernicus: On the revolutions of the heavenly spheres*, David & Charles, 1976.
5. A. Koyré, *The astronomical revolution*, trans. R.E.W. Maddison, Methuen, 1973, recounts that Georg Joachim Rheticus, a German Protestant, had visited him and consequently wrote a summary of Copernicus' theory 1539-40, and in 1542 produced an edition of Copernicus trigonometrical chapters.
6. M. Stupperich, *Osiander in Preussen, 1549-1552*, de Gruyter, 1973; B. Wrightsman, 'Andreas Osiander's contribution to the Copernican achievement', pp.213-243 of R.S. Westman, ed., *The Copernican achievment*, California U.P., 1975.
7. G. von Selle, *German thought in East Prussia*, Elwert Gräfe und Unzer, 1948, p.15. Cf. C.F. von Weizsäcker, 'Kopernikus, Kepler, Galilei', pp.376-394 of K. Oehler and R. Schaeffler eds., *Einsichten Gerhard Kruger zum 60 Geburtstag*, Klostermann, 1962.
8. *Cambridge history of Poland*. p.325. Cf. W. Hubatsch, trans. M. Barry, 'Albert of Brandenburg-Ansbach, Grand Master of the Order of Teutonic Knights and Duke in Prussia, 1490-1568' in H.J. Cohn ed., *Government in reformation Europe 1520-1560*, Macmillan, 1971.
9. E.H. Dunkley, *The reformation in Denmark*, S.P.C.K., 1948, p.42.
10. *Cambridge history of Poland*, p.399. Cf. F. Hipler ed., *Spicilegium Copernicanum. Festschrift des historisches Vereins für Ermland zum Vierhundersten Geburtstage der ermländischen Domherrn Nikolaus Kopernikus*, Peter, 1873, pp.215-222 describes the countryside and towns at this period.
11. F.L. Carsten, *The origins of Prussia*, Clarendon, 1954, p.160.
12. S.J. Baumgarten, *Geschichte der Religionsparteien*, ed. J.S. Semler, Halle 1766/0ims 1966 p.1240 f. Cf. Fr.U. Calixtus' compilation, *Via ad pacem inter Protestantes* of 1670, followed by his edition of his father's work, *De tolerantia reformatorum 1697*. A recent study of Calixt is that of H. Schüssler, *Georg Calixt: Theologie und Kirchenpolitik. Eine Studie zur ökumenizität des Luthertums*, Steiner, 1961,

especially pp 133-150 on the conflict over 'syncretism'. Further references are in the bibliography.
13. A. Foucher de Careil, *Oeuvres de Leibniz*, Firman Didot Frères, 1859, 1, xxxiii, 459; Schüssler pp. 157-171. Cf. M. Schmidt, 'Ecumenical activity on the Continent of Europe in the seventeenth and eighteenth centuries' in R. Rouse and S.C. Neill eds. *A history of the ecumenical movement 1517-1948*, S.P.C.K., 1954, pp.73-120.
14. Koch, p.56.
15. J.E. Erdmann, *History of philosophy*, trans. W.S. Hough,Sonnenschein, 1891, 2, 213f. Erdmann was Professor of philosophy at Halle when his *History* was published, and editor of Leibniz' work.
16. P.J. Spener, *Pia Desideria*, trans. T.G. Tappert, Fortress Press, 1977.
17. Cf. W.R. Ward, 'The relations of enlightenment and religious revival in central Europe and in the English-speaking world', pp.281-307 of D. Baker, ed., *Reform and Reformation: England and The Continent*, Blackwell, 1979, and S. Gilley, 'Christianity and enlightenment: an historical survey', *History of European Ideas*, 1:2, 1981, 103-121.
18. Haffner p.43. Cf. J.G. Herder, 'Preussische Krone', 455f. of 'Adrastea' in *Sämtliche Werke* ed. B. Suphan, Olms, 1967, (and on Leibniz as the genius of the century, pp.468f). The second of Frederick's wives was Sophia Charlotte, sister of the future George I of England, and like her mother Sophia (married to Ernest Augustus I, Duke of Brunswick-Kalenberg and Elector of Hanover) a friend of Leibniz.
19. C. Hinrichs, *Preussentum und Pietisimus*, Vandenhoeck & Ruprecht, 1971; H.-J. Schoeps, 'Christian Wolff-dreihundert Jahre alt', *Zeitschrift für Religions und Geistesgeschichte*, 31:2, 1979, 208-218. And for a discussion of Wolff, E. Gilson, *Being and some philosophers*, Pontifical Institute of Medieval Studies, 1949, pp.112-121.
20. L. Couturat, *La Logique de Leibniz d'après des documents inédits*, Alcan, 1901, Appendice 4, p. 501f 'Sur Leibniz foundateur d'Académies' and W. Dilthey, 'Leibniz und die grundung der Berliner Akademie', *Gesammelte Schriften*, Teubner, 1927, 3, 25f.
21. G. Zippel, *Geschichte des Königlichen Friedrichs-Kollegiums zu Königsberg*, 1898, Hartungsche Buchdruckerei, p. 35f.
22. G. Heinrich, 'Amtsträgerschaft und Geistlichkeit. Zur Problematik der secundären Führungsschichten in Brandenberg-Preussen, 1450-1786, pp.179-238 of G. Franz, ed. *Beamtentum und Pfarrerstand 1400-1800*, Starke, 1972.
23. G. Schmalenberg, *Pietismus-Schule-Religionsunterricht: Die christliche Unterweisung im Spiegel der vom Pietismus bestimmten Schulordnung des 18. Jahrhunderts*, Lang, 1974, p.207f. Cf. W.

Hubatsch, *Geschichte der evangelischen Kirche Ostpreussens*, Vandenhoek & Ruprecht, 1968, 1, 221.
24. G. Florey, *Geschichte der Salzburger Protestanten und ihrer Emigration 1731-1732*, Bohlaus, 1977, pp.172-183, 217-221. On a earlier incident, see G. Burnet, *Some letters, containing an account of what seemed most remarkable in travelling through Switzerland, Italy, some parts of Germany*, etc. In the years 1685 and 1686. Second edition, Acher, 1687, pp.85-87.
25. Hubatsch, 'Der Pietismus in Preussen zwischen Orthodoxie und Rationalismus', p.194f.
26. B. Erdmann, *Martin Knutzen und seine Zeit*, Voss, 1876; cf. F. Morrelle, 'Les idées religieuses de Kant en 1755-1760', *Revue Néo-Scholastique de Philosophie*, 30, 1928, 275-315.
27. Hubatsch, 'Der Preussische Kirche im ersten Regierungsjahrzehnt Friedrichs des Grossen', p.218f. Cf. W. Hubatsch, 'A variety of enlightened despotism', pp.67-80 of T.M. Barker ed., *Frederick and the making of Prussia*, Holt, Rinehart & Winston, 1972.
28. J.C. Gottsched, *Grund-Riss einer Lehr-Arth*, ordentlich und erbaulich zu predigen nach dem Innhalt der Königlich Preussischen allergnädigsten Cabinets-Ordre, 7 Marti entworften, Haude, 1740. The work was published anonymously and my attention was drawn to it by Professor P.M. Mitchell. Cf. W. Rieck, *Johann Christoph Gottsched. Eine Kritische Würdigung seines Works*, Akademie Verlag, 1972.
29. G. von Selle, *Geschichte der Albertus-Universität zu Königsberg in Preussen*, Hölzner-Verlag, 1956, p.131f.
30. J.C. Gottsched, *Ausgewählte Werke*, ed. P.M. Mitchell, de Gruyter, 1955, 7:3, 110-124; ed. J. Birke, de Gruyter, 1968, 1, 188-203. J.J. Brucker, *Historica critica philosophiae*, Breitkopf, 1733-1763, (ET W. Enfield, 1791). C. Kortholt, *Vir illustris Godefridi Guil. Leibnittii*, Epistolae ad diversos, Theologici, iuridici, medici, philosophici, mathematici, historici et philologici argumenti, E. misc. auctoris, cum annotationibus suis primum divulgavit, Breitkopf, 1734-35.
31. F. Gause, *Die Geschichte der Stadt Königsberg in Preussen, 11: von der Königskrönung bis zum Ausbruch der Ersten Weltkrieges*, Bohlau Verlag, 1968.
32. KW, 7, 120; ET M.J. Gregor, *Immanuel Kant, Anthropology from a pragmatic point of view*, Nijhoff, 1974, p.4.
33. H. Mortensen, 'Kants väterliche Ahnen und ihre Umwelt', *Jahrbuch der Albertus-Universität zu Königsberg*, 111, 1953, pp.25-57.
34. H. Motekat, *Ostpreussische Literaturgeschichte mit Danzig und Westpreussen*, p.177.
35. Motekat, p.177.
36. L.W. Beck, *Essays on Kant and Hume*, Yale U.P., 1978, p.189.
37. G. Meinhardt, *Die Universität Göttingen. Ihr Entwicklung und*

Geschichte von 1734-1974, Vandenhoeck & Ruprecht, 1977. Cf. B. Fabian, 'English books and their German readers', pp. 119-196 in P.J. Korshin ed., *The widening circle: essays on the circulation of literature in eighteenth-century Europe*, Pennysylvania U.P., 1976, includes information on the Göttingen library, which had 60,000 books by 1761.
38. Couturat, p.119f; J.P. Fleckenstein, *Gottfried Wilhelm Leibnitz: Barock und Universalismus*, Ott, 1958, pp.168-172.
39. K. Heussi, *Johann Lorenz Mosheim*, Mohr, 1906.
40. R. Cudworth, trans. J.L. Mosheim, *Systema Intellectuale huius universi seu de veris naturae rerum originibus*, Meyer, 1733.
41. J.L. Mosheim, *De odio Theologica*, Vandenhoeck, 1747, p.6.
42. J.L. Mosheim, *Institutiones Historicae Ecclesiasticae*, Weygard, 1755; ET *An ecclesiastical history, ancient and modern* trans. A. Maclaine, Cadell, 1826, though Maclaine added freely both to the text and to the notes.
43. Mosheim, *History*, 5, 851; ET 5, 66; cf. 5, 856-857, ET 5, 78-79.
44. Mosheim, *History*, 5, 929f, ET 5, 246f. Cf. E. Beyreuther, 'Halle und die Herrnhuter in den Rezensionen der Göttingischen Zeitungen von gelehrten Sachen auf dem Hintergrund niedersächsischer Religionspolitik zwischen 1739 und 1760', *Jahrbuch der Gesellschaft für Niedersächsisches Kirchengeschichte* 73, 1975, 109-134; and A. Buchholtz, *Die Geschichte der Familie Lessing*, Holten, 1909, 1, 109-129 on the work of G.E. Lessing's father.
45. Mosheim, *History*, 5, 939; ET 5, 269.
46. Meinhart, p.26f. O. Sonntag, 'Albrecht von Haller on Academies and the advancement of science: the case of Göttingen', *Annals of Science*, 32, 1975, 379-391; R. Toellner, *Albrecht von Haller:"Über die Einheit im Denken des letzten Universalegelerten*, Steiner 1971, pp.52-82; L.M. Price, 'Albrecht von Haller and English Theology', PMLA 41, 1926, 942-954.
47. J.A. von Haller, *A short account of His Majesty's late journey to Goettingen and the state of the new University there* 1748, ET of a German original, Schmidt.
48. P.H. Reill, *The German enlightenment and the rise of historicism*, California U.P., 1975, p.194; a useful source of information on such figures as Wolff, Baumgarten, Sulzer as well as Mosheim and Michaelis.
49. J.D. Michaelis, *Compendium Theologiae Dogmaticae*, Vandenhoeck, 1760. Cf. P. Kalweit, *Kants Stellung zur Kirche*. Schriften der Synodalkommission fur ostpreussische Kirchengeschichte 2, Beyers, Thomas & Oppermann 1904.
50. Michaelis, *Compendium* 4, 103-105, sections 55-56.
51. H. Schöffler, ed. G. von Selle, *Deutscher Geist im 18.Jahrhundert*, Vandenhoeck & Ruprecht, 1956, p.185 f.

52. E.J. Engel, 'Lavater, Mendelssohn, Lichtenberg', pp.187-205 of R.W. Last ed., *Affinities: essays in German and English Literature*, Oswald, 1971.
53. N.T. Phillipson, 'James Beattie and the defence of common sense', pp.145-154 of B. Fabian, ed., *Festschrift für Rainer Gruenter*, Winter, 1978m Cf. J. Beattie, *An essay on the nature and immutability of truth in opposition to sophistry and scepticism*, Kincaid & Bell 1770, (German trans. 1772) p.10, 448, 453. On p. 454 he remarked 'A metaphysician, exploring the recesses of the human heart, hath just such a chance for finding the truth, as a man with microscopic eyes would have for finding his way unable to make nothing of the face of nature only the cavernous yawning between the mountainous grains of sand that lie before him', and on p. 460 that 'the only thing that can enable sceptics to endure existence is insensibility'. cf. his *Evidences of the Christian religion briefly and plainly stated*, Strahan 1786 - he was the only philosopher of his group to produce a specifically Christian apologetic.
54. Schöffler, p.229f; and C. Brinitzer, *A reasonable rebel: Georg Christoph Lichtenberg*, trans. B. Smith, Allen & Unwin, 1960.
55. F.H. Mautner, 'Lichtenberg as an interpreter of Hogarth', *Modern Languages Quarterly* 13, 1952, 64-80; H. Schöffler ed. G. von Selle, *Lichtenberg: Studien zu seinem Wesen und Geist*, Vandenhoeck & Ruprecht 1956, p.74f.
56. W.J. Milch, 'Georg Christoph Lichtenberg: On the occasion of the two hundredth anniversary of his birth', (9 July 1942) *Modern Language Review*, 37, 1942, 335-355.
57. C.E. McClelland, *State, society and university in Germany*, Cambridge U.P., 1980, pp.39-40.
58. N.W. Wraxall, *Memoirs of the courts of Berlin* (written about 1777), second edition, Cadell & Davies, 1800, 1, 98f on the splendours of the garrison church in Berlin.
59. M. Schlenke, *England und das Friderizianische Preussen, 1740-1763*, Alber, 1963.
60. Koch, p.118f.
61. Koch, p.145f. Cf. J.A. Vann and S.W. Rowan, *The Old Reich: essays on German political institutions, 1495-1806*, Studies presented to the International Commission for the history of representative and parliamentary institutions, 48, 1, 1974; W.H. Mehl, *Germany in western civilisation*, Alabama U.P. 1979, p.252.
62. K.G. Jones, 'The observational basis for Kant's cosmogony', *Journal of the history of astronomy*, 2, 1971, 29-34.
63. Cf. W. Lepenies, 'Naturgeschichte und Anthropologie im 18. Jahrhundert' pp.211-226 and B. Fabian, 'Newtonische Anthropologie: Alexander Pope's *Essay on Man*' 99. 117-133 of B. Fabian, W. Schmidt-Biggemann and R. Vierhaus, eds. *Studien zum achzehnten*

Jahrhundert, Band 2/3, Kraus, 1980.
64. W. Dobbek, *Johann Gottfried Herders Jungendzeit in Mohrungen und Königsberg 1744-1764*, Holzner, 1961, p.91 f.
65. KW 8, 45-66; ET I. Kant, *On History* trans. L.W. Beck, R.E. Anchor, E.L. Fackenheim, Bobbs-Merrill 1979 pp.27-53. Cf. I. Berlin, 'Herder and the enlightenment', *Encounter* 25, 1965, 29-48 and 42-51 and M. Riedel, 'Historizismus und Kritizismus; Kants Streit mit G. Forster und J.G. Herder' pp.31-48 of B. Fabian etc. *Studien zum achtzehnten Jahrhundert*.
66. J.G. Herder, 'Briefe zur Beförderung der Humanität', 6, 79 in *Sämtliche Werke*, 17, 404. ET in *On History*, p.xxviii.
67. L.E. Borowski, *Darstellung des Lebens und Charakters Immanuel Kants* Nicolovius, 1804, p.85-86; cf. W. Wendland, *Ludwig Ernst von Borowski, Erzbischof der evangelischen Kirche in Preussen*, Schriften der Synodalkommission für ospreussische Kirchengeschichte 9, Thomas & Oppermann, 1910.
68. KW 5, 355; ET J.C. Meredith, *The critique of judgement*, O.U.P, 1969, p. 226. Hereafter C.A.J. or C.T.J, and page number. Cf. KW 8, 25. Reill p. 7 writes on the German Aufklärer: 'Still the image of the monad haunted them; the impetus to investigate a given entity as though it contained logical, epistemological and aesthetic categories that were harmoniously conjoined formed a starting point for most of their endeavours.'
69. H.H. Kaplan, *Russia and the outbreak of the Seven Years War*, California U.P., 1968, p.125.
70. KW 2, 34-35; ET G. Rabel, *Kant*, O.U.P. 1963, p.41. Cf. L.M. Kahl, *Vergleichung der Leibnitzischen und Newtonischen Metaphysik*, Vandenhoeck, 1741.
71. L.W. Beck, *Early German philosophy*, Harvard U.P., 1969 *Collection completes des oeuvres* de Jean-Jacques Rousseau, De la société Typographique de Geneve, 1782.
72. J.A. May, *Kant's concept of geography and its relation to recent geographical thought*, Toronto U.P. 1970.
73. C.F. Vaughan, *The political writings of Jean-Jacques Rousseau*, C.U.P., 1915, 1, 15.
74. Vaughan, 2, 37 and ET 1, 40.
75. J.L. Larson, 'Kant's Swedenborg', *Scandinavia: an international journal of Scandinavian Studies*, 14: 1, 1975, 45-51.
76. Voltaire, *Philosophical Dictionary*, trans. and ed. T. Besterman, Penguin, 1971, p.381.
77. KW 2, 34f; ET *Dreams of a Spirit-Seer illustrated by dreams of metaphysics* trans. E.F. Goerwitz, Sonnenschein 1900, p.121.
78. J. Carswell, *The Prospector: being the life and times of Rudolf Erich Raspe (1737-1794)*, Cresset Press, 1950.

79. Schreuder, 1765. The collection included the *Nouveaux Essais; Examen du Sentiment du Père Malebranche que nous voyons tout en Dieu; Dialogues de Connexione inter Res et Verba; Difficultates quaedam Logicae; Discours Touchant la Methode de la Certitude et l'Art d'inventer; Historia et Commendatio Characteristicae Universalis quae simul sit Ars Inveniendi.*
80. G.W. Leibniz, *New essays on human understanding*, trans. and ed. by P. Remnant and J. Bennett, C.U.P., 1981.
81. L. Dutens, *Memoirs of a traveller now in retirement. Written by himself. Interspersed with Historical, literary and political anecdotes, relative to many of the principal personages of the present age.* Translated from the French under the supervision of the author. 5 vols., Philipps & Dulan, 1806. J. Wesley, *A survey of the wisdom of God in the creation: or, a compendium of natural philosophy*, contains in 5, extracts from Dutens 'Enquiry into the origin of the discoveries attributed to the moderns'.
82. Dutens, *Memoirs*, 2. 77f. G. Tonelli, 'Leibniz on innate ideas and early reactions to the publication of the Nouveaux Essais (1765)' *Journal of the History of Philosophy*, 12, 1974, 437-454 reports p.449 on J.H. Formey, *Abrégé de toutes les sciences a l'usage des adolescents*, 1764 -1767, trans. into German as *Entwurf aller Wissenschaften*, reprinting the material of Diderot's article on Leibnizianism from the *Encyclopédie*, itself using material from Fontenelle's 1720 *Eloge* and Brucker's *History*.
83. Dutens, *Memoirs*, 2 199-200.
84. Dutens, *Memoirs*, 2, 244.
85. H.H. Kaplan, *The first partition of Poland*, Columbia U.P., 1962; W.W. Hagen, *Germans, Poles and Jews: the nationality conflict in the Prussian East, 1772-1914*, Chicago U.P., 1980, p.19.
86. Hagen, p. 45 remarks that the more strongly German protestantism embraced enlightenment and royal absolutism, the greater was the hostility to the Polish commonwealth. Only some poets and the journalist Christian Schubart in the 1774 *Deutsche Chronik* lamented the polish loss.
87. Vaughan 1, 359f.
88. KW 8, 24-25; *On history*, p.19. Cf. KW 8, 115-117; *On history* pp.60-62, and Reill, *German enlightenment*, p.75 f on 'Human origins and historical development'.
89. KW 8, 121; *On history* p.67.
90. Koch, p.136.
91. Wraxall, *Memoirs* 1, 145.

PART I
KANT's CONTEXT: ii

The period 1770-1780 was the so called 'silent decade' of Kant's life, when he was engaged in fundamental criticism of his early philosophy and theology with a number of projects in hand but not published until the 1780's.[1] In February, 1772, Kant (in a much-quoted letter) had written to Marcus Herz about a new project of which he had been thinking since well before his inauguration and the discussion of his public lecture. 'I am now in the position to present a critique of pure reason, containing the nature both of theoretical, as well as of practical knowledge, insofar as it is purely intellectual. I will first of all elaborate the first part containing the sources of metaphysics, its method and limits; after that, I will work out the pure principles of morality'.[2] Kant hoped to produce the first part of his work within three months, though given its complexity, it took him until 1781, two years after the publication of Hume's *Dialogues* and Lessing's *Nathan the wise*, and one year after the latter's *Education of the human race*, to get it through the press.[3] When it did appear,[4] it was dedicated to Baron K.A. von Zedlitz, minister responsible for culture and education 1771-1788, during the last fifteen years of Frederick's life and into the beginning of the reign of Frederick William II. It was he who tried to persuade Kant to move to Halle in 1777-1778. Kant had written to Herz about the problems arising out of his inaugural dissertation. He asked himself, 'on what basis rests the relation to the object of that which, in ourselves, we call representation?' One might suppose that the object is the cause of the effect, the representation, or one might suppose that that in us, which is called representation, is active with respect to the object:

i.e. if the object itself were produced by it, in the same way as divine knowledge is imagined as the prototype of things, the conformity of the representation to its object would be intelligible. The possibility, then, both of the archetypal intellect (*intellectus archetypus*) whose intuition is itself the ground of things, and of the derivative intellect (*intellectus ectypus*) which derives from sensible perfection the data for its logical treatment of things, is understandable at least.[5]

There was no simple solution to the problem posed by the alternatives, nor, when Kant did publish what he had to say, was it at all easy to assimilate. Kant's solution, his 'Copernican revolution', was expressed in difficult language in extremely complex sentences.[6] It was the result of his struggle to get to grips with what seemed to Kant to be two sources of knowledge for the human subject, the intelligible and the experienced world. L.W. Beck has succinctly explained Kant's solution thus: 'In order to know and to act, it is necessary both to see and to think', - in other words we can know only those objects given both to thought and to sense.[7] The revolution shifted attention to the way in which the human subject legitimately may claim to be cognisant of its proper objects of knowledge, and not be helpless in the face of its own discovery of the astronomic abyss of the world, which after all was man's own proper context.[8] He ascribed the character of knowable objects to the human intellect and its law-like operations, but within the boundaries of sense. The universe as he had described it in 1755 had been constituted by the deity to make itself, equipped with its own principles and elements cohering round a centre. Analogously, the human subject spontaneously organises the scaffolding of its experiences, by means of the organic interaction of its various capabilities, thereby itself instancing the harmonious order and systematic unity previously attributed to the fulcrum-centred universe. The human intellect was therefore more active, energetic and constructive than a sceptic such as Hume had thought, but in correction of Leibniz there could be no claim to knowledge of a transcendent deity. For the constructions of the intellect were the functional necessities of the time-bound and discursive mind, rather than corresponding to the inherent character of knowable objects let alone the character of the realm which transcends both human intuition and human intellect. For the intellect experiences the dialectic of reason as well as the achievement of the discursive mind. The recurring antinomies he recounted were the combat of reason with reason, arising from the overestimation of the power of reason to find solutions. Limitation as well as versatility were characteristic, and whereas some philosophers may have held that there was nothing more possible to know than certain alleged objects of the intellect, Kant would hold these to be inaccessible.

The *Prolegomena*[9] helpfully written after the first version of the *Critique*, and which marks the point at which Kant had really come to terms with Hume,[10] and then a second edition of the *Critique* in 1787, were produced during a period when Kant had to serve his first Rektorat at the Albertina in the summer semester of 1786, when he was re-reading Rousseau,[11] making his public contribution to 'enlightenment,'[12] and fulfilling the other part of the programme he had sketched to Herz. To state the principles of ethics and politics was also part of the projected revolution which Goethe put so precisely in one of his poems - 'Conscience is for right life the sun', for those who hold that the daily observance of difficult duties is all the revelation we need.[13]

Moral ideals in particular may cut through social and educational distinctions.

It was fortunate for Kant that in the 1780's two journals began publication, both of which were to prove extremely useful in explaining his ideas to his readers. C.G. Schütz, sometime professor of rhetoric at Halle, founded in 1785 the *Allegemeine Literatur-Zeitung* at Jena, where there was a small but distinguished theological college which later became the nucleus of a university close to the court of Weimar. The journal was a great success, and was almost as popular as *Der Teutsche Merkur* in being widely read outside the German states. According to Mosheim, the Jena divines had had an admirable record in the controversy over Calixtus and syncretism. Although they had confessed that 'all the sentiments of Calixtus were not of such a nature, as to be reasonably adopted without exception', yet with prudence and moderation they maintained that several of his tenets were admissable without damage to truth, and others were less dangerous than his accusers had thought.[14] This tradition of candid and impartial judgement seems somehow to have been maintained, for Jena was the first institution whose representatives unambiguously came out in support of Kant's philosophy. In 1785 the *Allegemeine Literatur-Zeitung* ran a favourable review article on a sympathetic treatment of Kant's philosophy as contained in the 1781 *Critique* and the 1783 *Prolegomena*.[15] The author of the work reviewed was J. Schultz, fifteen years younger than Kant and from 1776 minister at the castle church in Königsberg, then from 1787 a professor of mathematics at the Albertina. Apart from such support, K.L. Reinhold wrote some short papers on Kant's philosophy, just before he became professor of philosophy at Jena (moving on to Kiel in 1794).[16] He was obviously well equipped to discuss Kant's work as it was published in the 1780s and 1790s.

The advocates of 'enlightenment' in Berlin were to be of even greater service.[17] The *Berlinische Monatsschrift* began publication in 1783 (and ran until 1796) with a portrait of von Zedlitz in the first number helping to proclaim the journal as an organ of enlightenment. Working as editor at first with F. Gedicke and then on his own, J.E. Biester later consistently supported Kant's efforts to have his work published in the grim days after Frederick the Great's death when censorship of religious writing and teaching came into force. Biester, a classical scholar, was for a time von Zedlitz' secretary, and as well as being in charge of the royal library was also secretary of the Berlin 'Wednesday Society'. In the first year of publication of the *Monatsschrift* J.F. Zöllner, one of the ministers at the Marien Kirche had asked the question, 'Is it advisable to rescind the religious sanction of marriage?' (Representatives of 'Aufklärung' such as Lichtenberg had already decided this question for themselves). Zöllner had added a footnote asking 'What is enlightenment?' - a question almost as important as 'What is truth?' and certainly one that seemed to require an answer before one engaged in 'enlightening activity'. Kant of course was not a member of the society but had taken issue with Mendelssohn's answer to the question in September 1784. For Mendelssohn, the answer to the question was to advocate a system of philosophy deriving from Leibniz and systematized by Wolff, with assistance from English and Scots philosophy.[18] Furthermore, Mendelssohn had a radical answer to the question about 'enlightening activity' and was prepared to push ahead with change even if this meant violating existing laws. If the community did not approve such action, one would have to keep quiet, resign one's offices, or bear the consequences.

Kant wrote a brief postscript to Mendelssohn's answer to the question and then in December 1784 his own essay, with its motto 'Sapere aude' - have courage to use your own reason. This was a political document, though Kant had a horror of anarchy and an acute sense of the fragility of political institutions. It may be that his opening discussion of enlightenment as release from self-incurred tutelage was meant to recall *Emile* and the *Contrat Social*, for Rousseau had prized 'nature trained and disciplined by unflagging watchfulness'.[19] To begin with, the child's tutor, representative of the lawgiver and the state was responsible, but then the individual should get to the point at which he should find the resolution and courage to take that responsibility upon himself. Kant would argue that he need not be at the mercy of 'capricious will'[20] even though his will was to be independent alike of human weakness and theological derivation, but make himself worthy to be happy. He was contributing to a discussion of politics and education, of how the state's institutions could be rationalised and function humanely and make civilised life possible. New opportunities in government and commerce made those concerned with enlightenment involve themselves with questions about education, not just out of compassion for the poor. They seem not to have been interested simply in education to serve the needs of the state, however, least of all as those needs had been conceived in the twenty or more years earlier.[21] Von Zedlitz had written that 'the entire life of man is an education. Theology and politics contain the rules of this great process.'[22] Thus Kant:

> If we are asked, 'Do we now live in an *enlightened age?*' the answer is 'No', but we do live in an *age of enlightenment*. As things now stand, much is lacking which prevents men from being, or easily becoming, capable of correctly using their own reason in religious matters with assurance and free from outside direction. But, on the other hand, we have clear indications that the field has now been opened wherein men may freely deal with these things and that the obstacles to general enlightenment or the release from self-imposed

tutelage are gradually being reduced. In this aspect, this is the age of enlightenment, or the century of Frederick.[23]
The determination to put education within the reach of men without the advantages of aristocratic birth or wealth bore fruit in sometimes surprising ways. For instance, Kiesewetter, son of a sexton, had studied at Halle and done some work in Francke's orphanage there before turning up in Berlin. He then spent a period in Königsberg studying mathematics and philosophy as a pupil of Kant in order to be better equipped to teach in the 'Berlin Institute in the Military Sciences for Young Infantry and Cavalry Officers'. He was one of its two teachers when Scharnhorst arrived in 1801 to turn the Institute into an excellent training school. Scharnhorst kept him on primarily to teach mathematics and logic so he was able to teach the twenty one year old C.P.G. Clausewitz who arrived with Scharnhorst from a half-completed education in his regimental school, to leave in 1804 at the head of his class. The new regimental schools were themselves crucial to the progress of enlightenment in Prussia where political and military dimensions of the state were intricately connected.

Scharnhorst had himself left the service of Hanover at the age of forty-six when his promotion was blocked and no one would listen to what he had to say about the need to re-think military education. To begin with, he found himself as frustrated by the Prussian king and his advisers as he had been in Hanover and initially found real freedom only in the cause of military education in his Institute. In 1784, however, Scharnhorst was only twenty-nine, when Kant was himself expressing his awareness of the problem about military education:

Many affairs which are conducted in the interest of the community require a certain mechanism through which some members of the community must passively conduct themselves with an artificial unanimity, so that the government may direct them to public ends, or at least prevent them from destroying those ends. Here argument is certainly not allowed - one must obey. But so far as a part of the mechanism regards himself at the same time as a member of the whole community or of a society of world citizens, and thus in the role of a scholar who addresses the public (in the proper sense of the word) through his writings, he certainly can argue without hurting the affairs for which he is in part responsible as a passive member. Thus it would be ruinous for an officer in service to debate about the suitability or utility of a command given to him by his superior; he must obey. But the right to make remarks on errors in the military service and to lay them before the public for judgement cannot equitably be refused him as a scholar.[24]

To write as a scholar is to make public use of one's reason, and may not readily be approved by one's guardians, who may prefer the state of affairs in which 'domestic cattle' are incapable of taking a single step without the harness of their cart, each pretending to rely on books for their opinions and on their pastors for their consciences. Nevertheless, in a context in which civil order is not in doubt, people can learn to take responsibility for themselves. Kant wanted reformation in ways of thinking which would produce people capable of managing freedom and so, in time, greater civil freedom worthy of their dignity. The task of the ruler is twofold: on the one hand he must prevent his subjects from violently hindering one another in promoting their spiritual welfare. A particular aspect of this task is to make sure that he does not degrade his power 'by supporting the ecclesiastical despotism of some tyrants in his state over his other subjects'.[25] On the other hand he must positively respect his subjects and not merely tolerate them since from what they say he can evaluate himself and the performance of his government. Under such a ruler, 'venerable ecclesiastics are allowed, in the role of scholars, and without infringing on their official duties, freely to submit for public testing their judgements and views which here and there diverge from the established symbol. And an even greater freedom is enjoyed by those who are restricted by no official duties'.[26]

A society of clergy would never be justified 'in obligating itself by oath to a certain unchanging symbol in order to enjoy an unceasing guardianship over each of its members and thereby over the people as a whole, and even to make it eternal'.[27] Such a contract would be made only to shut out enlightenment, to prohibit the very possibility of extending knowledge and cleaning up error. No institution can be declared ''not subject to doubt'. For himself (and only for a short time) a man can postpone enlightenment in what he ought to know, but to renounce it for himself and even more to renounce it for posterity is to injure and trample on the rights of mankind'.[28] And it would prohibit any possibility of re-union between different church groups. Enough voices might bring a proposal to their ruler 'to take those congregations under protection which had united into a changed religious organisation according to their better ideas' - certainly a welcome point of view which would in years to come be implemented by Frederick William III and Borowski in the days of planning the Prussian church union.

The escape of men from self-incurred tutelage was in fact central to matters of religion for 'religious incompetence is not only the most harmful but also the most degrading of all'. What then was to be the role of ecclesiastics in the course of their official duties and as scholars, committed as they were to a religious compact 'for a short and definitely limited time, as it were, in expectation of a better'? Sermons and catechisms to a congregation (an example of the 'private' use of one's reason) must conform to the symbol of the church to which the cleric has committed himself and which has accepted him on that understanding. In this respect the role of the clergyman is analogous to that of the soldier on military exercises. The cleric will say: Our church teaches this or that - those are the proofs which it adduces'. He thus extracts all practical uses for his congregation from statutes to which he himself would not subscribe with full conviction but to the enunciation of which he can very well pledge himself because it is not impossible that truth lies hidden in them, and in any case, there is at least nothing in them contradictory to inner religion. For if he believed he had found such in them, he could not conscientiously discharge the duties of his office; he would have to give it up.[29]

The pattern is that of the person restricted by no official duties, to whom the soldier and the cleric can approximate within the restrictions of continuing in their posts, for 'as a scholar he has the complete freedom, even the calling, to communicate to the public all his carefully tested and well-meaning thought on that which is erroneous in the symbol and to make suggestions for the better organisation of the religious body and the church. In doing this, there is nothing that could be laid as a burden on his conscience'. A burden on his conscience might emerge in connection with the private use of his reason, if, as Kant said, he found in the statutes of his church something contradictory to 'inner religion'. The kind of clergyman who never thinks as a scholar, even if he does not produce writings which speak to his potentially world-wide public, is religiously incompetent. This for Kant would be an ultimate absurdity, because he sees that the kind of instruction this 'guardian' will give to his congregation will be destructive of the very possibility of their thinking for themselves. Kant consistently opposed servile belief in a despotic deity. For example, in his 1797 *Metaphysics of Morals* he warned against false humility, that is, kneeling or prostrating oneself before an idol. As he commented, whoever makes a worm of himself, cannot complain if he should afterwards be trodden upon.[30] Ecclesiastical claims to the possession of ultimate truth were as indefensibly pretentious as those of metaphysicians, supposedly devout people positively hindering the pursuit of such truth as lay within their reach. The impartiality and self effacement of the best natural philosophers in their investigation of nature were the appropriate model. One might not set bounds to the inquiry of nature by appealing to an arbitrary divine will, and the devout should not try to humble reason by such an appeal.[31]

The cluster of works produced between 1784-1788, which includes the exploration of fundamental moral principles and the publication of the second *Critique* - that of 'practical reason', together with the second edition of the first *Critique* exhibit Kant trying to integrate theory and practice, whether in the intellectual and scientific or in the ethical and political realms. He himself never had the experience of exercising political power beyond the structures of the Albertina, and the apparent formalism of some of his work could lead to a disastrous division between politics and practice in the achievements of German Kantians such as Ernst Cassirer in the first third of the twentieth century, like Kant a cosmopolitan humanist.[32] It could be argued that the habit of treating principles in such a way as to lead to political irrelevancy had its roots in nineteenth century political philosophy after Kant, since he paid attention to factors of many kinds which functioned as obstacles to the achievement of human dignity, aware as he was that it was by no means self-evident that reason could be brought to bear on human affairs, any more than it was self-evident that any particular individual could live in accordance with self-imposed moral principles.[23] To bring moral principle to bear on public life was problematic enough to require ready responses of hope and courage:

> A thoughtful person is acquainted with a kind of distress which threatens his moral fibre, a kind of distress of which the thoughtless know nothing: discontent with Providence which governs the course of this world. This distress he is apt to feel when he considers the evils which oppress the human species so heavily and, apparently, so hopelessly. It is true that Providence has assigned to us a toilsome road on earth. But it is of the utmost importance that we should nevertheless be content, partly in order that we may gather courage even in the midst of toils, partly in order that we should not lose sight of our own failings. These are perhaps the sole cause of all the evils which befall us, and we might seek help against them by improving ourselves. But this we should fail to do if we blamed all these evils on fate.[34]

Kant's exposition of the conjectural beginning of human history, using Genesis 2-6, helped his readers to see that we act exactly like our 'first parents'. Men want the satisfaction of their natural needs, universal human equality and perpetual peace, but will not achieve them by attempting to blame others for their own acts, nor indeed by dreams of 'paradise', a place of quiet inactivity and permanent peace, as much a creation of the imagination as Defoe's *Robinson Crusoe*.[35] The capacity to face up in the present to the often very distant future was, for Kant, the most decisive mark of human advantage. Recognition of this point helps man to mobilise himself away from misconceived goals as well as from moral passivity and the confusions of self-interest, in order to respect his neighbour and thereby glorify the deity.[36]

Frederick the Great died in August 1786 and his nephew Frederick William II[37] came to the throne at the age of forty two, at the time when Kant was still in his first period of office as the Albertina's Rector.

So he had the duty of welcoming the new king on behalf of the Senate on the occasion of the celebrations in the castle church, a duty that may have had a tinge of irony even at that stage, quite apart from the events of the reign which were to affect Kant so deeply. Two of Frederick William II's problems were his notoriously chaotic domestic affairs[38] and the fact that he allowed himself to get into the grip of a group of Rosicrucians. Both these factors added to the moral offence of the edicts concerning religion he was to promulgate during his brief reign and which in any case ran counter to the traditions of his ruling house. Mosheim had reported on the strange fantasies and society of the Rosicrucians of his day,[39] so at odds with enlightenment as Kant his group of acquaintances and correspondents understood it, or indeed the rising civil servants in the Prussian bureaucracy. The king had first been introduced to Rosicrucianism by J.R. Bischoffwerder, a Saxon who had like others made or recovered his fortune in the service of Prussia during or after the Seven Years War. In Bischoffwerder's case, he had served with the Prussian army in the last stages of the war, had later become one of Frederick William's circle, and took the king under the influence of J.C. Wöllner. Wöllner was born in 1732, the son of a pastor, a product of Halle, and a student of Wolffian philosophy.[40] Working as a pastor, then as a tutor, he had established a satisfactory reputation as an agriculturalist, and managed to marry a daughter of the noble family for whom he worked, though Frederick the Great, labelling him as deceitful and scheming, did not allow him to take his wife's rank. By 1770 he had a post with Frederick the Great's brother Henry, managing his estates, and had also become a Rosicrucian. Berlin Rosicrucian lodges were flourishing and Wöllner allegedly engineered at his own home séances for Frederick William at which the latter believed himself to receive intimations from personages as diverse as Marcus Aurelius, Leibniz and the Great Elector.[41]

Although in Berlin society interest in literature, music and philosophy was flourishing, there was one area in which enlightenment and free discussion were not to be allowed unlimited freedom in the new reign.[42] During the summer of 1788 Kant was in his second period as Rector of the Albertina and Wöllner had helped to dislodge von Zedlitz from office, though he was kept on in the ministry for education. Wöllner himself was made a minister of justice and head of the department to deal with the Lutheran church, its schools and charities. In July he put out the first of a series of edicts. The July 1788 'Religionsedikt' could be read as a direct reply to some of the points Kant had publicly made in 1784. The edict stated what had been accepted policy under the previous reign - that the three main Christian confessional groups were to continue to receive 'tolerance'. A believer had no problem with the state so long as he fulfilled his duty as a citizen. Proselytising was forbidden but Lutheran confessional orthodoxy was to be maintained, and freedom of discussion was restricted - especially on the part of ministers, professors of theology and schoolteachers, who must not deviate from the symbol formulated by Luther.[43]

There were immediate protests by Lutheran ministers themselves. Perhaps the most distinguished of the five 'Oberkonsistorium' members who protested as a group was J.J. Spalding.[44] In 1756 he had published the one and only German translation of Butler's 1736 *Analogy of Religion* together with Butler's two short essays on personal identity and the nature of virtue, not least as an antidote to the (1754) posthumously published works of Bolingbroke.[45] He had come to Berlin in 1764 as Provost, leading pastor of the Nikolai and Marienkirche and then 'Oberkonsistorialrat'. In 1788 Kant was sixty four, and though he was to find the whole series of edicts distressing he was less immediately in the forefront of the objectors than was the seventy-four year old Spalding. Whilst not himself a theologian or philosopher of the first rank he was a well known public figure who used his pulpit to criticize the edict as well as signing the protest that went to the king, before retreating into his family circle. Not wholly surprisingly, there were theologians - Semler in Halle for example, who were not antagonistic to the edict because of its defence of orthodoxy.[46] The protests in public, some of them in print, led to further restrictions, and came to limit the freedom of printers (with whom Frederick II had on the whole not interfered) so pamphlets poured in from presses outside Prussian jurisdiction. In May 1791 the Berlin Oberkonsistorium set up an 'Examinationskommission', to which were brought candidates for the ministry and already ordained pastors, if someone brought to the attention of the commissioners their suspicions of these men's understanding of Lutheran orthodoxy and pure Christian teaching. Similar measures were employed in other consistories. It was a not unexpected rear-guard phenomenon in a period in which there had been one major political upheaval in North America,[47] observed with an interest which sharpened perceptions of the greater upheaval in Europe inaugurated by the storming of the Bastille in July 1789.[48]

Kant was not without resources for meeting the new political challenges of his day, and whatever was to be the hurt to him personally, the effect of the edicts paled into insignificance with the imminent danger facing Prussia. He had the advantage of a growing reputation within Europe and was in the final throes of completing the third *Critique* - of aesthetic and teleological judgement, to be published in 1790. Not only in protestant but in Roman Catholic faculties of theology there was much discussion of Kant's 'natural' theology,[49] not least because of the problem, not unique to him, of how the 'historical' character of the distinctively Christian revelation was to be coped with, especially when the representatives of ecclesiastical institutions were themselves not ready to criticize their own organisations as shaped by particular historical and societal circumstances. Kant himself argued on the subject of 'theological geography' that 'Since theological principles suffer appreciable transformation because of differences in the land..., necessary information will have to be given about this. For instance, one has only to compare the Christian religion in the Orient with the Christian religion in the West, to observe, here as there, its finer shades. This is even more sharply noticeable with religions that differ in their basic principles'.[50] There was a particularly acute problem about the character of biblical theology when it became a manifestation of ecclesiastical authority exercised by theologians who did not think or speak or write like scholars prepared to make a 'public' use of their reason.[51] Kant was unlikely to accommodate his thinking so the prevailing spirit of the State or to ecclesiastical dogmatism in any form and those who learned from him would very probably fall foul of their own ecclesiastical authorities.

The nearest Roman Catholic seminary at which discussion could have taken place was that of Braunsberg in Ermland. Although Frederick the Great had refused to allow the papal dissolution of the Society of Jesus to take effect in Prussia,[52] the seminary programme in the aftermath of the partitions of Poland virtually collapsed.[53] By 1805 there were only three teachers and thirty four students, of whom sixteen were studying theology, and by 1811 the seminary was finished. The only possibility for its revival came when von Massow, Wöllner's replacement under Frederick William III suggested that there should be in Königsberg a catholic theological faculty drawing not only from Ermland but from the Polish territory Prussia acquired in the second and third partitions of Poland. Kant and C.J. Kraus, sometime his pupil, and currently professor of practical and political philosophy were on a small Senate committee to look into the matter. Kraus had been employed by the Keyserling family but had also worked in Halle and Göttingen. The Senate committee reported in March 1800 that there could be no academic objection to the proposal, but predictably, the plan ran aground and the end of the Braunsberg seminary was inevitable given the circumstances of the time.

Unfortunately for Kant during this period further criticism of him had been launched by a Halle-trained theologian, J.A. Eberhard. He had worked in Berlin as chaplain to a Prussian minister of state and had returned to Halle in 1778 to the chair which had been Wolff's, whose philosophy he wished to continue to promote. He thus occupied the chair which von Zedlitz had offered to Kant, and from it in 1788 founded and edited the *Philosophisches Magazin* which he used to tackle questions about the critical philosophy.[54] Eberhard's concept of deity was more akin to that of Kant in 1763, the concept related to that of Leibniz, of the deity as the knowable real ground of all possibility. He was able to appeal to Kant's pre-critical work in support of his own position, and then argue that Kant's work was superfluous to that of Leibniz.[55] Eberhard's attacks on Kant coincided with another Berlin Academy competition, a discussion of the progress made in metaphysics since the death of Leibniz. The competition ran from 1788 to 1795, the date of the peace of Basel by which Prussia temporarily extricated herself from war with revolutionary France. Kant composed three unfinished drafts for the competition and in the meantime tried to meet Eberhard on his own ground.[56] It was not his intention to emphasise his points of difference from Leibniz at this stage, but to justify his claim that his own work was indeed necessary. It was Kant, not Eberhard, who was capable of recognising what a philosopher of the past had meant beyond what he actually said.[57] In the middle of this philosophical controversy he continued to tackle the problem of Wöllner's edicts. He produced first of all another essay, published in the September 1791 number of the *Berlinische Monatsschrift* on the failure of all attempted philosophical theodicies, precipitating further discussion about Leibniz, and the value of theodicies and what they meant to people. He was also using the essay as an opportunity to voice his opinion on the subject of the religion-edict and connected the two topics together via a discussion of Job.[58] (The first censorship edict followed in December, and the second in the following March.) Hume's *Dialogues* were clearly a stimulus to the discussion, as was the argument of Butler's *Analogy*, to which Hume had offered a reply in his section of the *Enquiry*, 'Of a particular providence and of a future state', of which Kant could have been vigorously reminded by his reading of Beattie. The latter had drawn particular attention to Hume's essay and had commented: 'For an answer to the other cavills thrown out by Mr. HUME, in this flimsy essay, against the divine attributes, the reader is referred to the first part of Butler's Analogy of Natural and Revealed Religion. It need not be a matter of any surprise, that we name, on this occasion, a book which was published before Mr. HUME'S essay was written'.[59] It was not, he maintained, uncommon with infidels though less frequently with Hume, to deliver objections against religion which had already been refuted. There were other remarks of Beattie's which had already been of interest to Kant. For instance, Beattie had in effect recalled Butler's crucial paragraph in the preface to the *Analogy*[60] where he wrote that 'The highest degree of conviction in reasoning from causes to effects is called moral certainty; and the inferior degrees result from that species of evidence which is called probability or verisimilitude'.[61] Beattie had gone on to explain 'moral certainty' as judgement particularly concerned with the future, not susceptible of proof, and went on to indicate his interest in the connection between the problem of human free agency and love of political liberty, and between the character of the deity and virtue. Moreover, 'Revelation itself must be attended with evidence to satisfy conscience or common sense; otherwise it can never be rationally believed. By the evidence of the gospel, the rational Christian is persuaded that it comes from God. He acquiesces in it as truth, not because it is recommended by others, but because it satisfies his own understanding'.[62] Modern sceptics seemed to be ignorant that without belief in God and hope of immortality, the miseries of human life would often be insupportable.

Certainly Kant would differ from Beattie in the way he made these points, and would want to re-interpret them, the way he had interpreted the far greater Leibniz. It may be indeed that when he wrote the first edition of the first *Critique* he had already taken the measure of Butler's crucial introductory paragraph at the point where he was prepared to claim that his faith in the deity was a matter of moral certainty.[63] For Kant's faith in the deity had to do with hope for the future both in the course of human history and beyond death, and this contributed to his persuasion that he could recognise duties as divine commands and acknowledge an acceptable reason for worship: 'What if the final end of our true being is delineated to our minds quite freely, and in virtue of the precept of our own reason, by a reverence for the moral law? Why, then, we accept into our moral perspective a cause harmonising with that end and with its accomplishment and accept it with deepest veneration, wholly different from any pathological fear - and we willingly bow down before it'.[64] His position eliminated the dogmatism of rational theology as Eberhard for one had conceived it, as efficiently as it eliminated exclusive ecclesiastical claims to the possession of revealed truth. It was then not surprising that Fichte's anonymous critique of all revelation should have been attributed to Kant on its first appearance. The effect of the edict on religion had prevented the publication of Fichte's essay until a change of dean at Halle allowed its publication in 1792, and it may have been produced anonymously by the publisher's deliberate decision.[65]

Kant endeavoured to counter Hume's scepticism but would never have him silenced, and his essay is in its own way an apologia for Hume as well as for Leibniz. He had approved Hume's commendable frankness in his *Dialogues*[66] and had in a letter written of the man who believes that in the final moment, only the purest candor concerning our most hidden inner convictions can stand the test and 'who, like Job, takes it to be a sin to flatter God and make inner confessions, perhaps forced out of fear, that fail to agree with what we freely think'.[67] The crucial point about Job's discussion with his friends was the character which they exhibited when they reasoned with him. 'Job spoke as he thought, as he felt, and as every man in his position would feel'. His friends spoke 'as if they were overheard by the Almighty whose behaviour they were judging, as if they cared more for winning his favours by passing the right judgement than for saying the truth'. Kant's criticism was harsh, but it both expressed his central concern in religion and served his public, political purpose. 'The dishonesty with which they affirmed things of which they should have confessed that they had no knowledge and with which they feigned convictions which in fact they did not have, contrasts with Job's free and sincere outspokenness, which is so removed from lying flattery that it almost borders on temerity'.[68] The dénouement showed God honouring Job by showing him the wisdom of his creation and its unfathomable nature and Job for his part confessed that he had foolishly spoken abouth things beyond the reach of his understanding. God's condemnation fell on his friends, 'because, considered from the standpoint of conscience, they had not spoken of God as well as his servant Job did'.[69] So, 'If Job were to appear before some tribunal of dogmatic theologians, some senate or inquisition, some worthy presbytery or some high consistory of today (with the exception of one), he probably would have met with a worse fate'.[70] Kant had thus pilloried Wöllner and his supporters as well as making another comment on Leibniz and Hume.[71]

Some six months after Kant had published this essay another appeared in the *Berlinische Monatsschrift* which had moved to Jena to escape the rules of censorship (and then to Dessau) 'Concerning the indwelling of the Evil Principle with the Good, or, on the radical evil in human nature'which came out in April 1792, as it was judged not to be for the general reader. An essay which was to become the second of his *Religion within the limits of reasons alone*[72] 'Concerning the conflict of the good with the evil principle for sovereignty over man' was quickly finished and submitted to the censor in July, but permission to publish was refused, because the work was in part an attack on reactionary censorship related to a certain kind of theology. Eventually Kant obtained approval for the work from the theology faculty at Königsberg and the philosophy faculty of Jena and the whole work came out in 1793.[73] Kant made his views of censorship clear particularly in the preface to the first edition, and throughout the work.[74] His 1798 statement on *The conflict of faculties*[75] further fills in the background to the whole work.

> In religious matters the only thing that can interest the state is: to what doctrines it must bind teachers of religion to have useful citizens, good soldiers, and, in general, faithful subjects. Now if, to that end,it chooses to enjoin orthodox statutory doctrines and means of grace, it can fare very badly. For it is an easy thing for a man to accept these statutes, and far easier for the evil-minded man than for the good,

whereas the moral improvement of his attitude of will is a long and difficult struggle. And so, if a man is taught to hope for salvation primarily from these statutes, he need not hesitate greatly about transgressing his duty (though cautiously), because he has an infallible means at hand to evade God's punitive justice (if only he does not wait too long) by his orthodox belief in mystery and his urgent use of the means of grace. On the other hand, if the teaching of the church were directed straight to morality, the judgment of his conscience would be quite different: namely, that he must answer to a future judge for any evil he has done that he cannot repair, and that no ecclesiastical means, no faith or prayer extorted by dread, can avert this fate (*desine fata deum flecti sperare pecando* [cease hoping that you will alter the divine will by prayer]). With which belief, now, is the state more secure?[76]

It had become clear that 'a substantial measure of demystification was in store for Christian theology'[77] long before the actual publication of the *Conflict of the faulties* (dedicated to C.F. Staüdlin, Professor of theology at Göttingen).[78] His readers must somehow be enabled to take seriously the necessary difference between the professional cleric who works within limits and the professional critic who claims to work by reason alone. Beyond this too, they must come to appreciate the possiblity of change in the way they hold to their beliefs , given that it is the philosopher, rather than the cleric, who asks disturbing questions about truth. In the 'foreword' Kand had rehearsed in public the exchange of letters between himself and Frederick William II which to the distress of his friends[79] meant that Kant published no more on religion during the king's reign.

It was an essay of June 1794 on 'The end of all things' which provoked by the October of that year an edict specifically directed at Kant personally. Again Kant had more than one purpose in view. The essay reviewed the sense he could give to hope for eternity still meaningfully expressed for him in the poetry of Haller. As with the 1791 essay on theodicy, this essay also concerned itself with the theme of divine judgement, integral to Kant's moral certainty, and thence with the theme of eternal punishment, under review not least because of Lessing's discussion of Leibniz' views as expressed in the *Theodicy*.[80] It recapitulated in its own way Kant's abhorrence for any form or expression of Christianity which uses religious belief as a means of coercion and employs public power to do so. The founder of Christianity does not speak in the character of 'a dictator who impresses people by a will that demands obedience, but rather in the character of a humanitarian ... who brings to the heart of his fellowmen their own wellunderstood ... wills, according to which they would act spontaneously of themselves if they proved themselves fitting'.[81] He went further in his concluding paragraph by associating dictatorial authority with the reign of the Antichrist, since 'natural antipathy and insurbordination' to such authority would be bound to predominate. To his king he maintained that 'I have always and above all recommended to other believers a conscientious sincerity in not professing or obtruding on others, as articles of faith, more than they themselves are sure of, so, when composing my writings, I have always pictured this judge as standing at my side to keep me not only from error that corrupts the soul, but even from any careless expression that might give offence'. He was himself, in his seventy-first year, writing in the consciousness that 'I may well have to answer for this very soon to a judge of the world who scrutinizes men's hearts' - in which case he could offer his account of himself to his earthly king with conscientiousness.[82]

Kant's struggles with those who were responsible for the edicts may have seemed relatively unimportant in the light of the revolutionary struggle and war, not least when the Prussians had not been able to stand up to the French revolutionary army at Valmy. Although not publishing comments on religion, Kant was free to publish some pointed political statements, for the earlier predators of Poland had their eyes on the country still.[83] Frederick William II backed the party of constitutional reform in Poland, whereas Catherine of Russia supported the Polish conservative nobility. Confrontation between the rival parties was avoided by a second partition in 1793, increasing Russian territory particularly by the acquisition of the remainder of Lithuania. Prussia acquired Danzig, Thorn and related territory, and regions south of what she already possessed - purely Polish territory. With the third and final partition in 1795 Stanislaus was no longer king - a strange achievement for those allegedly at war because of the execution of Louis XVI in 1793.[84] Prussia this time took Warsaw and territory in the region of Cracow - another million population. Russia took twice as much again in the east, and Austria rejoined the predators to take two million more subjects, including Cracow itself and fertile land between the Bug, the Vistula and the Pilitza.

This latter partition took place in the immediate aftermath of signing the peace of Basel, the result of a French diplomatic triumph to separate Prussia from Austria, turning northern Germany into a zone under Prussian leadership. Hanover, Saxe-Weimar, Hesse-Kassel and Holland (where William V was married to Frederick William's sister Wilhelmina) followed Prussia's lead. Only Austria and England were left in the first coalition against France. Although the Prussian government had achieved a period of relative calm in a period of upheaval it remained ill at ease, and after Frederick William II's death in 1797, his sucessor Frederick William III[85] was in the end driven back into the fight with France by the unauthorised action of some of his commanders. Naturally Prussia had felt some relief from the cost of war, though some ten years were to elapse before constitutional reforms could begin effectively to be implemented. C.J. Kraus had been one of those responsible for the education of a new generation of civil servants, eager to launch themselves into every area of possible reform, from municipal statues to peasant smallholdings. After the struggle with Napoleon they were at the disposal of such men as Stein, educated in Göttingen, and who like Lichtenberg had learned a good deal from his visits to Britain.[86]

Kant's 1795 essay *On perpetual peace*, whilst by no means the last of his works had perhaps the most immediate major impact on the reading public, with a second edition containing two new appendices appearing a year later, translated immediately into English, and introduced into revolutionary France by Charles de Villers, who was also to produce his own introduction to Kant's philosophy.[87] Kant's essay has remained of interest to politicians even of the present century, not least because of Kant's focus on the dependence of everyone on common legislation for security, and the sheer rational vitality such security requires as a presupposition for its achievements.[88] As before, he argued that the principles of right are capable of implementation in practice, the fates leading the willing and dragging the unwilling.[89]

At any rate, the lull in hostilities so far as Prussia was concerned allowed Kant to see out his days in the calm pleasure of knowing that his merits were widely appreciated. Frederick William III in January 1798 issued his own cabinet order rescinding the religion-edict of his predecessor and by April had replaced Wöllner by von Massow, and Kant was able to publish without further interferences. He had the satisfaction of knowing that J.S. Beck[90] continued with his programme of providing critical introductions to the elements of Kant's philosophy, and that one of Beck's pupils, John Richardson, was to transmit not only Beck's work but many of Kant's essays to the English speaking world,[91] an important complement to the enterprising lecturing and writing of F.A. Nitsch and A. Willich.[92] When he died in February 1804 he was given a splendid funeral and was buried in the academics' vault of the cathedral. The Stoa Kantiana was later built over the place where he lay, with the words from his second *Critique*, 'The starry heavens above me, the moral law within me'[93] inscribed where everyone could read them. Less than three years later Königsberg was again in a war-zone and the aftermath of the battles at Jena and Auerstadt in October 1806 was a terrible time. So, in our own generation, were the closing years of the second world war. After that war, in the Federal Republic Gemany, the Albertina was given new commemoration in the Collegium Albertinum on Bonhoefferweg in Göttingen, and the writings of its greatest students have a world-wide reputation.

Notes

1. M.C. Washburn, 'Dogmatism, scepticism, criticism : the dialectic of Kant's "silent decade" ', *Journal of the history of philosophy*, 3, 1975, 167-176; W.H. Werkmeister, *Kants silent decade : a decade of philosophical development*, Florida U.P., 1979.
2. G.B. Kerferd and D.E. Walford, *Kant: selected pre-critical writings and correspondence with Beck*, Manchester U.P., 1968, p.114. Also in A. Zweig, ed., *Kant: philosophical correspondence 1759-99*, Chicago U.P., 1967, p.73.
3. As well as the studies by K. Aner and G. Pons, there is that of L.P. Wessell, *G.E. Lessing's theology: a reinterpretation*, Mouton, 1977.
4. KW 4(1781); KW 3 (1787); ET N. Kemp Smith, *Immanuel Kant's Critique of Pure Reason* Macmillan, 1964. Hereafter CPR and section number.
5. Kerferd/Walford p.112.
6. CPR B xvii; H. Blumenberg, *Die Genesis der Kopernikanischen Welt*, Suhrkamp, 1975, pp.64-80, 666-714. E.A. Blackall, *The emergence of German as a literary language, 1700-1775*, Cornell U.P., 1978, writes of the problem though naturally not with regard to the peculiar problems of specifically philosophical language.
7. Beck, *Essays on Kant and Hume*, p.18.
8. See essays two to four of K. Barth, *Protestant theology in the nineteenth century*, (trans. B. Cozens and J. Bowden), S.C.M., 1972.
9. KW 4, 255-384; ET P.G. Lucas, *Prolegomena to any future metaphysics that will be able to present itself as a science*, Manchester U.P., 1966.
10. D.-J. Löwisch, *Immanuel Kant und David Hume's Dialogues concerning natural religion*, Rheinische Friedrich Wilhelms Universität, 1964.
11. G.A. Kelly, 'Rousseau, Kant and history', *Journal of the history of ideas*, 29, 1968, 347-364; S. Ellenburg, discussed by R. Wokler, 'Rousseau and Kant: principles of political right', pp.3-35 of R.A. Leigh ed., *Rousseau after two hundred years*, C.U.P., 1982.
12. H. Brunschwig, 'Aufklärung in Preussen', vol.3, pp.1307-1327 of *Moderne Preussische Geschichte*, ed. O. Büsch and W. Neugebauer, de Gruyter, 1981; N. Hinske ed., *Was ist Aufklärung? Beiträge aus der Berlinischen Monatsschrift,* Wissenschaftliche Buchgesellschaft, 1973.
13. N. Boyle, 'Kantian and other elements in Goethe's "Vermächtnis" ', *Modern Language Review*, 1978, 532-549.
14. Mosheim, *History*, 5, 942; ET 5, 275.
15. 'Erläuterungen über des Herrn Professor Kants Critik der reinen

Vernunft', *Allegemeine Literatur-Zeitung*, 3-4, 1785, 42-44, 53-56, 117-118, 121-128.
16. KW 8, 183-4. Cf. Erdmann, *History*, 2,471-479; S. Atlas, *From critical to speculative idealism: the philosophy of Salomon Maimon*, Nijhoff, 1964, pp.284-301.
17. W. Dilthey, *Selected writings*, trans. H.P. Rickman, C.U.P., 1976, 99.35-77; K. Scholder, 'Grundzüge der theologischen Aufklärung in Deutschland', pp.294-318 of F. Kopitzsch, ed., *Aufklärung, Absolutismus und Bürgertum in Deutschland*, Nymphenburger, 1976.
18. A. Altmann, *Moses Mendelssohn*, Routledge & Kegan Paul, 1973, p.654 f. Cf. A. Menhennet, *Order and freedom: literature and society in Germany from 1720-1805*, Weidenfeld & Nicolson, 1973, p.14f, p.63.
19. Vaughan 2, 140.
20. Werkmeister, p.28, writes that Kant took 'Wilkür' to be equivalent to 'arbitrium', i.e. 'Arbitrary' will.
21. P. Paret, *Clausewitz and the state*, Clarendon, 1976, p.36f.
22. Paret, p..96.
23. KW 8,40; *On History* pp.8 9. Cf. KW 8, 144-147 of 'What is orientation in thinking?'
24. KW 8, 37; *On history* p.5.
25. KW 8, 40; *On history* p.8.
26. KW 8, 41; *On history* p.9.
27. KW 8, 38-39; *On history*, p.7. Cf. KW 8, 269 note.
28. Cf. R. Aris, *History of political thought in Germany from 1789-1915*, Allen & Unwin, 1965, p.103 on Kant's understanding of freedom as an ethical problem, having to do not so much with people's relationships to one another but to their better selves.
29. KW 8, 38; *On history*, p.6. Cf. D.F. Strauss, *The life of Jesus critically examined*, (trans. G. Eliot), ed. P.C. Hodgson, S.C.M. 1973, pp.781-784, on the relation of critical and speculative theology to the life of the church.
30. KW 6 437; ET J. Ellington, *The metaphysical principles of virtue*, Bobbs-Merrill, 1964, p.100.31.
31. KW 2, 119; cf. Altmann, *Mendelssohn*, p.175f.
32. D.R. Lipton, *Ernst Cassirer: the dilemma of a liberal intellectual in Germany, 1914-1933*, Toronto U.P., 1978.
33. Lipton, *Cassirer*, p.175.
34. KW 8, 121; *On history*, p.66. Cf. J. Passmore, *The perfectibility of man*, Duckworth, 1970, pp.216-221; J.A. Bernstein, 'Ethics, theology and the original state of man: an historical sketch', *Anglican theological review*, 61:2, 1979, 162-181.
35. KW 8, 114-115, 112; *On history*, p.59. p.68. In *Emile* Rousseau had recommended that the child's library should for a long time

be composed only of *Robinson Crusoe;* cf. *Emile* trans. B. Foxley, Everyman's, 1969, p.147f; P. Earle, *The world of Defoe,* Weidenfeld & Nicholson, 1976.
36. Cf. S.B. Thomas, 'Jesus and Kant: a problem in reconciling two different points of view', *Mind,* 79, 1970, 188-199; A. Koutsouvilis, 'Kant and the Christian command', *Heythrop Journal,* 14m 1973, 190-194.
37. Frederick William II's father was Augustus William, brother of Frederick the Great, who had died as a result of his terrible experiences during the Seven Years War. Augustus' wife was the sister of Frederick's own queen.
38. Frederick William's first wife was Elizabeth of Brunswick, divorced after the birth of her daughter, Frederika, herself later married to the Duke of York, son of George III. Frederick William's second wife was Frederika of Hesse-Darmstadt, and her first son survived to become Frederick William III, who came to the throne in 1797. In the meantime Frederick William had educated Wilhelmina, later Countess Lichtenau; the king also became entangled with Julie Voss, who contracted a form of 'marriage' with the king, and there was another such marriage with Sophie, countess von Dönhoff. Cf. Koch, pp.146-148; Zweig, *Correspondence,* pp.162-165.
39. Mosheim, *History,* 5, 852f; ET 5, 69f.{
40. W. Schrader, *Geschichte der Friederichs-Universität zu Halle,* Dummlers, 1894, pp.118-128 on the theological faculty begun with Francke, pp.168-196 on Wolff and p.513f on Wöllner.
41. G. Stanhope, *A mystic on the Prussian throne: Frederick William II,* Mills & Boon, 1912; H. Brunschwig, *Enlightenment and romanticism in eighteenth century Prussia,* (trans. F. Jellinek), Chicago U.P., 1974, pp.164-170.
42. E.J. Feuchtwanger, *Prussia: myth and reality,* Wolff, 1974, pp.78-87, Dutens, *Memoirs,* 3, 160, 259 on the Parisian view of the merits of philosophy and religious belief.
43. F. Valjavec, 'Das Woellnersche Religionsedikt und seine geschichtliche Bedeutung', *Historisches Jahrbuch der Görres-Gesellschaft,* 72, 1953, 386-400; Hubatsch, 'Die Wirkungen der Ära Wöllner auf Ostpreussen', 1, 246f. of his *Geschichte der evangelischen Kirche Ostpreussens.*
44. R. von Thadden, *Die Brandenburgisch-Preussischen Hofprediger im 17 und 18 Jahrhundert,* de Gruyter, 1951, p.126.
45. J. Schollmeier, *Johann Joachim Spalding: ein Beitrag zur Theologie der Aufklärung,* Mohn, 1967, pp.168-183; and for the wider context, F. Lötzsch, *Vernunft und Religion im Denken Kants: Lutherisches Erbe bei Immanuel Kant,* Böhlau, 1976.
46. Schrader, *Halle,* p.518.

47. H. Dippel, *Germany and the American revolution, 1770-1800*, (trans. B.A. Uhlendorf), North Carolina U.P., 1977. Cf. KW 6, 350-351; T. Bruns, *Kant et l'Europe*, Saarlandes Universität, 1973.
48. Cf. Beck *Essays on Kant and Hume*, p.171-187; P. Burg, *Kant und die Französische Revolution*, Dunker & Humbolt, 1974; S. Axinn, 'Kant, authority and the French revolution', *Journal of the history of ideas*, 32, 1971, 423-432.
49. J.A. Dörner, *History of Protestant theology particularly in Germany*, trans. G. Robson and S. Taylor, T & T Clark, 1871, 2, p.272d; W. Maurer, *Aufklärung, Idealismus und Restauration: Studien zur Kirchen und Geistesgeschichte in besonder Beziehung auf Kurhessen, 1780-1850*, Topelmann, 1930, pp.24-41; and W. Heizmann, *Kants Kritik spekulativer Theologie und Begriff moralischen Vernunftglaubens im Katholischen Denken der später Aufklärung*, Vandenhoeck & Ruprecht, 1976.
50. May, *Geography*, p.264 translates KW 9, 165, para. 5 on 'theological geography'.
51. K.-H. Crumbach, *Theologie in kritischer Öffentlichkeit: Die Frage Kants an das kirchliche Christentum*, Kaiser, 1977.
52. W. Hubatsch, *Frederick the Great: absolutism and administration*, (trans. P. Doran), Thames & Hudson, 1975, p.198.
53. B. Stasiewski, 'Die geistesgeschichtliche Stellung der katholischen Akademie Braunsberg, 1568-1945', pp.41-58 of W. Hubatsch *et al.*, *Deutsche Universitäten und Hochschulen im Osten*, West Deutscher Verlag, 1964. Cf. H. Preuschoff, 'Hohenzollern auf dem ermländischen Bischofsthron', *Kauskal*, 88, 1955, 27-51.
54. Also other related topics e.g. *Philosophisches Magazin* 1791, 4:1, 84f discusses Pyrrhonism and Hume. Cf. J.A. Eberhard, *Deutsche Pantheon*, 2, 1795 on Leibniz, especially 142f; *Philosophisches Archiv*, 1793, 2:1, 1-16, on Kantian teleology.
55. H.A. Allison trans. and ed., *The Kant-Eberhard controversy*, Johns Hopkins, 1973.
56. H.-J. de Vleeschauer, *The development of Kantian thought*, (trans. A.R.C. Duncan), Nelson, 1962, p.140-165.
57. CPR A 314, b 862; KW 8, 250 on Kant's 'genuine apologia' for Leibniz.
58. KW 7, 253-272; ET by M Despland, pp.283-297 of his *Kant on history and religion*, McGill-Queen's U.P., 1973; this is the first modern translation of this essay; the first was by John Richardson in 1798.
59. Beattie, *Essay*, p.115, p.120.
60. J. Butler, *The analogy of religion*, (1736), the introduction, para.4: '... it follows, that in questions of difficulty, or such as are thought so, where more satisfactory evidence cannot be had, or is not seen; if the result of examination be, that there appears upon the whole, any of the

lowest presumption on one side, and none on the other, or a greater presumption on one side, though in the lowest degree greater; this determines the question, even in matters of speculation; and in matters of practice, will lay us under an absolute and formal obligation, in point of prudence and of interest, to act upon that presumption or low probability, though it be so low as to leave the mind in very great doubt which is the truth. For surely a man is as really bound in prudence to do what upon the whole appears, according to the best of his judgement, to be for his happiness, as what he certainly knows to be so. Nay further, in questions of great consequence, a reasonable man will think it concerns him to remark lower probabilities and presumptions than these; such as amount to no more than shewing one side of a question to be as supposable and credible as the other: nay, such as but amount to much less even than this. For numberless instances might be mentioned respecting the common pursuits of life, where a man would be thought, in a literal sense, distracted, who would not act, and with great application too, not only upon an even chance, but upon much less, and where the probability or chance was greatly against his succeeding'.

61. Beattie, *Essay*, p.121-2.
62. Beattie, *Essay*, p.389.
63. Cf. CPR B850-B859; H. Scott Holland, 'The optimism of Butler's 'Analogy'; Romanes Lecture, Clarendon, 1908.
64. KW 5, 481; Meredith C.T.J. p.159.
65. J.G. Fichte, *Critique of all revelation*, (trans. G. Green), C.U.P., 1978.
66. KW 18, 6087.
67. Zweig, *Correspondence*, pp.79-80.
68. KW 7, 265-266; Despland p.292.
69. KW 6, 185-190, 'Concerning the guide of conscience in matters of faith', which includes, p.186 an allusion to Bayle's problem' text, Lk.14, 23, 'Go out into the highways and compel them to come in'. ET T.M. Greene and H.H. Hudson, *Religion within the limits of reason alone*, Harper, 1960, pp.173-178.
70. KW 8, 266; Despland p.293.
71. One of the most interesting reactions to Kant on the subject of theodicy at this point came from Salomon Maimon; cf. ed. B. Verra, his *Gesammelte Werke*, Olms, 1965, 3, 309-332. As well as Atlas' book on Maimon, cf. that of S.H. Bergman, *The philosophy of Salomon Maimon*, Goldberg, 1967. And Brunschwig, *Enlightenment and romanticism*, pp.249-282; E. Sagarra, *A social history of Germany, 1648-1914*, Holmes & Meier, 1977, pp.156-163; J. Allerhand, *Das Judentum in der Aufklärung*, Fromann-holzboog, 1980, p.51f.
72. Cf. Eberhard's comments in the *Philosophisches Archiv*, 1793, 1:2,

34-47 on Kant's failure to make an alliance between Protestantism and philosophy.
73. Book three is entitled 'The victory of the good over the evil principle, and the founding of a kingdom of God on earth'; and book four, 'Concerning service and pseudo-service under the sovereignty of the good principle, or, concerning religion and clericalism', in which occurs the subsection on conscience.
74. Cf. Zweig, *Correspondence*, pp.205-206, Kant's spirited letter to Staüdlin.
75. KW 7, 1-116. The ET by M.J. Gregor, *The conflict of the faculties*, Abaris 1979 gives the translation on the page facing the reprinted German text.
76. KW 7, 60.
77. S.W. Sykes, p.101 of his essay 'Theological study: the nineteenth century and after', pp.95-118 of B. Hebblethwaite and S. Sutherland eds., *The philosophical frontiers of Christian theology: essays presented to D.M. MacKinnon*, C.U.P., 1982.
78. Crumbach records him with J.F. Schleussner as editing the *Göttingische Bibliothek der neuesten theologischen Literatur*, 1794-1801. Cf. O. Kaiser, 'Kants Anweisung zur Auslegung der Bibel: Ein Beitrag zur Geschichte der Hermeneutik', pp.75-90 of G. Müller and W. Zeller, eds., *Glaube, Geist, Geschichte:* Festschrift für Ernst Benz, Brill, 1967.
79. E.g. Zweig, *Correspondence* p.220 from Biester; cf. his 1766 letter to Mendelssohn, p.54; Reiss p.2 gives other references.
80. H.A. Salmony, *Kants Schrift'Das Ende Aller Dinge'*, Evz-Verlag, 1962; KW 7, 325-40; ET in *On history*, pp.69-84.
81. KW 7, 338; *On history*, pp.82-3.
82. KW 7, pp.9-10.
83. KW 8, 273-313, especially part 3, 'On the relation of theory to practice in international law - a general-philanthropic, i.e. cosmopolitan view'; ET E.B. Ashton, *On the old saw: that may be right in theory but it won't work in practice*, Pennsylvania U.P., 1974; and in H. Reiss, ed., *Kant's political writings*, (trans. H.B. Nisbet) C.U.P., 1979. Cf. Hagen, *Germans, Poles and Jews*, p.48f; N. Davies, *God's playground: a history of Poland*, Clarendon, 1981, 1, 519-546: G. Ritter, 'The Prussian statesmen of the reconstruction era and the Polish question', pp.201-213 of A. Brackmann ed., trans. S.M. Bouton, *Germany and Poland in their historical relations*, Oldenbourg, 1934.
84. KW 6, 320-322; ET J. Ladd, *The metaphysical elements of justice* (part 1 of *The metaphysic of morals* of 1797) Bobbs-Merrill, 1965, pp.87-88. Cf. KW 6, 188; Greene/Hudson, pp.176-177; H. Arendt, *On revolution*, Penguin, 1973, pp.21-58.
85. W. Hubatsch, *Hohenzollern in der Deutschen Geschichte*,

Athenaum, 1961, p.60-77.
86. G. Ritter, *Stein: eine politische biographie*, Deutsche-Verlags-Anstalt, 1958, p.74f; W. Hubatsch, *Die Stein-Hardenbergschen Reformen*, Wissenschaftliche Buchgesellschaft 1977; W. Hubatsch, Der Reichsfreiherr Karl vom Stein und Immanuel Kant', pp.1328-1345 of *Moderne Preussische Geschichte*, 3; for Kant's influence on Clausewitz cf. Paret, p.149f; and on the reform from a different point of view, H. Rosenberg, *Bureaucracy, aristocracy and autocracy : the Prussian experience 1660-1815*, Harvard U.P., 1958, p.190f.
87. There is a U.S. Library Association 1932 edition of the first London translation, with a short preface by N.M. Butler. Cf. Bruns, *Kant et l'Europe*, p.248; Charles Villers (de la Societé royale des sciences de Göttingue) *Philosophie de Kant, ou principles fondamentaux de la Philosophie Transcendentale*, Collignon, 1801. He had also in 1798 published his translation of Kant's 1784 *Idea for a universal history* from the *Berlinische Monatsschrift*, and later wrote the introduction to a new edition of Mme. la Baronne de Staël-Holstein's *de l'Allemagne*, Brockhaus, 1814. Cf. p.81, p.177f for its recommendation of what Kant had to say about moral dignity and the accord of all the faculties, and E. Cassirer, *Rousseau, Kant, Goethe*, trans. J. Gutmann, P.C. Kristeller, J.H. Randall, Princeton U.P. 1963, p.64f on Goethe's reactions to the *Critique of Judgment*.
88. W.B. Gallie, *Philosophers of peace and war; Kant, Clausewitz, Marx, Engels and Tolstoy*, C.U.P., 1978; K. Jaspers, 'Kant's "Perpetual Peace" ', pp.88-125 of *Philosophy and the world*, Gateway, 1963; F.H. Hinsley, *Power and the pursuit of peace*,C.U.P., 1963, pp.62-80.
89. KW 8, 313; ET of 'Perpetual peace: a philosophical sketch' is in Reiss, pp.93-130. Cf. K. Löwith, *Meaning in history*, Phoenix Press, 1967, p.119.
90. It was Beck to whom Kant sent the first version of the introduction to the *Critique of Judgement*, Zweig, *Correspondence*, p207-8. E.T. is by J. Haden, *First Introduction to the Critique of Judgements* Bobbs-Merrill, 1965. Cf. M.E. Mayer, *Das Verhältnis des Sigismund Beck zu Kant, Winter, 1896*. Beck ended up as a professor of metaphysics in Rostock, where W. Dilthey identified the Kant material forty-nine years after Beck's death: 'Die Rostocker Kanthandschriften', *Archiv für Geschichte der Philosophie*, 2, 1889, 592-650. Cf. R.A. Makkreel, *Dilthey: philosopher of the human studies*, Princeton U.P., 1975, p.224f; G. Lehmann, *Beiträge zur Geschichte und Interpretation der Philosophie Kants*, de Gruyter, 1969, pp.3-26.
91. R. Wellek, *Immanuel Kant in England*, Princeton U.P., 1931, pp.3-21.
92. A. Poschmann, 'Die Ersten Kantianer in England', pp.470-486 of ed. E. Bahr, *Studien zur Geschichte des Preussenlandes: Festschrift für*

Erich Keyser, Elwert, 1963.
93. KW 5, 161. ET T.K. Abbott, *Kant's Critique of practical reason and other works on the theory of ethics*, Longmans, 1967.

PART II : 1
BAYLE AND LEIBNIZ

To appreciate Kant's concern with the topic of theodicy it is useful to be reminded of some of the sources of stimulus to the debate about it during his lifetime,[1] for the enterprise of writing a justification of the deity's dealings with his creation has rarely lacked those who would undertake it and those who would criticise the very possibility of such an undertaking. Pierre Bayle was one of the most significant of these critics at the end of the seventeenth century.[2] Bayle was living in Rotterdam as a French Calvinist refugee when he produced the notorious *Dictionnaire Historique et Critique*[3] (1697). Some of the articles of the *Dictionary* were to prompt the production of Leibniz' *Théodicée*[4] (1710). The latter word itself seems to have been coined by Leibniz to refer to the cluster of arguments marshalled from a diversity of sources in response to Bayle. Bayle had been interested in Leibniz' work at least since 1686, and the two had communicated their views to one another not only through the obvious means of private correspondence but also through the journals which were already an important feature of intellectual exchange.

Much of the discussion had been about Leibniz' metaphysical worldview, which seemed to Bayle to defeat both intellect and imagination. Although reflected in the *Theodicy*, this was not there Leibniz' main concern. Both shared an interest in William King's *De Origine Mali*[5] of 1697. However, for Leibniz, it was Bayle's *Dictionary* articles which had to be discussed, since material could be drawn from them which entirely dissolved rationally grounded confidence in the deity. Bayle was already well-known as a critic by the time the *Dictionary* came out, and his work had established some features of his critical method, especially his determination to clarify what purported to be evidence in relation to the particular questions under discussion. He was determined not to say more than was warranted by the evidence, and was deeply suspicious of systematization, hating both dogmatism, and the cruelties of some dogmatic men. Certainly he was aware that any work he produced would be thoroughly scrutinised, since Jurieu the theologian who was originally his patron, had become his major enemy, and was alert to the damage which Bayle's scepticism might do to the orthodoxy Jurieu represented.

In 1693, Jurieu had managed to dislodge Bayle from his teaching position at the Protestant Academy in Rotterdam, using material culled from some of Bayle's earlier work to support a charge of atheism. Jurieu had some support from the civil authorities because of what he was able to interpret as Bayle's dangerous political ideas. Jurieu was busy promoting the image of William of Orange as a second David, whereas Bayle and his friends saw Jurieu as someone who was destroying the distinctive character and achievement of seventeenth-century French Calvinism, increasingly attached as it was to an interpretation of Scripture which would not allow scriptural warrants to be employed to serve current political and military adventures. A major point for Bayle in the article on 'David' was that it was 'of great concern to true religion that the lives of the Orthodox be judged by the general concepts of right and order'.[6] Jurieu's attacks on Bayle had turned the *Dictionary* into an instrument of controversy, hence the appearance of the articles on 'David' the 'Manichees', 'Paulicians' (other Manichees), and 'Pyrrho', concerned with a method of disputation which issued in suspense of judgment. Reason might be weak for the purposes of speculative reason and for the construction of systematic theology, but it was to remain a satisfactory guide where morality was at stake. Attempts were made to get Bayle to revise these articles, but he maintained that his subscribers would not buy the second edition unless they could purchase the original articles included in the first edition. The only major concession he made was to cut the article on 'David', and to add four clarificatory articles to the second edition.

Extracts from the *Dictionary* reveal Bayle's distress over the way in which evil is woven into the entire cosmic texture. The exercise of making the extracts needs care because of Bayle's peculiar literary tactics. If he were to write in such a way as to deprive the orthodox of their theological comforts and make them re-think the character of their faith he had both to say enough to erode received opinion and also to protect himself from those who would harass him.[7] Having selected his topic, he presented his readers with his article, sometimes very briefly, added extensive footnotes, and cross-referenced both article and notes to other material in the volumes. It is not always easy to be entirely certain that it is Bayle's own opinion that is being cited. However, one may start with the assumption that God detests what Bayle detested, that God is good as Bayle understood the word. Thus Bayle wrote in 'Pyrrho':

our theologians tell us that God, having to choose between a world perfectly regulated, adorned with every virtue, and a world like ours, where sin and disorder predominate, preferred ours to the other as suiting better the interest of his glory. You are going to tell me that the duties of the creator should not be measured by our standards.

But if you do this, you fall into the nets of your adversaries. This is where they want you. Their major aim is to prove that the absolute nature of things is unknown to us and that we can know them only relatively. We do not know, they say, if sugar is sweet in itself. We know only that it appears sweet when it is placed on our tongues. We do not know if a certain action is righteous in itself and by its nature. We only believe that with regard to such a person, with respect to certain circumstances, it has the appearance of righteousness. But it is something in other respects and other relations.[8]

The 'orthodox' position was that 'The most certain and the clearest ideas of order teach us that a Being who exists by himself, who is necessary, who is eternal, must be one, infinite, all-powerful, and endowed with every kind of perfection'.[9] A further point related to this may be picked up from 'Paulicians', that 'since God gave being to his creatures as an effect of his goodness, he also gave them, in his role as a beneficent cause, all the perfections proper to each species'.[10] If that were true, the fact that there is opposition among the entities of the world 'fortified as much as one likes by what are called variations, disorders, irregularities of nature, cannot make half an objection against the unity, simplicity, and immutability of God',[11] since the created order declares God's glory, his power and his unity. However, Manicheism derived from what Bayle called a deep meditation on the state of man[12] in which suffering could be held to be the punishment for moral evil, a punishment which, 'far from being incompatible with the supremely good principle, necessarily flows from one of God's attributes, I mean that of justice, which is no less essential to man than God's goodness'.[13] Thus in 'Paulicians' one finds the proposition that God prepared 'all the misfortunes that can be conceived for the human race in this lifetime - plague, war, famine, pain, trouble - and after this life a hell in which almost all men will be eternally tormented in such a way that makes our hair stand on end when we read descriptions of it'.[14] There seemed for Bayle, to be no rationally satisfactory explanation of why man should sin, or of why his sin should involve such consequences as extreme physical pain.

In their perplexity, the Manicheans had proposed two principles of explanation rather than the one of Christian tradition. These principles have made an agreement that reciprocally limits their operations. The good one cannot do us all the good that it wishes to. It was necessary that in order to do us much good, it consented that its adversary do us as much harm; for without this agreement chaos would always have remained chaos, and no creature would ever have experienced what is good. Thus, the supreme goodness, finding a better means of satisfying itself in seeing the world sometimes happy and sometimes unhappy than in never seeing it happy, made an agreement that produced the mixture of good and evil that we find in the human world.[15]

Bayle's assessment was that 'the Manicheans, with a completely absurd and contradictory hypothesis, explain experiences a hundred times better than do the orthodox, with their supposition so just, so necessary, and so very true of an infinitely good and all-powerful first principle'.[16] The Manicheans' 'explanation' of experience is 'better' in the sense that they were not compelled, as the orthodox seemed to be, to compare God either 'to a father who allows his children to break their legs so that he can show everyone his great skill in mending their broken bones, or to a king who allows seditions and disorders to develop through his kindom so that he can gain glory by overcoming them'. For Bayle, the major issue was clear: 'The conduct of this father and this monarch is so contrary to the clear and distinct ideas by which we judge goodness and wisdom and in general all the duties of a father and a king, that our reason cannot conceive how God could act in this way'. Consequently to say 'the ways of God are not our ways'[17] was helpful only insofar as it directed attention to the fact that reason alone could not cope with the Manicheans. The orthodox position was to be considered

> as a truth of fact, clearly revealed; and since it must finally be admitted that the causes and the reasons for it cannot be understood, it would be better to say this from the outset, and stop there, and allow the objections of the philosophers to be considered as vain quibblings, and to oppose nothing to them but silence along with the shield of faith.[18]

Human experience, and a dualistic theology related to that experience, were not to be allowed to have the last word. But the orthodox could learn from the Manicheans, for example in assessing the notion that the suffering of pain, including the pains of hell, were of a short duration. He explained what he thought a Manichean would make of the suggestion.

> The first thing he might say is, that we do not find in our minds the idea of two sorts of goodness; one of which consists in making a present, whose bad effects are foreseen, without preventing them, though that is in the power of the giver; the other, in granting a favour of such a nature as will always be advantageous to the receiver. It is needless to observe, that by the idea of goodness we do not understand an imperfect sort of goodness, such as we meet with in the heart of a sinner; but a goodness which in a logical abstracted sense is clear of all failure. This ideal goodness is not a genus containing under it the two species just described. Its essential and distinguishing attribute is so to dispose its subject as to bestow favours, which by the shortest and surest means it can make use of, may render the condition of the receiver happy.[19]

So if God can abate man's punishment by pain, of which torment in hell is the extreme example, he can abate it immediately and not simply halve its duration or diminish it in some other proportion. As Bayle wrote, 'we can never rise from cruelty to infinite goodness by a bare diminution of cruelty'. There could not, in the infliction of such punishment, be any mistake on God's part.

We commend the exactness of a Clockmaker, if his pendulum does not err above two or three seconds in a year. But the exactness of an artificer infinitely perfect, absolutely excludes all exceptions; his holiness, his wisdom etc. are absolutely simple, and without any mixture of contrary qualities; I say, without the least mixture which can be conceived, or which can possibly exist in the nature of things.

On the other hand, Bayle would have no truck with any talk about God which, as he said, adopted the Manichean error of saving God's goodness at the expense of his power. He concluded that

both the ideas of experience and metaphysics concur in demonstrating, that to hurt anyone, though itbe for never so short a portion of time, and in order to procure him the greatest benefit is altogether incompatible with goodness, unless it be absolutely impossible to find out a straightpath to lead him from good to good in a constant and invariable manner.

If anyone were to enquire why this was not possible for the deity, Bayle would cite the 'maxim of Christian humility', that 'metaphysical notions ought not to be the rule, by which we are to judge of the conduct of God; but that we ought to conform ourselves to the oracles of the scripture'.[20] Rather Bayle would rely on those principles which could be extracted from scripture which laid 'the solid Foundation of the Providence, and Perfection of God'. The foundation principle was that God was creator of all things, and to this principle three subsidiary principles were to be connected. 'I. That with the most lawful Authority that can be, he disposes of the Universe as he thinks fit: II. That he needs only a single Act of his Will to do whatever he pleases: III. That nothing happens but what he has placed in the Plan of his work'. Whatever happens is subservient to 'the Ends he has proposed to himself from all Eternity, and which are the greatest Mysteries of the Gospel'.[21] This must indicate the character of his reply to Chrysippus' question, 'Did the Nature of Things, or the Providence that made the World and human kind, make also the Diseases, to which Men are subject?'[22] Thus he wrote with approval of Anaxagoras' inability to supply Socrates with what he described as absurd explanations, or explanations which would depend upon man's having insight into God's reasons for making the world as it is.

All that the greatest Philosophers can say upon this Occasion, amounts to this: That, since The Earth is round, and situated at such a Distance from the Sun;This figure and Situation were necessary to the Beauty and Symmetry of the Universe; the Author of this vast Machine having an infinite Intelligence, and Wisdom. From hence we know, in general, that everything is right in this Machine, and that there is no Defect in it: But, if we should undertake to make it appear, Piece by Piece, that everything is in the best State it could possibly be in, we should infallibly assign very wrong Reasons. As a particular illustration he noted, 'Would Sir Isaac Newton who has discovered so many Mathematical and Mechanical Beauties in the Heavens, pretend to warrant, that, if Things were not such, as he supposes them, as to Magnitude, Distances, and Velocities, the World would be an irregular Work, ill built, or ill contrived?'[23] For as Bayle asked 'Is not the Divine Understanding infinite? God has therefore the Ideas of the Infinity of Worlds, different from each other, all of them Beautiful, regular, and Mathematical, to the last Degree'. Creation is as it ought to be, but is one of a number of alternatives which would have been possible. It was precisely from what he took to be a correction of this point that Leibniz was to draw conclusions different from Bayle's about how much could be done to justify the deity's dealings with his creation.

Leibniz attempted to tackle the apparent absurdities of the othodox position, finding it a great fault in Bayle, gifted though he was,[24] that he not only chose to demonstrate the folly and pretension of humanity in his role as historian and critic, but also that he did not elaborate a justification of the deity in the face of evil as part of his recommendation of trust in divine providence. Leibniz' exposition depended above all upon a grasp of the 'rapport' which the divine attributes enjoyed one with another in creation. He did not see the deity of rationally defensible theology as a sort of cosmic Nero,[25] an aesthete who enjoyed the spectacle of pain. He wanted to banish this nightmare, and console Bayle for his grief over human life, which Bayle had expressed when he wrote that

> We are subject to pain and sorrow, two such terrible afflictions, that it is not to be decided which is most dreadful. The most vigorous health does not secure us from grief. For grief flows in upon us through a thousand channels, and is of the nature of *dense* bodies: it comprises a great deal of matter in a very small compass; evil is heaped up, crowded and pressed close in it. One hour's grief contains more evil, than there is good in six or seven pleasant days.[26]

Leibniz must have regretted that Bayle died before the publication of the *Theodicy*, of which Barth wrote that hardly 'a hundred years after the horrors and miseries of the Thirty Years War, there is sounded and sung to a finish a hymn in praise of the Creator' which had its part to play in relating the ecclesiastical and secular history of the day to the 'radiance of God'.[27] It is clear that the *Theodicy* was of particular importance for Leibniz, since it was the one major work of the many he produced by which he chose that his contemporaries and successors should remember him. It was the expression of his conviction that the deity in his goodness was to be adored without hesitation. It probably remained the most widely read of his works, even after more of his writings had been discovered and published or re-printed in the course of the century.[28]

Leibniz' response to the problem of theodicy was like that of Bayle a response of religious conscience, but was informed by what he believed to be a rational apprehension of the deity. He wanted intelligent and sensitive men to see the world as he believed the deity sees it. Certainly he enjoyed the exercise of 'the power of discursive, logical thought, of searching and of examination, of abstraction, of definition and drawing conclusions', but he also sought for 'understanding' in the sense of 'the simple vision to which truth offers itself like a landscape to the eye'.[29] In the search for that understanding, Leibniz maintained that there were three philosophical topics for examination, i.e., those of necessity, freedom, and the origin of evil, and three theological topics (by which he seems to have meant topics derived directly from reflection on scripture) - original sin, grace, and predestination. On careful examination one sees that it was his discussion of the first group which provided him with his method of dealing with the second group,[30] that is, none of the three theological topics seem to have been essential to theodicy so far as he himself was concerned, though their presentation in correlation with the philosophical triad was a necessary feature of his work as presented to the public.[31] There is no reason to doubt his intention to promote devotion to the deity, since he refers to the divine being in terms of delight, beauty, charm and great pleasure.[32]

Leibniz' view of things was of a reality which, contrary to Bayle, could be experienced and appreciated by man as an ordered goodness, a creation worthy of the deity of Christian faith. The world was not in itself a sufficient object of attention, but physical reality provided the data on which the mind reflected in order to understand certain principles, and in the light of these the world could be adequately described in a way which would give delight and satisfaction. To look at 'the structure and economy of the universe'[33] was but a preliminary which would lead to man's recognising things in all their intelligibility, in relation to the mind of God. To 'see' was to know *a priori* by 'cause'[34] for 'the mind is elevated by true reason to that which to us is invisible, but none the less sure'.[35]

To view the world in relation to the mind of God implies a confidence in the power of human reason of a kind which now seems impossible to sustain. For Leibniz, however, such confidence was integral to giving assent to the principle of the rationality of God, for man's rationality is a perfection 'shared' with God, from whom it is derived. Man's reason differs from God's 'as a drop of water differs from the ocean',[36] but 'the perfections of God are those of our souls'.[37] So Leibniz could speak of 'a close contemplation which grants us an enjoyment, so to speak, of the vision of the ideas of God'.[38] Faith, on this analysis, is the issue of the exercise of reason, for it is the 'assurance ... wherewith we can and ought to say that God has done all things well'.[39] There is an area of 'mystery', truth ultimately above man's reason, such as 'the miracles reserved for God alone, as for instance Creation; such is the choice of the order of the universe, which depends upon universal harmony, and upon the clear knowledge of an infinity of things at once'.[40] But given man's capacity to reflect on the truth of things he can think through to the eternal verities, which include first of all those truths which have a logical, metaphysical, or geometrical necessity, which cannot be denied without contradiction.[41] He can further analyse reality in terms of the principle of efficient causality,[42] and this leads him to realise that the existence of things as they are is not determined solely by logical reason, but by other considerations, both moral and teleological which can also be seen to be included in the concept of the 'eternal verities'. More specifically, the principle of determinant reason,[43] the principle of the best, was for Leibniz a simple but fruitful means of explaining why the things that now exist are what they are and why they occupy their place in the scheme of things.[44] It is the foundation of 'an infinitude of very just and very profitable arguments'.[45] Its application will eliminate any appearance of instability in the world, and any hint that anything exists by chance and is not controlled by God's creative providence.

Leibniz' God delights in his own self-sufficiency, for 'his bliss is ever perfect and can receive no increase, either from within or from without'.[46] In designing to create the world, he 'purposed solely to manifest and communicate his perfections in the way that was most efficacious, and most worthy of his greatness, his wisdom and his goodness'.[47] It is especially true that goodness will characterise his creatures, for 'God, as well as every wise and beneficent mind, is inclined towards all possible good, and ... this inclination is proportionate to the excellence of the good'.[48] This appetite to produce what is excellent results in the production of the world, 'the whole succession and the whole agglomeration of all existent things'.[49] The love of the best is for Leibniz 'the only impulse whose very exercise is absolutely infinite',[50] and if God did not make the best world, 'he would not himself be satisfied with his work, he would blame himself for its imperfection; and that conflicts with the supreme felicity of the divine nature'.[51]

God's goodness is the perfection of one of the three principles of the divine nature, will, understanding and power.[52] Just as God's will, with its perfection of goodness,[53] in relation to creation is determined by the best, so his understanding, with its perfection of wisdom, guides him 'to produce as much reason and knowledge in the universe as his plan can admit'.[54] God's consideration of the 'ideas' which have their source 'in' him[55] is an important matter for Leibniz. Leibniz does not endeavour to describe how God forms or thinks the vast range of ideas, all of which he thinks distinctly all the time,[56] but maintains only that 'the choice of the order of the universe'depends first of all upon 'the clear knowledge of an infinity of things at once'.[57] God's vision of unlimited possibility includes his being able to think of the 'possibles' intensively, making 'infinitely infinite combinations'[58] of them when considering the pattern of his creation. In other words he calculates and ponders on the best sequence of things, a whole set of creatures at once. His idea of one thing is brought to bear on his idea of another, for 'each thing *as an idea* has contributed, before its existence, to the resolution that had been made upon the existence of all things'.[59] It is in connection with God's sifting of the 'possibles' that Leibniz reached a crucial point in his attempt to construct a theodicy. He is clear that what he is offering is a re-interpretation of Platonism, and he therefore noted that 'the Region of the Eternal Verities must be substituted for matter when we are concerned with seeking out the source of things'.[60] He was consequently forced to say, that God's understanding 'furnishes the principles of evil, without being sullied by it, without being evil; it represents natures as they exist in the eternal verities; it contains within it the reason wherefore evil is permitted'.[61] So of the possibles Leibniz wrote that God 'penetrates them, compares them, weighs them one against the other, to estimate their degrees of perfection or imperfection, the strong and the weak, the good and the evil'.[62] What God seeks is a 'compossible' sequence of ideas, which means that not all the possibles will be actualised, not because some of them are unquestionably 'evil', but because they are not all compatible in one world order.

Clearly, it is Leibniz' understanding of this concept of the region of the Eternal Verities which is fundamental to his defence of God, and his explanation of how it is that God tolerates what seems to men to be outrageous and detestable. The status of the eternal verities in relation to God is ambiguous. Whilst they are in some undefined sense not identical with any of the principles of the divine being, it is on the other hand not appropriate to speak of them as created. They have no existence which could be said to be independent of God either before he considers them or in order that he may consider them. They are nevertheless meant to represent that which is right and valid for every possible world irrespective of whether God creates anything to correspond to them, i.e. truths which cannot be denied without contradiction. They are also, as already indicated, characterised by 'value' as well as by logical necessity.[63] The values that are maintained by Leibniz are those which are derived from his analysis of 'the principles of morals under terms that imply an obligation'.[64] It is justice that helps to interpret the meaning of God's goodness.[65] Riley[66] has drawn attention to the importance of this for Leibniz and writes of Leibniz' view of justice as charity tempered by a knowledge of what is deserved.[67] Charity, Riley maintains with reference to many of Leibniz' writings, is a habit of loving. Loving is understood as a feeling of perfection in others, perfection being both the cause of love and the reason that regulates that love.[68] God's generous benevolence, which Leibniz advocates for men in imitation of God, is inevitably an active benevolence. This raises a problem for Leibniz in that a justice which is the result of rationally informed choice, and the action consequent upon that choice is not altogether consistent with his notion of 'harmony' in so far as he interprets that in terms of proportion, of 'ratios as precise as any in mathematics'.[69] Consistency would require that all the eternal verities would have to be of the first group mentioned above - i.e. those truths which cannot be denied without contradiction. But as Riley points out, 'a justice of harmony and proportion alone presupposes an aesthetic passivity which fails to take Christian voluntarism into account'. However, justice is not simply a relation but an action, and action for Leibniz is an activity of a being whose choice has been rationally determined by the best that is in view.[70]

A serious problem here is the question of whether or not Leibniz so described the next 'stage' in God's deliberations as to result in his offering a re-construction of Manicheism in his efforts to cope with the problem as Bayle set it. In a sense it reflects the religious courage of those who cannot, and would not wish to, deny the presence of evils in the world. Such men are bold enough to attribute them to God in some sense, as part of the consequence of belief in his omnipotent creator, and yet want to maintain that the word 'good' when used of God is not purely equivocal.[71] Perhaps this was Leibniz' way of coping with what seems to have been one of Bayle's major points - that *a priori* argument alone was without force when confronted with the facts of physical evil. Certainly Leibniz was not trying to defend an *a priori* argument which would purport to show that evil was impossible in a world which was God's work. The reverse is true - what he offered was an *a priori* argument which maintains that evil, understood in a certain kind of way, is necessary to a world which is God's work. What is involved in God's deliberation leading to the choice of the best sequence is the interaction of the principles of God's being with the reign of the eternal verities and the consequent production of the universe, - the eternal verities regulate divine as well as creaturely thought and action. Leibniz' difficulties were evidenced when he wrote that 'as soon as God has decreed to create something there is a struggle between all the possibles, all of them laying claim to existence, and that those which, being united, produce most reality, most perfection, most significance carry the day'. The position is hardly helped when he immediately endeavoured to avoid the 'region' metaphor and went on: 'It is true that this struggle can be only ideal, that is to say, it can only be a conflict of reasons in the most perfect understanding, which cannot fail to act in the most perfect way, and consequently to choose the best'.[72] But he usually wrote as though God's choice of the best is determined by something other than himself, with the 'possibles' providing their own reason for actualisation, when considered as included in a particular sequence or system as compared with other sequences. This is despite his having also to maintain that the essences do not contain within themselves their own springs of productive power and self-movement, which are the marks of a created being, separate from the being of God. He could then be criticised with some justice for including in the very concept of godhead the conflict between originative principles which was characteristic of Manicheism.

There seem, indeed, to be two kinds of conflict going on in connection with God's creative activity. One is the conflict among the possibles, and the other, to be looked at shortly, is a conflict in the very will of God, and this especially lends weight to the accusation that what he is offering is a kind of Manicheism. The fact that there is any conflict is what makes the difficulty, and it is reasonable to ask whether Leibniz ever satisfactorily resolved the problem he set himself. It is questionable whether any resolution of the problem as he posed it is possible, and whether he would not have done better to abandon the discussion when it reached this particular stage of intractibility. However, to conclude the description of what he says about the conflict amongst the 'possibles' one must also notice that Leibniz has both to deny that he must admit 'a brute and blind necessity in the cause of the existence of things'[73] and assert that God acts from necessity. This alone guarantees the goodness of the world and will silence those who think that God could have done better. The necessity which determines God is a 'happy' or 'moral' necessity. 'God chose between different courses all possible: thus, metaphysically speaking, he could have chosen or done what was not the best; but he could not morally speaking have done so'.[74] So freedom for Leibniz is not the licence to be unreasonable,[75] but to be wise enough to will only the good, and powerful enough to give effect to that will. 'The wise mind wills only the good: is it then a servitude when the will acts in accordance with wisdom? And can one be less a slave than to act by one's own choice in accordance with the most

perfect reason?'[76] And of God he wrote:
> For either God will act through a vague indifference and at random, or again he will act on caprice or through some other passion, or finally must act through a prevailing inclination of reason which prompts him to the best. But passions, which come from the confused perception of an apparent good, cannot occur in God; and vague indifference is something chimerical. It is therefore only the strongest reason that can regulate God's choice. It is an imperfection in our freedom that makes us capable of choosing evil instead of good, a greater evil instead of the lesser evil, the lesser good instead of the greater good. That arises from the appearances of good and evil, which deceive us; whereas God is always prompted to the true and the greatest good, that is, to the absolutely true good, which he cannot fail to know.[77]

God is therefore essentially free either to create or not to create, and effectively free in that there is no imbalance between his knowledge and his power.[78]

God's toleration of such evils in the world is therefore not to his discredit, and Leibniz' boldness in being prepared to make this point at least protects him from the charge of offering a facile optimism. For the moment one can note one important analogy he offered as an alternative to some of Bayle's to help his readers, though he knew how dangerous such analogies can be. Leibniz considered that

> there are causes where one will justifiably prefer beauty of construction in a palace to the convenience of a few domestics. But I admit that the construction would be bad, however beautiful it might be, if it were a cause of diseases to the inhabitants; provided it was possible to make one that would be better, taking into account beauty, convenience and health altogether. It may be indeed, that one cannot have all these advantages at once. Thus, supposing one wished to build on the northern and more bracing side of the mountain, if the castle were then bound to be of an unendurable construction, one would prefer to make it face southward.[79]

What this means in terms of an explanation of God's toleration of evil in his original creative act, emerges in his distinguishing a threefold function of God's will. The result of this distinction is to make evil an integral part of the pattern of things, though Leibniz was somewhat uneasy with the result of his discussion. He distinguishes between God's antecedent, mediate, and consequent will. God's antecedent will considers 'each good separately in the capacity of a good'.[80] Acts of his antecedent will are described as 'love of virtue and hatred of vice, which tend in an undefined way to bring virtue into existence and to prevent the existence of vice'.[81] To produce the decision on the basis of a defined choice seems to be the function of the 'mediate' will, which operates at an intermediate stage between God's consideration of things separately and his willing the best sequence into existence.[82] At this stage in the creative programme God compares all the possible combinations of essence and chooses the best sequence. He thereby excludes an infinite number of essences from actualisation and opts for a sequence in which there is a concomitance[83] of what is good, to which God is 'antecedently' attracted, together with some of the essences from which he is antecedently averted. 'The supreme goodness of God causes his antecedent will to repel all evil, but moral evil more than any other: it only admits evil at all for irresistible superior reasons, and with great correctives which repair its ill effects to good advantage'.[84] Of this 'decree to create the best'[85] Leibniz wrote: 'success entire and infallible belongs only to the *consequent will*, as it is called. This it is which is complete; and in regard to it this rule obtains, that one never fails to do what one wills when one has the power. Now this consequent will, final and decisive, results from the conflict of all the antecedent wills, of those which tend towards good, even as of those which repel evil; and from the concurrence of all these particular wills comes the total will'.[86]

Despite the conflict in the region of the verities, and the conflict in the will of God in relation to the verities, there are no flaws in the actual production of the world. 'It is therefore not to be wondered at that he who penetrates all things at one stroke should always strike true at the outset; and it must not be said that he succeeds without the guidance of any cognition. On the contrary, it is because his knowledge is perfect that his voluntary actions are also perfect'.[87] The flawless production of the world depends upon the exercise of God's power, the third principle of God's being, on the basis of which the other two have their efficacy. Power 'precedes even understanding and will, but it operates as the one displays it and the other requires it'.[88] It is indeterminate, and God's goodness and wisdom combined determine him to produce the best.[89] Leibniz emphasised this when he wrote, 'I set no bounds to God's power, since I recognize that it extends *ad maximum, ad omnia*, to all that implies no contradiction; and I set none to his goodness, since it attains to the best, *ad optimum*'.[90]

To conclude what he had to say about God's power, one may return to his analogy, where he remarked that God is

> like a great architect whose aim in view is the satisfaction of the glory of having built a beautiful palace, and who considers all that is to enter into this construction: the form and the material, the place, the situation, the means, the workmen, the expense, before he forms a complete resolve. For a wise person laying his plans cannot separate the end from the means; he does not contemplate any end without knowing if there are means of attaining thereto.[91]

One may note in passing that since actual existence is not an essence which God 'saw' in the region of the eternal verities and, as it were, added to a sequence of essences,[92] God's creative act of will rather transposes the chosen sequence into a new mode of being, separate from the existence which he himself enjoys, and this therefore defines the chosen sequence as 'imperfect'. 'Existence' is not finally intelligible to man because of its necessary connotation of 'imperfection'. This coheres with the one other way in which it is not intelligible, which arises from Leibniz' more *a posteriori* description of the world. Neither from an *a priori* approach nor from the *a posteriori* description of things which coheres with that *a priori* view would Leibniz concede a point to anyone who wishes to argue that it is by no means clear that the existing world is all right because of the evils found in it. He wanted to maintain, that it is all right, despite what seem to us to be outrageous evils, - not that it has been all right, has gone wrong, and will be put right again; nor that it is not all right but will be made so at some future time. With regard to this very last point he may be said to have left himself some loopholes, which will be noticed later, though he could hardly make much of them in the light of what he maintained as the major points of his defence of God.

A.O. Lovejoy in his book *The great chain of being*[93] retrieved for modern readers a traditional way of looking at the world which was still familiar to Leibniz and open to be rephrased by him. M.-D. Chenu has written more about it, especially in its medieval flowering when it suited admirably the needs of the contemplative and scientist alike. He quotes A.J. Festugière, on the world as

> truly an 'order', a kosmos. To be sure, disorder is found within it, not, however, as an essentially evil thing, but only as a lesser good. There could be no 'order' without a multiplicity of beings, each consequently limited; or without a diversity of beings, each consequently endowed with a greater or smaller share of goodness. If, therefore, one considers only a part of the whole, one necessarily discovers limits or privations of goodness, disorders. But this is precisely because one is looking only at a part, not the whole. If one makes the effort to comprehend the whole into a single view, the disorder disappears; it becomes explicable within the whole and becomes absorbed into the total order. Always look to the whole - such will be the rule of this self-consciously optimistic philosophy.[94]

When Leibniz looks to the whole, his *a posteriori* examination of the things in the world is a complement to that inspection of things which enables us to recognise them in their intelligibility. For him, the distinct knowledge which alone satisfies is not knowledge of the material and changeable as such but of the causes or principles of things, of 'what is always'. To describe the world in terms of an *a posteriori* theology is merely to 'believe', to judge by effects,[95] in contrast with 'seeing', which is to know *a priori*, by cause. A satisfactory justification of God produced by the true correlation of the intellect with the world must involve sustained thinking in this *a priori* mode, and for Leibniz this takes shape in his 'monadology'. Things are pre-established by God, in this presentation, to exist in harmony with one another as a single whole, composed as they are of an infinity of individual substances or 'monads' variously arranged so as to represent to the human mind the variety, order and beauty we are moved to acknowledge. Leibniz' vital clue to the construction of this *a priori* intelligible world is rational human self-conscious individuality. Given the text of the *Monadology* (published in 1714) it is perfectly possible to work through the text of the *Theodicy* and put together the material which one recognises as corresponding to the *Monadology*, but in the *Theodicy* this material is somewhat in the background and appears there as an accidental result of Bayle's interest in this area of Leibniz' philosophy. So although Leibniz would finally want to rest his case on his demonstration of nature as made up of individual substances arranged to form the hierarchy of being, thereby understanding the world in detail as a world worthy of God, one sees that in the *Theodicy* this is not the kind of justification of God of which Leibniz preferred to make use in this 'public' work. One would have to say of him that he rather had recourse to what for him were inevitably more superficial arguments, *a posteriori* arguments.

With regard to his *a posteriori* argument, as with his *a priori* argument, one finds that it is closely underpinned by his trust in God at points where argument could do no more. In the light of what he has said about the concomitance of the possibles God has chosen, Leibniz could therefore emphasise the evidence of the co-existence of things. 'For it must be known that all things are *connected* in each one of the possible worlds: the universe, whatever it may be, is all of a piece, like an ocean: the least movement extends its effect there to any distance whatsoever, even though this effect becomes less perceptible in proportion to the distance'.[96] The harmony of things led him to say that God is therefore 'infinitely more skilful than a watchmaker, who himself makes machines and automata that are capable of producing as wonderful effects as if they possessed intelligence'.[97] God has made of matter 'the most excellent of all possible machines'[98] but it is not a machine properly speaking,[99] nor does God abandon it to its own devices. Leibniz maintained that 'there is organism everywhere in a matter whose disposition proceeds from God',[100] and the nature of every creature is that 'which God conveys to it in creating it always'.[101] This relationship of dependence Leibniz also described as 'continued creation'[102] maintaining that 'God gives ever to the creature and produces continually all that in it is positive, good and perfect, every perfect gift coming from the Father of Lights'.[103]

There is rich variety of creatures in God's world and this is also a reflection of God's ingenuity and wisdom. 'To multiply one and the same thing only would be superfluity, and poverty too. To have a thousand well-bound Vergils in one's library, always to sing the airs from the opera of Cadmus and Hermione, to break all the china in order to have cups of gold, to have only diamond buttons, to eat nothing but partridges, to drink only Hungarian or Shiraz wine - would one call that reason'?[104] The variety of things is, however, ordered hierarchically. 'There are degrees among creatures. The general order requires it'.[105] To quote Chenu again: 'The key to the understanding of the universe and of man in the universe, was taken to be the ordered, dynamic, and progressive chain of all being, - a chain in which causality and meaning fall together, and in which each being is a 'theophany', a revelation of God'.[106] What Leibniz understood by the 'chain' of things he spelled out by saying that 'The connexion and order of things bring it about that the body of every animal and of every plant is composed of other animals and of other plants, or of other living and organic beings: consequently there is subordination, and one body, one substance serves the other: thus their perfection cannot be equal'.[107] The division of the continuum to infinity[108] as he put it, ensured that he could rule out a defect which would be called the *'vacuum formarum*, a gap in the order of species'.[109]

A reading of Chenu once more makes it clear that Leibniz is still very much a representative of an influential tradition of interpretation. Chenu writes of the continuity of beings that it is

at once dynamic and static in principle. Between each of these beings in their separate ranks exists an intimate bond: the greater intensity of the superior being exerts an attractive force upon the one next below it and draws it upward toward its own higher level; and out of this attraction arises the fulfilment of the lower being ... We are far from a discontinuous universe in which each being possesses its dynamism and intelligibility wholly and only within itself ... such continuity in the universe does not compromise the intrinsic law operative at each level, the proper autonomy of each being: it does not infringe the purity of natures of essences.[110]

When one returns to the *Theodicy* one finds that Leibniz picked up part of one of Bayle's discussions with an opponent about whether creatures are 'eternally, immutably and essentially as perfect and as good as they can be'.[111] Leibniz insisted that things are different in their degree, i.e. in their place in the hierarchy of things, but would not want to say that 'a thing cannot change its kind in relation to good or evil'. So he could say, 'Thus the best may be changed into another which neither yields to it nor surpasses it; but there will always be an order among them, and that the best order possible'. Whereas the whole sequence may be the best possible, 'what exists through the universe in each portion of time' may not be the best. 'It might be therefore that the universe became even better and better, if the nature of things were such that it was not permitted to attain to the best all at once', but sensibly concluded, 'these are problems of which it is hard for us to judge',[112] though was prepared to concede that 'It is perhaps not impossible that there be somewhere a species of animals much resembling man and more perfect than we are. It may be even that the human race will attain in time to a greater perfection that that which we can now envisage'.[113]

Whilst the universe as a whole is stable, this stability is not displayed in a rigid pattern, since it is essentially organic in character:

As for the so called creation of the accidents, who does not see that one needs no creative power in order to change place or shape, to form a square or a column, or some other parade-ground figure, by the movement of the soldiers who are drilling; or again to fashion a statue by removing a few pieces from a block of marble; or to make some figure in relief, by changing, decreasing or increasing a piece of wax? The production of modifications has never been called *creation*, and it is an abuse of terms to scare the world thus. God produces substances from nothing, and the substances produce accidents by the change of their limits.[114]

In connection with 'substance' Leibniz stressed 'action' - the striving peculiar to it, 'called 'force' , 'effort', 'conatus', from which action itself must follow if nothing prevents it'.[115] This striving seems to be relevant to the empirical-metaphysical analysis of creatures that corresponds to the struggle amongst the possibles in God's understanding, before his choice of the best sequence for creation. The degree of striving proper to each creature is one of the characteristics which places it in its position in the hierarchy of being, because it relates to its degree of perfection. Hence Leibniz employed the Aristotelian term 'entelechy'[116] meaning by it in Farrer's words: 'active principle of wholeness or completion in an individual thing'.[117]

Leibniz had to turn from his fascinated contemplative vision of the world teeming with God's creatures in their hierarchy to focus on some analysis of evil. Whilst Leibniz in some respects cut man down to size in his estimate of his position and importance in the order of things,[118] he made a revealing comment when he said that 'an evil will is in its department what the evil principle of the Manicheans would be in the universe; and reason, which is an image of the Divinity, provides for evil souls great means of causing much evil. One single Caligula, one Nero, has caused more evil than an earthquake. An evil man takes pleasure in causing suffering and destruction, and for that there are only too many opportunities'.[119] He was deeply perturbed by the evil perpetrated by human beings, and sought for explanations in terms of metaphysical evil which would provide the context for his discussion of moral evil as well as for the discussion of physical evil. Metaphysical evil is simply to fall short of divine perfection,[120] to be less wise, less good, less powerful than God - i.e. to be a creature. Leibniz alludes briefly to the 'explanation' of evil as 'privation'[121] relating this to the scholastic description of evil as 'deficient'[122] in order to rule out the possibility of giving some sort of 'status' to the evil principle of the Manicheans. He developed a 'parable' about evil understood as 'imperfection', of boats going downstream with the current, some more heavily laden than others, therefore travelling down river at varying speeds. The sluggishness and inertia of the various vessels are compared with the 'natural imperfection' of creatures, essential to their location in the order of things.[123] This kind of parable is particularly helpful when he came to tackle the question of moral evil in so far as that can be attributed to ignorance, though such human frailty need not lead to offences against God.[124] Human happiness and indeed virtue are only two of the many goods which attract God, and Leibniz was driven to say that virtue 'is not the only good quality of creatures. There are innumerable others which attract the inclination of God: from all these inclinations there results the most possible good, and it turns out that if there were only virtue, if there were only rational creatures, there would be less good.[125]

From this point of view, the cause of physical suffering in men is first of all their own moral evil. 'One suffers because one has acted; one suffers evil because one does evil'.[126] Physical evil is a penalty established by God as part of the harmony of all things. Yet Leibniz had to face the problem of 'innocent' suffering:[127] 'It is true that one often suffers through the evil actions of others; but when one has no part in the offence one must look upon it as a certainty that these sufferings prepare for us a greater happiness'.[128] The fundamental point for which Leibniz was prepared to argue was that according to his view of God's plan, it was essential that 'there should not be lacking here on earth a rational animal clothed in flesh and bones, whose structure involves susceptibility to pain'.[129] Leibniz stressed often enough that God could never be described as negligent or casual in his dealings with his creation, even with those parts of it which are not conscious of him: 'God does not neglect inanimate things: they do not feel, but God feels for them ... He would reproach himself for the slightest actual defect there were in the universe even though it were perceived of none'.[130] God feels concern for animals also, though their pleasures and pain are not so keen as they are in man. According to

Leibniz, it is reflection that makes pain a misery, and without it pain is inconsiderable.[131] But he commented: 'When God justified to the Prophet Jonah the pardon that he had granted to the inhabitants of Nineveh, he even touched upon the interests of the beasts who would have been involved in the ruin of this great city'.[132] His attitude was that since susceptibility to pain is a consequence of enjoying existence in a material universe, and since we have been given this kind of existence as a gift of God, we must conclude that to be without it would have involved the presence of a still greater evil, or of a greatly diminished capacity for pleasure. He wrote of the 'pleasures of the senses when these are mingled with that which borders on pain':

> A little acid, sharpness or bitterness is often more pleasing than sugar; shadows enhance colours; and even a dissonance in the right place gives relief to harmony. We wish to be terrified by rope-dancers on the point of falling and we wish that tragedies shall well-nigh cause us to weep. Do men relish health enough, or thank God enough for it, without ever having been sick? And is it not most often necessary that a little evil render the good more discernible, that is to say, greater?[133]

The very pain of physical creatures, together with monstrosities and apparent irregularities;[134] is an indispensable feature of God's ordering of things. It is therefore not in itself, anymore than is anything else that could be cited, an indication that the world is not worthy of God as Leibniz believed him to be. Just as a mathematician can make sense of a series of apparently irregular numbers, and give the equation and construction of a twisting and turning line, so the order of creatures is within God's comprehension and intention.[135] Leibniz' brief references in the *Theodicy* to the study of geology and astronomy made his point that even various disasters in fact were for the purpose of making the globe fit for occupation by man.[136] He did not, however, make the mistake of trying to account for every particular evil, except in so far as he argued that it was sufficient for him 'to point out that there is nothing to prevent the connexion of a certain individual evil with what is best on the whole'. However, he added that 'This incomplete explanation, leaving something to be discovered in the life to come, is sufficient for answering the objections, though not for a comprehension of the matter'.[137]

He also endeavoured to put evil as he understood it into perspective in an aesthetic sense. God turns everything, even human evil, to serve his ends. 'God, by a wonderful art, turns all the errors of these little worlds to the greater adornment of his great world. It is as in those devices of perspective, where certain beautiful designs look like mere confusion until one restores them to the right angle of vision or one views them by means of a certain glass or mirror. It is by placing and using them properly that one makes them serve as adornment for a room'.[138] The power of this kind of argument has been well expressed by Richard Rees:

> The painter has to go out and meet and make contact with something that is not himself. This attempt to react to one's visual impressions has a strangely cleansing and releasing effect, because it seems to transport one into a world beyond good and evil, a world in which everything has equal value because everything is equally worth reacting to and studying. This is not literally true of course. Some things are more interesting and beautiful to look at than others. Nevertheless, it is roughly true that almost anything is worth drawing or painting.[139]

Leibniz' final position was expressed when he affirmed that 'One must judge the works of God as wisely as Socrates judged those of Heraclitus in these words: What I understood thereof pleases me: I think that the rest would please me no less if I understood it'.[140]

Allen has distinguished between Leibniz' overall theodicy which rests on his argument that this is the best of all possible worlds[141] and Leibniz' specific arguments and distinctions to rebut various objections to the divine credit. As Allen comments, these arguments and distinctions are no more than a miscellany serving the purpose of enabling someone to retain the conviction of the divine wisdom and goodness. Such a conviction is in part prompted and supported by appreciation of the complexity, variety and order of the universe, and is not destroyed by the evaluation of experience in tems of good and evil. Further, as Ahern noted,[142] both the Jewish and Christian revelations leave solutions to the intellectual problems raised by evil shrouded in mystery, and insofar as Leibniz too simply trusts to the divine being at the points where arguments can do no more, he also, despite his rationalism, relies on revelation. Indeed, he makes some appeal to a feature of specifically Christian theodicy, in the 'reduction' of his whole work to formal arguments,[143] in giving a particular focus to the divine permission of evil for the sake of the logically higher order good-the best world. 'I have shown that among older writers the fall of Adam was termed *felix culpa*, a fortunate sin, because it had been expiated with immense benefit by the incarnation of the Son of God: for he gave to the universe something more noble than anything there would otherwise have been amongst created beings'.[144] Leibniz here was indicating by means of the Latin tag a passage from the Paschal vigil of 'Holy Saturday',[145] celebrating Christ's victory over the powers of darkness, though from the text of the *Theodicy* Christ is little better than the best of philosophers.[146] As Farrer put it:

> Leibniz ... writes with perfect seriousness and decency about the Christian scheme of redemption, but it hardly looks like being for

him a crucial deliverance from perdition. It is not the intervention of Mercy, by which alone He possesses himself of us: it is one of the ways in which supreme benevolence carries out a cosmic policy; and God's benevolence is known by pure reason, and apart from Christian revelation.[147]

Insofar as this appeal to revelation is important to him, one would then place Leibniz in the line of tradition represented by for example Duns Scotus. The latter had maintained an optimistic view of nature, 'bound to the theology of Creation',[148] and developed on that basis a concept of incarnation as the crown of the doctrine of creation. Knowles wrote of Duns Scotus that he maintained that God first of all loves himself; then he desires to love and be loved by others; finally he desires to be loved by the One who can love Him to the limit, and so he willed from all eternity the union of His Son with the created nature that was fitted so to love Him.[149] Thus Barth could commend Leibniz for at least once finding a place for 'looking at creation through the message of Good Friday and Easter',[150] though maintained that as with other optimists of this period Leibniz was unable to exploit this message as Barth would do - defending the position that 'it is in relation to Christ, to His position as Member and Head of creation, as Lord and Saviour and Hope of the world, that God chose this world as the best; and it is in the divinity and humanity of Christ that we are to recognise the *maxima ratio* as the supreme principle of the perfection of the universe and therefore of the perfection of God himself'.

The comments by Farrer and Barth indicate the possible scope of theological controversy as to how the incarnate God could be a 'solution' to the problem of theodicy, and Leibniz saw his position as freeing his readers from being embroiled in such controversy. Berger also, and not writing as a theologian, has remarked on the shift in specifically Christian theodicy from the question about the justice of God to that about sinfulness of man.[151] Leibniz had done no more than indicate what Christian theology seemed to offer him at one crucial point, though without needing to modify his overall programme. Barth's reference in fact was not to the 'reduction' of the work but to the Latin summary, 'Causa Dei asserta per justitiam eius', a translation of which was omitted from Farrer's edition but made available in a selection of Leibniz' work by the Schreckers.[152] Paragraph 49 of what amounts to a summary legal brief prepared by Leibniz runs:

> The strongest reason for the choice of the best series of events (namely, our world) was Jesus Christ, God become Man, who as a creature represents the highest degree of perfection. He had, therefore, to be contained in that series, noblest among all, as a part, indeed the head, of the created universe. To him also all power has been granted in heaven and on earth, in him all the peoples were to be

blessed, and through him every creature will be freed from servitude and corruption to enjoy the liberty and glory of the children of God. And as in the *Theodicy*[153] Leibniz quoted Christ's words of Jn.12:24, that 'if the grain falling to the soil did not die, it would not bear fruit', as one of his ways of alluding to the theme of the hoped for logically higher order good. However, its importance for the present purpose lies in that, as Loemker has suggested,[154] it may be that Kant's 1791 essay on the failure of theodicy takes its particular form from the style of the 'Causa Dei', though Kant's 'case' for the divine being rests on different lines of argument. He too wanted to maintain human resources of patience amd courage, but not by means of Leibniz' theological rationalism and the argument that this is the best of all possible worlds. Not the least of Kant's problems was to ponder Leibniz' view that 'It is an imperfection in our freedom that makes us capable of choosing evil instead of good',[155] and to think carefully about the value of freedom in a pre-established, harmonious, Leibnizian world. For part of his career, he developed a modified Leibnizian theodicy, then virtually left the topic alone whilst he worked out his particular philosophical viewpoint, until able to summarise his views on theodicy towards the end of his career.

NOTES

1. For example, P. Hazard, 'Le problème du mal dans la conscience européenne du dix-huitième siècle', *The Romanic Review*, 32, 1941, 147-170: cf. *La crise de la conscience européene, 1680-1715*, of 1935 and *La pensée européene au XVIIIe siècle: de Montesquieu à Lessing*, of 1946, both available in English translation. Cf. J. McManners, 'Paul Hazard and the 'Crisis of the European Conscience'', *Arts: The Proceedings of the Sydney university arts association*, 2, 1962, 73-68.
2. Cf. O. Lempp, *Das Problem der Theodicee in der philosophie und Literatur des 18. Jahrhunderts bis auf Kant und Schiller*, (1910) reprinted by Olms, 1976, begins with Bayle. R.P. Sertillanges, *Le Problème du Mal: L'Histoire*, Aubier 1948 groups him with Descartes, Pascal, Malebrance and Spinoza together with Leibniz as representing the problem-area in 'L'ère Cartésienne' pp.207-237.
3. The second London edition (1734) is a translation from Bayle's second edition (1702). It included Bayle's introduction to his own first and second editions, his life by Des Maiseaux, and a full account of the controversies in which he was engaged. Citations will be from this text and from recent selections.

4. G.W. Leibniz, *Essais de Théodicée, sur la bonté de Dieu, la liberté de l'homme et l'origine du mal*, ed. C.I. Gerhardt/J. Jalabert, Aubier 1962; ET G.W. Leibnitz, *Theodicy: Essays on the goodness of God, the freedom of man and the origin of evil*, trans. from the Gerhardt edition of the collected works, by E.M. Huggard, ed. A.M. Farrer, Routledge & Kegan Paul, 1951. All references are to Huggard.
5. Cf. W. King, *An essay on the origin of evil*, E. Law ed. and trans., 1731; Sir Charles Simon King, ed., *A great archbishop of Dublin, William King D.D. 1650-1729. His autobiography, family, and a selection from his correspondence*, Longmans, Green, 1906, p.402: 'In the year 1697 I produced a book entitled 'De Origine Mali'. Mr. Bayle published strictures on it before he had read it; it will not seem wonderful that they were marked neither by sense nor force of argument, when the book was not otherwise known to him than from a summary, an abridged narration of it which Mr. Bernard, a learned man, contributed to a certain French work ...' Bernard's summary appeared in the May-June, 1703 number of the journal Bayle had promoted, the *Nouvelles de la République des Lettres*. Leibniz' comments on King appear in the *Theodicy*, pp. 274-5, pp.292-3, p.340f, and principally pp.405-442. Cf. J. Hick, *Evil and the God of love*, Macmillan, 1966, pp.154-160: A.O. Lovejoy 'Optimism and romanticism', pp.319-343 of J.L. Clifford ed., *Eighteenth century English literature: Modern essays in criticism*, O.U.P., 1959 on King.
6. R.H. Popkin, *Pierre Bayle: Historical and Critical Dictionary: Selections*, with Craig B. Brush, ed. and trans., Bobbs-Merrill, 1965, p.53. Other selections available are by K.C. Sandberg, trans. and ed., *The great contest of faith and reason*, Ungar 1968; E.A. Beller and M. du P. Lee, trans. and ed., *Selections from Bayle's Dictionary*, Princeton U.P. 1952.
7. L. Strauss, *Persecution and the art of writing*, Free Press, 1952; L. Strauss, *What is Political philosophy?* Free Press, 1959, chapter 9, 'On a forgotten kind of writing'.
8. Popkin, p.203.
9. Ibid., p.145.
10. Ibid., p.188.
11. Ibid., p.145.
12. Ibid., p.146.
13. Ibid., p.149.
14. Ibid., p.185.
15. Ibid., p.173.
16. Ibid., p.173.
17. Ibid., p.176.
18. Ibid., p.193.
19. *Dictionary*, IV 'Origen', p.416.

20. Ibid., pp.418-419.
21. Ibid., II 'Epicurus' p.789.
22. Ibid., II 'Chrysippus' p.496.
23. Ibid., I 'Anaxagoras' p.310-11.
24. *Theodicy*, 2, 148-149 'Preface' p.62.
25. Ibid., 'Preface' p.53, p.59.
26. *Dictionary*, V, 'Xenophanes' p.579.
27. Karl Barth, *Church Dogmatics*, trans. J.W. Edwards, O. Bussey H. Knight, T. & T. Clark, 1958, 3:I, pp.404-5. The whole section on Leibniz runs from pp.388-414. For the stimulus given by a representative of a different element in the Christian tradition see G. Stieler, *Leibniz and Malebranche und das Theodiceeproblem*, Reichl, 1930; A. Robinet, *Malebranche et Leibniz: relations personelles*, Vrin, 1955, pp.403-425. And cf. P. Siwek, 'Optimism in philosophy', *New Scholasticism*, 22:4, 1948, pp.417-439.
28. P. Des Maiseaux's *Recueil de diverses pieces* of 1720 was one of the most influential and widely read of the early collections, and as it happened, helped to publicize Shaftesbury's work, cf. 1740 edition, Changuion, 2, 311-353. Cf. D.B. Schlegel, *Shaftesbury and the French deists*, N. Carolina U.P., Johnson reprint 1956; S. Green, *Shaftesbury's philosophy of religion and ethics*, Ohio U.P., 1967, pp.73-88 on 'Optimism and evil'. Another collection in the second half of the century was that of J.A. Emery, *Esprit de Lebnitz, ou Recueil de pensées choisies, sur la religion, la morale, l'histoire, le philosophie* etc. Bruyset, 1772.
29. J. Pieper, *Leisure the basis of culture*, trans. A. Dru, Fontana 1965, pp.27-28. Cf. D. Emmet, 'Theoria and the way of life', *Journal of theological studies*, N.S. 17:1, 1966, 38-52.
30. Leibniz, *Theodicy*, 'Preface' p.59; 1, 163.
31. Cf. L.E. Loemker, 'Leibniz's conception of philosophical method', and 'The ethical import of the Leibnizian System', pp.135-157 and 207-223 of I. Leclerc, ed., *The philosophy of the modern world*, Vanderbilt U.P. 1973.
32. Leibniz, *Theodicy*, 'Preface', p.51; 'Preliminary dissertation' 30, 81; 3.297. Cf. J. le Brun, 'Leibniz', columns 548-557 of the *Dictionnaire de Spiritualité*, 9, Beauchesne, 1976, Cf. the concluding paragraphs of the 1678 'Two dialogues on religion', and the last three paragraphs of the 1714 'Principles of nature and of grace', pp.213-220 and 636-642 of L.E. Loemker, trans. and ed., *G.W. Leibniz: philosophical papers and letters*, Reidel, 1956, And F. Sontag, *Divine perfection*, SCM 1962 pp.64-68.
33. Leibniz, *Theodicy*, 2, 201.
34. 'Preliminary dissertation', 44.
35. 'Preliminary dissertation', 81.
36. 'Preliminary dissertation', 61.

37. 'Preface' p.51; 'Preliminary dissertation', 4.
38. 3, 242; cf. 3, 257.
39. 'Preliminary dissertation', 37; 45.
40. 'Preliminary dissertation', 23; 77.
41. 'Preliminary dissertation', 2; 3, 282.
42. 'Preliminary dissertation', 59.
43. 1, 44.
44. 2, 208. Cf. 'The novel of the enlightenment', pp.37-72 of W.H. Marshall, *The World of the Victorian novel*, Yoseloff 1967, especially pp.37-47 relating to 'Robinson Crusoe'.
45. Leibniz, *Theodicy* 1, 44.
46. 2, 217; 165.
47. 1, 78. Cf. p.412 on King's book, 'He wished to communicate himself at the expense of a certain fastidiousness which we assume in God, imagining that imperfections offend him'.
48. 1, 80; 1, 22.
49. 1, 8.
50. 2, 117.
51. 2, 201.
52. 2, 149.
53. 1, 7.
54. 2, 119.
55. 3, 335.
56. 2, 124.
57. 'Preliminary dissertation', 23.
58. 2, 225.
59. 1, 9. Cf. L.E. Loemker, 'Leibniz doctrine of ideas', pp.28-51 of Leclerc, *Leibniz*.
60. Leibniz, *Theodicy* 1, 20. Cf. P. Schrecker, 'Leibniz and the Timaeus', *The review of metaphysics*, 4:4, 1951, 495-505 which is particularly concerned with Leibniz' 1697 'De rerum originatione radicali', E.T. in Loemker, *Philosophical papers* pp.486-491. The same work of Leibniz is discussed as posing significant religious questions in D. Allen, 'Leibniz' two questions in De rerum originatione radicali', pp.226-230 of *Theoria cum Praxi: zum verhältnis von Theorie und Praxis im 17 und 18 Jahrhundert*, 3: Logik, Erkenntnistheorie, Wissenschaftstheorie, Metaphysick, Theologie, Steiner, 1980, (Proceedings of the third international Leibniz-congress, Hanover 12-17 November, 1977). Cf. D. Allen, 'Leibniz' relevance for today's Christianity', *Princeton seminary bulletin*, 1:1, 1977, 13-20.
61. Leibniz, *Theodicy*, 2, 149.
62. 2, 225.
63. 2, 183.
64. Cf. J. Hostler, *Leibniz' moral philosophy*, Duckworth, 1975, p.53f

on 'caritas sapientis' and God as the instantiation of the concept of a good man.
65. 2, 179.
66. P. Riley, *The political writings of Leibniz*, C.U.P. 1972.
67. Riley, p.4.
68. Riley, p.17-18.
69. Riley, p.4.
70. Riley, p.5.
71. Cf. G. Stanley Kane, 'The concept of divine goodness and the problem of evil', *Religious Studies*, 11:1, 1975, 49-71.
72. Leibniz, *Theodicy* 2, 201. Cf. K. Barth, *Church Dogmatics*, trans. G.W. Bromily and R.J. Ehrlich, T & T Clark, 1966, 3:3, 316-319.
73. Leibniz, *Theodicy*, 2, 168.
74. 2, 234.
75. 1, 45.
76. 2, 228.
77. 3, 319.
78. 3, 290. J. M. Hostler, 'Some remarks on "omne possibile exiget/ existere" ', *Studia Leibnitiana*, 5, 1973, 281-285, defends Leibniz as having given a metaphorical description of certain and predictable choice given God's wisdom and goodness.
79. 2, 215.
80. 1, 22.
81. 2, 222.
82. 2, 119.
83. 2, 119.
84. 2, 114.
85. 2, 222.
86. 1, 22.
87. 2, 192.
88. 2, 149.
89. 2, 130.
90. 2, 227.
91. 1, 78.
92. 1, 52.
93. A.O. Lovejoy, *The great chain of being*, Harper, 1960. Important criticisms of Lovejoy are indicated in for instance J. Hintikka's discussion of 'Leibniz on plenitude, relations, and the 'reign of law', pp.259-286 of S. Knuuttila, *Reforging the great chain of being: studies in the history of modal theories*, Reidel, 1981.
94. M. - D. Chenu, *Nature, man and society in the twelfth century*, trans. J. Taylor and L.K. Little, Chicago U.P., 1968, p.21. Cf. Leibniz, *Theodicy*, 2, 182.
95. Leibniz, *Theodicy*, 'Preliminary dissertation', 44. Cf. Loemker,

'Leibniz and the limits of empiricism, in Leclerc, *Leibniz*, pp.158-175.
96. 1, 9.
97. 2, 188.
98. 2, 130.
99. Cf. H.W.B. Joseph, *Lectures on the philosophy of Leibniz*, O.U.P. 1949, p.2.
100. Leibniz, *Theodicy*, 'Preface' p.64.
101. 3, 388.
102. 1, 27.
103. 1, 31.
104. 2, 124.
105. 2, 120.
106. Chenu, *Nature*, p.23.
107. Leibniz, *Theodicy*, 2, 200.
108. 2, 195.
109. 1, 14.
110. Chenu, *Nature*, p.24.
111. Leibniz, *Theodicy*, 2, 198.
112. 2, 202.
113. 3, 341. Cf. N. Rescher, *Leibniz*, Prentice-Hall 1967 pp.157-159 on 'Cosmic evolution and melioration'.
114. Leibniz, *Theodicy*, 3, 395.
115. 1, 87.
116. 'Preface' p.69.
117. Farrer's introduction, p.13.
118. Leibniz, *Theodicy*, 2, 119, 194; 3, 262-3. Cf. D. Allen, 'The theological relevance of Leibniz' 'Theodicy", pp.83-90 of *Akten des II. Internationalen Leibniz-Kongresses, Hannover, 17-22 Juli, 1972*, 3: Metaphysik-Ethik-Asthetik-Monadenlehre, Steiner, 1975, especially pp.89-90.
119. Leibniz, *Theodicy*, 1, 26.
120. 1, 21, 31.
121. 1, 33; 2, 153.
122. 1, 20; for criticism see C.D. Broad ed. C. Lewy, *Leibniz: an introduction*, C.U.P. 1975, pp.159-165.
123. 1. 30.
124. 1, 20f.
125. 2, 124.
126. 3, 241.
127. 1, 16.
128. 3, 241.
129. 3, 343.
130. 3, 246.
131. 3, 250.

132. 2, 118.
133. 1, 12.
134. 3, 241.
135. 3, 242.
136. 3, 245.
137. 2, 145.
138. 2, 147.
139. R. Rees, *A theory of my time*, Secker & Warburg, 1963, p.82.
140. Leibniz, *Theodicy*, 2, 146.
141. Allen, as in note 118. Cf. K.E. Yandell, *Basic issues in the philosophy of religion*, Allyn & Bacon, 1971, in particular p.51 on how the question as to whether the concept of a best logically possible world is or is not incoherent is undecided.
142. M.B. Ahern, *The problem of evil*, Routledge & Kegan Paul, 1971, p.79.
143. *Theodicy*, pp.377-392.
144. *Theodicy*, p.378; cf. 1, 84. Cf. C.D. Zangger, *Welt und Konversation: Die Theologische Begründung der Mission bei Gottfried Wilhelm Leibniz*, Theologischer Verlag, 1973, pp.51-70.
145. H.A. Schmidt ed., *Hebdomada Sancta, volumen alterum: Fontes historici, commentarius historicus*, Herder, 1957, p.639f.
146. *Theodicy*, 'Preface' pp.49-51, p.54; 1, 15; 1, 84.
147. *Theodicy*, Farrer's 'Introduction', pp.9-10.
148. P. Vignaux, *Philosophy in the middle ages*, trans. E.C. Hall, Meridian, 1959, p.212; cf. *Theodicy* 'Preliminary dissertation', 55.
149. D. Knowles, *The evolution of medieval thought*, Longmans, 1962, p.308.
150. Barth, *Church Dogmatics*, 3:1, p.413.
151. P. Berger, *The social reality of religion*, Penguin, 1967, pp.83-87.
152. P. and A.M. Schrecker, *Leibniz: Monadology and other philosophical essays*, Bobbs-Merrill, 1965, pp.114-117.
153. *Theodicy*, 1, 23; 'Causa Dei' paragraph 54.
154. L.E. Loemker, in P. Wiener ed., *Dictionary of the history of ideas*, Scribners, 1973, 4, 378-384 on theodicy, p.382.
155. *Theodicy*, 3, 319 as note 77.

PART II: 2
SOME CONTROVERSY ABOUT LEIBNIZ

Apart from the *Theodicy* much of Leibniz' work had been relatively unknown until the middle years of the century. To give one example, 1749 saw the publication of the full text of the *Protogaea* known hitherto in abstract in the Leipzig *Acta Eruditorum*, the first major literary and scientific review published in the German states;[1] and as already noticed, important collections of his work appeared in the 1760's.[2] Leibniz' opinions were also kept in the public eye because of certain controversies in which the supporters of his reputation found themselves in open conflict with his detractors. The significance of some of Kant's work from the first half of his professional career becomes clearer if it is seen in reflection to these conflicts. For instance, there was the great controversy which attracted attention all over Europe about whether Leibniz or Maupertuis had been the first to enunciate the 'principle of least action', a principle taken to be an expression of the ultimate rationality of nature in its dependence upon the wisdom of the deity. We recall that the Berlin Academy had been fostered at the turn of the century by Leibniz, reformed by Maupertuis at the instigation of Frederick II, and Maupertuis was its president at the time of this controversy. To appreciate the importance of the principle or 'law' of least action it is worth paying attention to Erich Frank's citation of the Göttingen Nobel prizewinner, Max Planck:

> It strikes us most surprisingly that an entirely adequate formulation of this law gives every unbiased person the impression that nature is governed by a reasonable purposeful will ... This principle of the least action is the principle from which the elementary effect quantum later received its name ... To the causa efficiens, the cause which acts out of the present into the future, now comes the causa finalis, which reversely takes the future as its hypothesis and derives from it the cause of events. In its historical development theoretical physical research has been led to a formulation of physical causality which possesses a definitely teleological character.[3]

The principle suggests that maximum effect is associated with minimum effort in the transition from the mere possibility in the divine mind of things as they might be to whatever reality and perfection they may have as actual creatures. Thus in the *Theodicy* Leibniz had written of God: 'It is therefore not to be wondered at that he who penetrates all things at one stroke should always strike true at the outset; and it must not be said that he succeeds without the guidance of any cognition. On the contrary, it is because his knowledge is perfect that his voluntary actions are also perfect'.[4] One might well ask how there could be any dispute about priority, but Maupertuis was engaged in an attack on the use of ill-defined principles of explanation, of which the principle of least action was but one example. He had discussed the use of the principle of continuity in physics before the Berlin Academy in 1746 and again in his essay on cosmology,[5] and this latter principle had been used with ill-defined meaning in psychology, biology, metaphysics and logic as well as physics. Its usefulness in biology, when the continuity of species was being considered, did not mean that it would be equally helpful in each of these other areas of study.[6] His particular contribution, so he thought, was to be the first to use the principle of least action in relation to the laws of motion and rest. So an exposition of his version of the principle read:

> Everything in the universe, wherever it may be, shows its dependency upon and need of the presence of its author. Moreover, it is seen that this author is a Being, not only infinitely powerful, but also infinitely wise. The forces he reintroduces again and again into nature are always dispersed with the greatest economy, the action by which all the motions are produced and distributed is always the least possible.[7]

Koenig, a professor in Holland and a member of the Berlin Academy since 1749, was a Leibnizian who had introduced Leibniz' thought to Voltaire and some of his circle of friends at Cirey. Zealous for the reputation of the Academy's founder, he precipitated the crisis with Maupertuis by going to see him with information about a letter of Leibniz' which purported to establish the latter's priority in the precise usage claimed by Maupertuis. (The latter did indeed exist, though in it Leibniz had done no more than reassert the axiom). Koenig followed up the visit by writing in the *Acta Eruditorum*, but since he could not produce the actual letter when required to do so, he left himself vulnerable to accusations of acting dishonestly, and to condemnation at the Academy, in April 1752. Voltaire had recommended Maupertuis as president of the Academy to Frederick, but now saw Maupertuis as using his powerful position to persecute a vulnerable man who could be held to represent the right to raise such a fundamental question without being threatened by ostracism or persecution. Although by this time Voltaire was more sympathetic to Newtonian theism than to Leibnizian theism, he engaged himself with Koenig's defence. His diatribe on the history of Dr. Akakia, completed at the end of 1754, was contrived exactly to pillory the pride and ambition of Maupertuis.[8] Moreover, fresh interest in the *Theodicy* was prompted by the publication of Pope's *Essay on Man*,⁹ translated into German in 1740 by the Hamburg poet Barthold Heinrich Brockes whose work was akin to that of H.S. Reimarus.¹⁰ Published anonymously in 1733-1734, Pope had acknowledged authorship in 1735. The *Essay* was supposed to be part of a philosophical framework for some of Pope's satires, a matter of which most of his pious readers would hardly be aware. The *Essay* inspired the Berlin Academy to ask candidates for one of its essay competitions to tackle a comparison of Pope's position as indicated in the phrase 'Tout est bien' with the system of optimism, or choosing what is best. In other words, the competition's subject provided another opportunity to disparage Leibniz. That this was clear from the outset is demonstrated by the way in which Sulzer, one of Leibniz' admirers, opposed the setting of the competition subject. Gottsched too, was clear about how the wording of the competition subject could be read as an implicit invitation to denigrate Leibniz' position. Gottsched was emphatic that Leibniz' position could by no means be summarised by 'All is well'.¹¹ The very choice of the subject at this date necessarily meant that the discussion could be seen as a continuation of the debate about the value of Leibniz' work which the acrimonious controversy between Koenig and Maupertuis exemplified. The essay prize went to Reinhard, attempting to refute optimism, but attention was drawn away from his piece to an essay originally projected as a contribution to the competition, but now published anonymously as 'Pope, ein Metaphysiker!' The writers were two young authors preoccupied to varying degrees throughout their careers with Leibnizian thought.¹² Mendelssohn and Lessing had put their heads together for its concoction shortly after their first meeting. Lessing had been a student at Leipzig, the base of some of Leibniz' stalwart defenders. Essentially, the essay made Gottsched's point, that the sophistication of Leibniz' position could not be reduced to Pope's aphorism.¹³ Of their later discussions, one should note that Lessing in 1772 engaged in debate with Eberhard about Leibniz' position with regard to the orthodox doctrine of eternal punishment. Lessing was clear that Leibniz had supported the orthodox doctrine, and this was evident not only from the text of the *Theodicy*, but also from Des Maiseaux's *Recueil*. As Lessing saw, Leibniz supported orthodox formulae if he thought they expressed some truth he believed to be important, in this case, the point that in a harmonious world, every action has its consequences.

Evidence of interest in theodicy can be gathered from a variety of sources, but it was Voltaire above all who was especially provocative in his writings about the problem of evil, and who fought hard to get others to see the problem as he saw it, and to admit the moral offensiveness of some of the elements of theodicies: 'My poor Pope, my poor hunchback, whom I have known, whom I have loved, who told you that God was unable to form you without a hump?'[14] Voltaire's campaign on Koenig's behalf was but one example of how he could fight to avenge those who suffered most cruelly at the hands of the powerful, and theodicies sometimes were verbal cruelties. Above all, Voltaire did what he could to make people acknowledge the wickedness of themselves and of their fellows in a supposedly 'best' world. So fresh from the writing of 'Dr. Akakia', he was more than ready to continue to try to get others to see evil as he saw it, without benefit of theistic solutions. His interest in the various facets of the topic of evil had already come to the surface in his philosophical tales, beginning with *Zadig* in 1747. The tale employed the literary device, perhaps inspired in part by the reading of the book of Job itself, of a revelation which silences those who would query the goodness, wisdom and power of the deity in relation to their experiences.[15] In any case, Leibniz himself, at the very end of the *Theodicy*,[16] wrote of the experience of a character in a fable he developed, who slept in the temple of Pallas. In a dream the goddess revealed to him all that he had wanted to understand of the goodness of the deity. The angel Jesrad in *Zadig* repeated the stock arguments of theodicy, and counselled submission. Zadig retained some urge to question the angel but nevertheless worshipped Providence on his knees. But in *Memnon* of 1750, the principal character was counselled by his angelic visitor to believe that 'all is well', despite the misfortunes of his family, and his own loss of an eye. So like Bayle, Voltaire was for time driven to consider the possibility that the dualist, Manichean position would be more tolerable. After Bayle, I. de Beausobre's *Histoire de Manichée et du Manichéisme*[17] of 1734 had revived interest in this possibility. However, the events of the 1750's impelled Voltaire to dispense with all alleged solutions, whether those of the Manicheans, of Leibniz, or of Pope, let alone the submission of 'faith' apparently recommended by Bayle. The earthquake of November and December 1755 which destroyed Lisbon and badly affected other cities prompted Voltaire to compose his poem on the disaster. Although Voltaire at the last seemed to counsel submission to the way things go, at least he insisted that 'all is well' obscured the truth of the human situation, that moral and physical evil was all-pervasive.[18] The poem (and its accompanying one on natural law) received an 'answer' from Rousseau in August 1756.[19] Rousseau tried to get Voltaire to engage in a public discussion of the issue, but in vain. So Rousseau allowed his letter to be copied and it was printed for publication somewhere in Germany. It came out in 1759, the year of the publication of *Candide*, and was published in France the following year. The first point clearly mattered a great deal to Rousseau. An optimism to be expressed in the civilised practice of justice was not identical with the kind of optimism which Voltaire found so cruel, but helped to sustain Rousseau in his own sufferings and griefs. Voltaire had aggravated his sense of ill-usage and self-pity, incited him to complain, shattered his hope and thereby reduced him to despair. His hope depended upon belief in the existence of a perfect God, wise, powerful and just, and in his own possession of an immortal soul. He exhibited his faith again in *Emile*, written between 1757-1760, in 'The Creed of a Savoyard Priest', the faith of a man endeavouring to live without allegiance to any ecclesiastical institution. His experience of persecution after the publication of *Emile* drove him temporarily to Neuchâtel under the protection of Frederick the Great and eventually to England in 1766, at David Hume's invitation.[20]

1756 had also seen the beginning of the Seven Years War, bringing further ruin to parts of France and the German states. *Candide* mocked the pretensions of an optimist still further, since for Voltaire, speculation about the intentions of the deity in producing the world of human experience helped to stifle whatever initiative human beings might retain to help one another to manage their lives tolerably well. One might entertain the notion of the world as the harmonious creation of a supremely powerful and good being, but it was experienced as producing evils which human beings could neither understand, not in many cases even hope to control. By this time, Voltaire could only counsel silence.[21] So at the end of *Candide*, Martin argued that we should work without reasoning, since it was the only way to make life endurable, and any further attempts at a solution of the problem of evil by the windbag, Pangloss, were overcome by the plea of the innocent Candide to cultivate the garden.[22] Incidentally, there is a certain irony worth noting at this point, in that Bolingbroke had provided material for both Pope and for Voltaire. Pope's *Essay* was dedicated to Bolingbroke, who had tutored Pope in the philosophy expressed in the *Essay*.[23] Bolingbroke may have relished the knowledge that it was published in the thick of Pope's attacks on other people. Furthermore, Bolingbroke had been a friend to Voltaire when the latter had visited England in 1723-4, a friendship recalled to mind by the publication of Voltaire's defence of him, begun shortly after the latter's death in 1751, and completed just before *Dr. Akakia*. A letter of Bolingbroke's may well be one of the sources of Candide's position at the end of the tale.[24] Bolingbroke had arranged for the posthumous printing of his collected works (1754) so that he would not suffer the opprobrium which the expression of his views might have elicited. Their publication showed him to give some minimal acknowledgement to the existence of the deity, but he saw no reason to suppose that such a belief could in any way be relevant to the solution of problems of morality and human well-being. Voltaire continued to endeavour to puncture insensitive complacency in his 1764 *Philosophical Dictionary*,[25] in one of the articles suggesting that writers of theodicy are like convicts who play with their chains, perhaps a suitable comment on his own earlier attempts at theodicy.

Although it would seem that in the latter part of his life Voltaire was again prepared to concede that the world was the best achievable, as distinct from the best conceivable, this was not likely to be known to most of his readers.[26] And Voltaire's strictures were certainly not taken to heart in every quarter, least of all after the publication of Raspe and Dutens' collections of Leibniz' works in the 1760s. For example, Charles Bonnet, a friend of Haller, was to recommend the reading of the *Theodicy* as a book of devotion, and supplemented his reading of it by judicious selections from the newly available material.[27] However, hostility to theodicy was lively in the person of another acute critic, David Hume, whose work became increasingly popular in France and the German states. To say the least, Hume wanted to discredit the fanatical and superstitious, and an analysis of different modes of theism was indispensable to his working out of his own attitude to religious conviction. It is known that Hume received some stimulus towards formulating his own distinctive ways of tackling theism from Bayle, for he made careful extracts from the *Dictionary*, not least on theodicy, and took upon himself Bayle's role of sceptic.[28] He acquired a reputation for atheism based on his 1739-40 *Treatise of human nature*,[29] a reputation which the 1748 *Enquiry concerning human understanding*[30] helped to foster. The first part of this latter work was to a certain extent a reworking of the first book of the *Treatise*, but with some material new to the public, though not to Hume, in which he began to destroy the arguments of eighteenth century theism. His tactics included those which he was to develop in an extended form in his *Dialogues* - the narration of an imaginary conversation in the course of which the selective anthropomorphism of much theology could be exhibited for criticism.[31]

Some members of the Berlin Academy, notably Formey, Mérian and Sulzer, were quick to appreciate and try to dispose of the sceptical challenge revived by Bayle of which Hume was now a most lively and talented exponent.[32] The 1757 *Natural history of religion* was translated by Mérian at Maupertuis' request, and first Sulzer and then Formey translated the *Enquiry*. Maupertuis himself, in his philosophical examination of the proof of the existence of God, indicated that he had paid attention to Hume's discussion of causality, and Kant seems to have followed Maupertuis' lead here, when he in turn came to re-examine his own understanding of the limits of argument in enabling him to affirm God's existence.[33] Kant's acquaintance with Hamann, a pupil of Rappolt's in the 1730's, and perhaps the finest Lutheran theologian of his day, ensured that Hume's work would not be overlooked. Hamann wrote to Kant of Hume in 1759, that 'All his errors aside, he is like Saul among the prophets'. He quoted the concluding remarks from the essay on miracles in the *Enquiry* to show that 'one can preach the truth in *jest* and without awareness or desire, even if one is the greatest doubter and, like the serpent, wants to doubt even what God said'.[34] Hamann's own translation of book I of the *Treatise* was published in a Königsberg periodical in 1771.[35] The following year (when eastern Prussia linked up with western Prussia as a result of the first partition of Poland) a translation of Beattie's *Nature and immutability of truth* appeared. This work further emphasized the relevance of what Hume had said about causality to his analysis of allegedly rational theism, a topic which preoccupied Kant in the writing of his first *Critique*.[36] Another writing available for discussion was the text of Hume's *Dialogues concerning natural religion*, written up during the course of continuing controversies of one sort and another, such as that following the publication of the first volume of his *History of Great Britain* in 1754, which gave offence not least because of Hume's opinions on the religious fanaticism characterising the political struggles of the previous century and a half. The general assembly of the church of Scotland were dissuaded from holding an enquiry into his writings probably because there seemed sense in the suggestion that such an investigation would give Hume's writings even greater notoriety. Hamann gave Kant part of his version of the *Dialogues* to read no earlier that August 1780, when Kant was in the last stages of producing the first *Critique*. Hamann had intended to append his own critique of Hume to his translation completed by January 1781,[37] but Schreiter published his own translation of the *Dialogues* before Hamann could get his out, and the critique was soon to be undertaken by Kant, though undoubtedly not as Hamann would have done it. The *Dialogues* were given substantial reviews in the *Göttingische Gelehrte Anzeigen* and in the *Brittisches Museum für die Deutschen*, and Kant tackled points made in the *Dialogues* particularly in the *Prolegomena* and then in his *Critiques*, as well as in his lectures from 1783 onwards.[38]

Hume had given the literary form of the *Dialogues* careful thought, skilfully developing techniques already employed with a degree of success. A dialogue was well suited to the examination of problematical topics such as belief in the deity of the Christian tradition. Hume could deploy the various participants to express his own opinions, without it being possible conclusively to identify him as an unbeliever according to some preconceived position. Much as Bayle at the last had remained within the French Calvinist community of belief, Hume made his points about the extreme difficulty of justifying the form of theism he was analysing, and yet, as at the conclusion of the essay on miracles apparently preferred to protect himself by having the sceptic give up his argument.[39] His particular model may well have been Cicero's *De natura deorum*, enjoying a modest popularity in the eighteenth century, in which Cicero searched for a theism which enabled him to affirm some significance for his life. Parts of Bayle's *Dictionary* could well have been read as a commentary on some of the arguments Cicero had employed. As Hume wrote to his friend Elliot, 'What Danger can ever come from ingenious Reasoning & Enquiry? The worst speculative Sceptic ever I knew, was a much better Man than the best superstitious Devotee & bigot.'[40] Despite his own pleasure in his achievement, Hume chose to make arrangements for posthumous publication (his nephew brought the *Dialogues* out in 1779) and perhaps for that reason they were less controversial that his friends had feared, and it took time for readers to see that what Hume had to say outweighed the design theology of someone like Paley.[41]

One attractive feature of Hume's writings in the *Dialogues* was his unambiguous embrace of the newer cosmology, re-appropriating with self-confidence the extraordinary dimensions of the universe as a human discovery. Hume explicitly reminded his readers of the proposals of Copernicus and of Galileo's achievements, followed up by Newton, which had confirmed the heliocentric understanding of the discernable universe.[42] In doing so, Hume was making the point that theologians employed analogies in the service of their theology, but that analogical argument in theology did not produce results comparable in success and prestige with those of the natural philosophers. The new cosmology had achieved a gain in intelligibility, but there was no comparable gain achieved by a theistic hypothesis.

It is clear that Hume was familiar with Leibnizian theology and criticized it with confidence, not least on the mistake of imagining oneself to understand the actions of God.[43] As well as the *Theodicy*, there was Samuel Clarke's 1717 production of *A Collection of papers which passed between the late learned Mr. Leibniz and Dr. Clarke in the years 1715 and 1716 relating to the principles of natural philosophy and religion*,[44] printed in French with the parallel text in English, to which Clarke added his translation of some extracts from the *Theodicy*. Clarke's theology was to be one of Hume's targets in its own right,[45] quite apart from the points of reference he provided for Leibniz' own philosophy and theology. Unfortunately, given the dispute between the Newtonians and Leibniz, the latter's views were unlikely to commend themselves to the English-speaking public. For example when Raspe published the *New Essays*, *The Monthly Review*[46] inevitably advocated Locke's epistemology in his *Essays concerning human understanding*.[47] The first major book on Leibniz published in England was to be that of Bertrand Russell in 1900.[48]

Prior to the Lisbon earthquake, Londoners had had a foretaste of clerical animadversions on the subject of the minor earthquakes of 1750, treated by some as a special visitation by God on London's sins, with varieties of theodicy promulgated from fashionable London pulpits.[49] Hume had reason to be scathing about the way in which the clergy played on people's fears,[50] and not surprisingly, was delighted with *Candide*, which he said was 'full of Sprightliness & Impiety, & is indeed a Satyre upon Providence, under Pretext of criticising the Leibnitian System.'[51] Certainly his unambiguous reference to Leibniz in the *Dialogues* suggests that he cared little for what he knew of the *Theodicy*. In the *Dialogues* Demea says that a look around Cleanthes' library would show that 'there is scarce one of those innumerable writers, from whom the sense of human misery has not, in some passage or other, extorted a complaint and confession of it. At least, then, chance is entirely on that side; and no one author has ever, so far as I can recollect, been so extravagant as to deny it'. But Philo corrects Demea, and affirms that 'LEIBNITZ had denied it; and is perhaps the first, who ventured upon so bold and paradoxical an opinion; at least, the first, who made it essential to his philosophical system'. Hume's footnote to this remark reads: 'That sentiment had been maintained by Dr. King and some few others, before LEIBNITZ, though by none of so great fame as that GERMAN philosopher', as though to offer an editorial correction of Philo's error.[52] In fact, Hume's views of the torments of mind and body to which men may be subject, seems to have changed little between writing the *Enquiry* and the *Dialogues*.[53] Whereas in writing the *Enquiry* he may perhaps be said to express some dissatisfaction with his own scepticism, in the *Dialogues* he was prepared to let it have full reign, in order to provoke his combatants. He clearly sided with Bayle in his analysis of human ills and human folly, and as with Bayle his main theological problem was the moral attributes of the deity:

> The true conclusion is, that the original source of all things is entirely indifferent to all these principles, and has no more regard to good above ill than to heat above cold, or to drought above moisture, or to light above heavy. There may *four* hypotheses be framed concerning the first causes of the universe; *that* they are endowed with perfect goodness, *that* they have perfect malice, *that* they are opposite and have both goodness and malice, *that* they have neither goodness and malice. Mixt phenomena can never prove the two former unmixt principles. And the uniformity and steadiness of general laws seem to oppose by far the most probable.[54]

Unlike Bayle, however, Hume preferred to suspend judgement on the whole issue: 'But there is a species of controversy, which, from the very nature of language and of human ideas, is involved in perpetual ambiguity, and can never, by any precaution or any definitions, be able to reach a reasonable certainty or precision'.[55]

It is not to the purpose here to give more than an indication of the arguments of the *Dialogues* to make clear Hume's criticism of Leibniz in particular, throughout the ongoing conversation, as well as where he chose to name Leibniz. In part X, for instance, Leibniz' *a priori* theology was invoked when Cleanthes said, 'This world is but a point in comparison of the universe; this life but a moment in comparison of eternity ...'[56] a position mocked in *Candide*. More substantially, Hume dealt with what he took to be the non-sense of Leibniz' theology as he went along, and cleverly parodied some of Leibniz' favourite analogies which the latter had offered as alternatives to those produced by Bayle. His basic point, as he had indicated in the *Enquiry*,[57] was the folly of allowing ourselves to indulge in what he called 'the unbounded licence of conjecture,' - that of tacitly considering ourselves 'as in the place of the Supreme Being'. His view of man was that he is not equipped to discuss with assurance the origin of worlds.[58] Given the agreement between the participants in the *Dialogues* that they were going to argue not in terms of 'possibility' but of 'experience',[59] Hume raised a question which applied to theology of any variety, whether *a priori* or *a posteriori*, - 'What peculiar privilege has this little agitation of the brain which we call *thought*, that we must thus make it the model of the whole universe?'[60] Even if agreement could be reached on the point that ideas in a human mind fall into order of themselves,[61] it did not follow that it was possible to give 'precise meaning' to something similar said of the deity. In particular:

> If *Reason* (I mean abstract reason, derived from inquiries *a priori*) be not alike mute it will venture to pronounce, That a mental world, or universe of ideas, requires a cause as much, as does a material world, or universe of objects; and if similar in its arrangement must require a similar cause. For what is there in this subject, which should occasion a different conclusion or inference? If an abstract view, they are entirely alike; and no difficulty attends the one supposition, which is not common to both of them.[62]

So Hume wanted to draw particular attention to what he called the 'inconvenience' of the anthropomorphism involved: 'there is no ground to suppose a plan of the world to be formed in the divine mind, consisting of distinct ideas, differently arranged; in the same manner as an architect forms in his head the plan of a house which he intends to execute'.[63] Nothing was gained by such a supposition, since as he understood it, the ideal universe and the universe of experience were both exactly alike.[64] And he went on to affirm that it was merely arbitrary to say 'We must stop somewhere' in reply to the man who insisted on asking the question about the 'cause' of God or of the ideal world. As Hume said, 'if we stop and go no farther; why go so far?

Why not stop at the material world? How can we satisfy ourselves without going on *in infinitum*? And after all, what satisfaction is there in that infinite progression? Let us remember the story of the INDIAN philosopher and his elephant. It was never more applicable than to the present subject'.[65] For Hume, talk about the ideas in the divine mind was to double the problem, not to simplify it or solve it. 'An ideal system, arranged of itself, without a precedent design, is not a whit more explicable that a material one, which attains its order in a like manner; nor is there any more difficulty in the latter supposition than in the former'.[66] And there was another problem to be faced: 'In all instances which we have ever seen ideas are copied from real objects, and are ectypal, not archetypal, to express myself in learned terms: You reverse this order, and give thought the precedence'.[67] His view of reality enabled him to produce a rather different version of some of Leibniz' analogies. 'A builder is never esteemed prudent, who undertakes a plan, beyond what his stock will enable him to finish'.[68] So:

> Did I show you a house or palace, where there was not one apartment convenient or agreeable; where the windows, doors, fires, passages, stairs, and the whole oeconomy of the building were the source of noise, confusion, fatigue, darkness, and the extreme of heat and cold; you would certainly blame the contrivance, without any farther examination. The architect would in vain display his subtilty, and prove to you, that if this door or that window were altered, greater ills would ensue. What he says, may be strictly true: The alteration of one particular, while the other parts of the building remain, may only augment the inconvenience. But still you would assert in general, that, if the architect had had skill and good intention, he might have formed such a plan of the whole, and might have adjusted the parts in such a manner, as would have remedied all or most of these inconveniences. His ignorance, or even your own ignorance of such a plan, will never convince you of the impossibility of it. If you find any inconveniences and deformities in the building, you will always without entering into any detail, condemn the architect.[69]

Through the characters in the *Dialogues,* Hume suggested that one could be satisfied with 'an eternal inherent principle of order',[70] an immanent structuring power. He asked whether there was not 'a certain degree of analogy among all the operations of Nature, in every situation and in every age, whether the rotting of a turnip, the generation of an animal, and the structure of human thought be not energies that probably bear some remote analogy to each other'?[71] His recommendation was not to look beyond the present material world. 'By supposing it to contain principle of its order within itself, we really assert it to be God; and the sooner we arrive at that divine Being, so much the better. When you go one step beyond the mundane system, you only excite an inquisitive humour, which it is impossible ever to satisfy'. This preference for non-theistic explanation changed the significance of the maxims which sometimes had been found to lay a 'strong foundation of piety and religion, such as the maxim '*Nature acts by the simplest methods, and chuses the most proper means to any end*'.[72] At best, nature is indeed frugal: 'So well adjusted are the organs and capacities of all animals, and so well fitted to their preservation, that, as far as history or tradition teaches, there appears not to be any single species, which has yet been extinguished in the universe. Every animal has the requisite endowments; but these endowments are bestowed with so scrupulous an oeconomy, that any considerable diminution must entirely destroy the creature'.[73] Beyond nature's calculation of necessities, there seems no evidence of care or concern for the happiness of the members of the universe: 'No resource for this purpose: no machinery, in order merely to give pleasure or ease: no fund of pure joy and contentment: no indulgence without some want or necessity accompanying it. At least, the few phenomena of this nature are overbalanced by opposite phenomena of still greater importance'.[74] Indeed, it is precisely the 'contrivance of oeconomy of the animal creation, by which pains, as well as pleasures, are employed to excite all creatures to action, and make them vigilant in the great work of self-preservation'.[75]

If, with the writers of theodicy, one were to propose in advance of this sample of experience, 'a very powerful, wise, and benevolent Deity', then some features of human experience may be consistent with such a supposition. However, when the whole range of human experience is taken into consideration, it does not afford us an inference to the existence of such a deity. 'A perpetual war is kindled among all living creatures. Necessity, hunger, want, stimulate the strong and courageous: Fear, anxiety, terror, agitate the weak and infirm. The first entrance into life gives anguish to the new-born infant and to its wretched parent: Weakness, impotence, distress, attend each stage of that life: and 'tis at last finished in agony and horror'.[76]

Hume was especially concerned with human endowments, with particular application to the need to develop a cultured and prosperous society. Such a society depends on continued efforts, 'But as industry is a power, and the most valuable of any, Nature seems determined, suitably to her usual maxims, to bestow it on men with a very sparing hand; and rather punish him severely for his deficiency in it, than to reward him for his attainments'. So Hume insisted that 'it is hard, that being placed in a world so full of wants and necessities; where almost every being and element is either our foe or refuses its assistance ... we should also have our own temper to struggle with, and should be deprived of that faculty, which can alone fence against these multiplied evils'.[77]

Thus there was a variety of prompting for Kant in the course of his reflections on human experience, presenting him with a range of responses from the enthusiastic advocacy of theodicy to deep suspicion of theodicy, and of contemporary forms of theism. Kant shared some of these responses on the way to affirming his own eventual position in relation to the distinctive features of human living as he appreciated it. Although he came to share Hume's sympathies, he did not agree that responsible affirmation of faith in the deity of the Christian tradition depended philosophically solely upon causal inference. He was to suggest that Hume had omitted some of the most important characteristics of rational and sensitive humanity from the 'facts' which were to be explained, characteristics which themselves contributed to the explanation. This did not mean that he thought human beings were equipped to describe and comment on the life of the deity in his creative activity, as Leibniz had proposed. Nor could he, as one of the philosophers of nature of his day, write theology as though what they said was irrelevant to the style of operation of those propounding arguments for religious conviction.

Notes

1. *Acta Eruditorum*, 1693, pp.40-43, *Protogaea*, autore G.G.L. For the stimulus this work gave to de Buffon, see J. Piveteau, *Oeuvres philosophiques de Buffon*, Presses Universitaires de France, 1954, 41:1, 87.
2. See p. 17-18 of 'Kant's context', part 1.
3. E. Franck, *Philosophical understanding and religious truth*, O.U.P., 1963, p.47. Cf. J.R. Lucas, *A treatise on time and space*, Methuen, 1973, p.190: 'We anticipate nature, and in our anticipations show our belief that ours is, if not the best of all possible worlds, at least one of the most rational ones ...'; and S. Brown, 'The 'principle' of natural order: or what the enlightened sceptics did not doubt', pp.56-76 of ed. S.C. Brown, *Philosophers of the enlightenment: Royal Institute of Philosophy Lectures*, 12, 1977-78, Harvester, 1979.
4. *Theodicy* 3, 192.
5. *Oeuvres de Maupertuis*, Lyon, 1768, 4, 31f, 'Recherche des lois du movement' and E. Callot, *Maupertuis: le savant et le philosophe*, M Rivière et Cie., 1964, pp.95-106 on the 1749 'Essai de philosophie morale'. The 1750 'Essai de Cosmologie', (pp.107-119), 'Première Partie, ou l'on examine les preuves de l'existence de Dieu, tirées des merveilles de la nature', was followed by the 1757 'Examen philosophique de la preuve de l'existence de Dieu employée dans l'Essai

de Cosmologie'. These essays are presupposed in some of Kant's work of the 1750's and 1760's.
6. G. Tonelli, 'The law of continuity in the eighteenth century', *Studies on Voltaire*, 27, 1963, 1619-1638.
7. Cited in I. Polonoff, *Force, cosmos, monads and other themes of Kant's early thought*, Bouvier, 1973.
8. C. Fleischauer, 'L'Akakia de Voltaire', *Studies on Voltaire*, 30, 1964, 7-146. Maupertuis' *Oeuvres* vol.1 contains an introduction by Maupertuis giving his account of the controversy with Koenig.
9. J. Reeves, *The reputation and writings of Alexander Pope*, Heinemann, 1976, pp.212-228. Cf. A. Harnack, *Geschichte der Königlich Preussischen Akademie der Wissenschaften zu Berlin*, 1:i, 404f.
10. Brockes had published the first volume of his 'Irdisches Vergnügen in Gott' in 1719 (Brockes' text was used by Händel for his 'Nine German arias'). See his *Auszug vornehmsten Gedichte aus dem Irdischen Vergnügen in Gott*, Faksimile of 1738 ed., Metzlersche Verlagsbuchhandlung, 1965, especially pp.113-114, the poem 'Der gestirnte Himmel'. His *Versuch vom Menschen vom Alexander Pope*, Herold, 1740, has the English facing the German translation, and also includes Thomson's 'Love' from his *Seasons*, selections from Milton's *Paradise Lost* and p.180f translations of Addison's hymns, 'When all thy mercies, O my God! and 'The spacious firmament on high'. Cf. D.F. Strauss, *Gesammelte Schriften*, Strauss, 1876, 2, 1-16; H.M. Wolff, 'Brockes' Religion', *Publications of the Modern Language Association of America*, 62, 1947, 1124-1152; W.F. Maitland, 'Brockes and the limitations of imitation', pp.101-117, and P. Böckmann, 'Eighteenth century German hymnic verse', pp.121-135 of A. Close ed., *Reality and creative vision in German lyrical poetry*, Butterworth, 1963; Barth, *Church Dogmatics*, 3:1, 399-402. On Reimarus see the introductory essay, pp.9-16 of W. Schmidt-Biggemann, ed., *Hermann Samuel Reimarus: Handschriften verzeichnis und Bibliographie*, Vandenhoeck & Ruprecht, 1979; and on Haller and Brockes, K.S. Guthke, *Literarisches Leben in Achtzehnten Jahrhundert in Deutschland und in der Schweiz*, Francke, 1975.
11. Cf. Th. W. Danzel, *Gottsched und seine Zeit. Auszüge aus seinem Briefwechsel*, Dyk'sche, 1848, p.60f. I.O. Wade, *Voltaire and Candide*, Princeton U.P., 1959, pp.23-34 gives details of various books published discussing Leibniz' views on theodicy.
12. *Pope, ein Metaphysiker!* Schuster, 1755. Cf. Altmann, *Mendelssohn*, p.46f, p.112f; and A. Altmann, *Studies in religious philosophy and mysticism*, Routledge & Kegan Paul, 1969, pp.246-274. O. Chadwick, *Lessing's theological writings*, A. & C. Black, 1956, pp.99-102; H.E. Allison, *Lessing and the enlightenment: his philosophy of religion and its relation to eighteenth century thought*, Ann Arbor, 1966. In

connection with the revival of the contrast between a rationalist, Leibnizian understanding of religious belief and that which had been represented by Bayle, cf. Erich Beyreuther, 'Zinzendorfs Verhältnis zu Pierre Bayle und zur Aufklärung', pp.354-394 of M. Greschat ed., *Zur Neueren Pietismus-Forschung*, Wissenschaftliche Buchgesellschaft, 1977. H.D. Nisbett writes on Bayle and Lessing with particular reference to Bayle's advocacy of tolerance, pp.13-29 of C.P. Magill, B.A. Rowley, C.J. Smith eds., *Tradition and creation : essays in honour of Elizabeth Mary Wilkinson*, Maney, 1978.
13. Cf. Warburton's commentary on Pope's works (Nine volumes complete, together with the commentary and notes of Mr. Warburton, Knapton, 1752) 3,12,23.
14. Voltaire's *Correspondence*, ed. T. Bestermann, Institut et Musée Voltaire, 1957, 29, 72. Cf. *Theodicy*, 3, 241, and Montesquieu, *Oeuvres Complètes*, Nagel, 1950, the *Lettres Persanes*, esp. no.97, pp.193-195, and no.113, pp.224-226; Diderot, *Selected philosophical writings*, ed. J. Lough, C.U.P. 1953, p.30f. 'Pensées sur l'Interpretation de la Nature'; E.B. Hill, 'The role of 'le Monstre' in Diderot's thought', *Studies on Voltaire*, 97 1972, 147-258.
15. Voltaire, *Candide, Zadig and selected stories*, trans. D.M. Frame, Signet, 1961; A. Foulet, 'Zadig and Job', *Modern language notes*, 75, 1960, 421-423.
16. *Theodicy* 3. 414-417. Cf. 'Leibniz' philosophical dream' in *Leibniz: philosophical writings*, trans. M. Morris, Dent, 1968, pp.253-257.
17. R.H. Popkin, 'Manicheanism in the enlightenment', pp.31-54 of *The critical spirit: essays in honor of Herbert Marcuse*, ed, K.H. Wolff and Barrington Moore, Beacon, 1967, provides an account of de Beausobre's work.
18. Voltaire, *Oeuvres Complètes*, Garnier, 1877, 60 433-479.
19. R.A. Leigh, 'Rousseau's letter to Voltaire on optimism, 18th August, 1756', *Studies on Voltaire*, 29, 1964, 247-309; *Voltaire's Correspondence*, 30, 102-115. And see the 'Lettre à M. Philopolis', 1, 223-4 of Vaughan, *Political writings*.
20. J.J. Rousseau, *Emile*, trans. B. Foxley, p.228f. Cf. R. Grimsley, *Rousseau and the religious quest*, Clarendon, 1968, pp.52-58; and *The philosophy of Rousseau*, O.U.P., 1973, pp.70-88. Also Vaughan, 1,15.
21. Vol.21 of the complete works contains the texts of Voltaire's tales which discuss evil, including 'Plato's dream', and 'White and black', where the discovery that there are no 'solutions' is compared to the awakening from a dream. Cf. H. Mason, 'Voltaire and War', *The British Journal for Eighteenth-Century Studies*, 4:2, 1981, 125-138.
22. KW 2, 373, Mme de Staël was to refer to *Candide* as 'Cet ouvrage d'une gaieté infernale', p.42 of *De l'Allemagne*.
23. Maynard Mack, ed., *Alexander Pope: an Essay on Man*, Methuen,

1958, pp.xii-xiv- J. Laird, *Philosophical incursions into English literature*, C.U.P., 1946, pp.34-51; D.G. James, *The life of reason*, Longmans, 1949. pp.174-267.
24. W.F. Bottiglia, 'Voltaire's Candide: analysis of a classic', *Studies on Voltaire*, 7, 1959, 101-102.
25. Voltaire, *Philosophical dictionary*, p.73-4.
26. G.R. Havens, 'Voltaire and Alexander Pope', pp.124-150 of J. Papas, ed., *Essays on Diderot and the enlightenment in honor of Otis Fellows*, Droz, 1974. Dr. Johnson also had a jaundiced view of Pope's essay: 'Never was penury of Knowledge and Vulgarity of sentiment so happily disguised. The reader feels his mind full, though he learns nothing', Reeves, *Pope*, p.226. Cf. R.B. Schwartz, *Samuel Johnson and the problem of evil*, Wisconsin U.P., 1975.
27. *La Palingénesie philosophique, ou idées sur l'état passé et sur l'état futur des Êtres vivans*, 1770; and *La contemplation de la nature*, Amsterdam, 1764, ET 1766, 1, 3: 'The DIVINE MIND, which at once comprehends all the combinations of possible beings, saw from all eternity the true good, without deliberation. It has acted, it has displayed its sovereign liberty, and the universe its being. So that the universe has acquired every possible perfection from a Cause in whom wisdom is one of his chief attributes, and in whom goodness is also wisdom'. The study of nature was useless, did it not lead us 'to aspire incessantly after this adorable BEING, by endeavouring to acquire a knowledge of him from that immense chain of various productions wherein his power and wisdom are displayed with such distinguished truth and undiminished lustre'.
28. L.P. Courtines, 'Bayle, Hulme and Berkeley', *Revue de Littérature Comparée*, 1947, 416-428; E.C. Mossner, 'Hume's early memoranda: the complete text', *Journal of the history of ideas*, 9, 1948, 492-518, especially p.501, sections 19-20. Hume also used Law's introduction to King's work.
29. Ed. E.C. Mossner, Penguin, 1969.
30. Ed. L.A. Selby-Bigge, 3rd edn., Clarendon, 1975, Section viii, 'On liberty and necessity' included remarks on moral and physical evil, and p.226-7 of the 'Principles of morals' on the Manicheans. Section xi, 'Of a particular providence and a future state' further attempts to corrode the cautiously expressed theism of Bishop Butler. For a recent recommendation of Butler, cf. J.R. Lucas, *Butler's philosophy of religion vindicated*, Durham Cathedral Lectures, 1978.The importance of two sections on miracles and on providence, etc. taken together, was spotted in the nineteenth century, the heyday of enthusiasm for the reading of Butler, by L. Stephen, in his 1876 *History of English Thought in the Eighteenth Century* I, ch. vi.
31. E.g. *Enquiry* section XI and the 'dialogue' at the end of the

'Principles of morals', pp.324f.
32. R.H. Popkin, 'Scepticism in the enlightenment', *Studies on Voltaire* 25, 1963, 1321-1345.
33. Polonoff, p.165; KW 2, 160.
34. Zweig, *Correspondence*, pp.41-2.
35. C.W. Swain, 'Hamann and the philosophy of David Hume', *Journal of the history of philosophy*, 5,1967, 343-351. Cf. I. Berlin, 'Hume and the sources of German anti-rationalism', pp.162-187 of ed. H. Hardy, *Against the current: essays in the history of ideas*, Hogarth, 1979.
36. B 20, B 233. Cf. A. Seth, *Scottish philosophy: a comparison of the Scottish and German answers to Hume*, Blackwood, 1907, K.E. Yandell argues that '*The Natural History of Religion* contains the key to Hume's position, and that the *Dialogues* must be read in the light of the *Natural History*. Or, to be more accurate, the *Natural History* expresses straightforwardly theses which the *Dialogues* expresses only by implication', p.111 of his essay 'Hume on religious belief', pp.109-125 of D.W. Livingston and J.T. King eds. *Hume: a re-evaluation*, Fordham U.P., 1976.
37. J.G. Hamann, *Werke*, Herder, 1951, 3, 245-274.
38. Löwisch, p.28f; Immanuel Kant, *Lectures on philosophical theology*, trans. A.W. Wood and G.M. Clark, Cornell U.P., 1978, pp.99-108 on 'Physicotheology'.
39. *Hume on religion*, ed. R. Wollheim, Collins, 1966, p.203 (all citations from the *Dialogues* will be taken from this edition.
40. J.Y.T. Grieg, ed., *The Letters of David Hume*, O.U.P., 1932, 1, 154. The sort of argument Elliot might have produced may be found in *Encyclopedia Britannica: or, a Dictionary of Arts and Sciences, compiled upon a new plan, by a Society of Gentlemen in Scotland*, J. Donaldson, 1773, 3, 'Metaphysics', p.175f.
41. Cf. J.H. Newman, *University Sermons*, S.P.C.K., 1970, p.70 of 1831 on 'some unsoundness in the intellectual basis of the argument' from design, and p.194-5 of 1839, on 'the practical safeguard against Atheism in the case of scientific enquirers' being 'the inward need and desire, the inward experience of that Power, existing in the mind before and independently of their examination of His material world'.
42. Wollheim, *Hume*, pp.108-10, p.124-5.
43. *Enquiry*, p.54-5, p.145-6.
44. S. Clarke, *Works*, 1738, 4, and H.G. Alexander, ed., *The Leibniz-Clarke Correspondence*, M.U.P., 1956, Cf. L.M. Teeter, 'Albrecht von Haller and Samuel Clarke', *Journal of English and German Philology*, 27:4, 1928, 520-523.
45. Wollheim, *Hume*, p.161f.
46. *The Monthly Review*, 32, 1765, 497f.
47. James, *The life of reason*, two chapters.

48. B. Russell, *A critical exposition of the philosophy of Leibniz*, Allen & Unwin, 1900.
49. T.D. Kendrick, *The Lisbon earthquakes*, Methuen, 1956, p.15.
50. *Letters*, 1, 141.
51. R. Klibansky and E.C. Mossner, eds., *New letters of David Hume*, Clarendon, 1954, p.53.
52. Wollheim, *Hume*, p.166-7.
53. Ibid., part x of the *Dialogues*, compared with the latter part of the secion 'Of liberty and necessity' in the *Enquiry*.
54. Wollheim, *Hume*, p.186-187.
55. Ibid., p.193.
56. Ibid., p.173; *Theodicy*, 'Preliminary Dissertation', 82; 1, 19.
57. *Enquiry*, p.145.
58. Wollheim, *Hume*, p.103, p.107.
59. Ibid., p.118-119.
60. Ibid., p.121-2.
61. Ibid., p.119.
62. Ibid., p.134.
63. Ibid., p.133.
64. Ibid., p.134.
65. Ibid., p.135.
66. Ibid., p.137.
67. Ibid., p.159 R. Wegener, *Das Problem der Theodicee in der Philosophie und Literatur des XVIII Jahrhunderts*, Niemeyer 1909, p.48 remarked on Leibniz' Faust-like talent for giving reality to phantoms.
68. Ibid., p.178; Leibniz, *Theodicy*, 3; 215.
69. Ibid., p.148.
70. Ibid., p.193-4.
71. Ibid., p.135.
72. Ibid., p.189-90.
73. Ibid., p.181-2.
74. Ibid., p.172, cf. p.186.
75. Ibid., p.179.
76. Ibid., p.167.
77. Ibid., p.183-4.

PART III
KANT'S OPTIMISM BEFORE 1781

Kant put himself on record as an optimist in the 1750's. Like other young men seeking to establish their literary and philosophical reputations, he responded to Berlin Academy competitions. One was set for 1754 on the question as to whether, since the first period of its origin, the earth had undergone any alteration in its rotation round its axis.[1] The other was the one about the distinction between the positions of Leibniz and Pope. Kant thought of drafting an essay for this competition[2] but preferred to develop his theology in conjunction with his cosmological speculations. Here he followed the example of Maupertuis,[3] and also responded to the stimulus of the work of Thomas Wright of Durham.[4] He announced his new work as a 'cosmogony', but when it appeared in the year of the competition, it was with the title, *Universal Natural history and theory of the heavens*. Copernicus' achievement had been sufficiently to demonstrate that absolute primary motion was to be attributed to the earth, and Newton's achievement to formulate the general law of attraction which determined the primary factor. For present purposes, the concentration must be on the way in which the essay contributes to the expression of optimism. Even to the most casual reader, Kant's optimism was signalled by his quotations from Brockes' translation of Pope's *Essay*, and from the work of von Haller. The latter was back in Switzerland flourishing as a didactic poet after an outstandingly successful career. Indeed, Kant's whole stance is informed by his preoccupation with a theological concept of creation. He had satisfied himself that his speculation was in accordance with a principle which could be drawn from 'revelation', that is, that the universe depended upon a creator, that it had a 'beginning'. For him, the result of his struggle for comprehension was that he saw the glory of the supreme being 'break forth with the brightest splendour'.[5] Paying attention to the laws of matter in motion elaborated and explained by Newton, he found the confidence to go further than had Newton in utilising his understanding of these laws to serve his religious apologetic. Already, in his 1747 'Thoughts about the true estimation of living forces', Kant had reported that 'Leibniz thought it was not seemly for God's power and wisdom that He should be incessantly compelled to renew the motion which He had implanted in His creation, as Newton imagined'. For 'God saves Himself as much activity as He can afford to do without damaging the world-machine. Instead, he makes nature as active and effective as possible'.[6] The fundamental forces of nature serve the very plan which the supreme wisdom has set itself. Whilst at this stage he entirely agreed that arguments drawn from the beauty and perfect arrangement of the universe established the existence of a supremely wise creator for all but the most obstinately stupid, he himself preferred to start with arguments drawn from the analysis of 'physics' as Newton had expounded it. He would develop further arguments to do with 'finality', holding the opinion that mechanism and finality would in any case be found to be coherent.

Kant's scheme was indeed ambitious: to 'discover the system which binds together the great members of the creation in the whole extent of infinitude, and to derive the formation of the heavenly bodies themselves, and the origin of their movements, from the primitive state of nature by mechanical laws'.[7] The principles of physics seemed to entitle him to say, 'with intelligent certainty and without audacity: '*Give me matter and I will construct a world out of it!*' i.e. give me matter and I will show you how a world shall arrive out of it'.[8] Kant did not think it entirely beyond the bounds of credibility to suppose that the production of a single herb or caterpillar would be distinctly and completely understood. However, he advised himself as apologist to cope with subjects which seemed to him to be manageable and relatively less obscure.[9] Thinking about a nature characterised by its own 'inherent essential striving' he was inescapably driven to think about the all-sufficient supremely wise power, the 'Infinite Intelligence, an Understanding in which the essential properties of all things have been relatively designed'.[10] Only in a 'reflection'[11] did he express his perplexity over the status of the eternal verities and their 'independence' of the deity, representing a necessity in conflict with the divine will which the deity nevertheless authorises. In his essay he remarked that without such a divine origin for things of such a diverse nature,[12] 'what an impossibility would it be that they should so exactly fit into each other with their natural activities and tendencies, just as if a reflective prudent choice had combined them!' From elemental chaos (in the primitive state of this world, not in the mind of the deity) has arisen the ordered variety which so delighted Kant as observer.

Kant suggested that his readers ought to begin with chapter eight, the last chapter of the second main part, probably because this chapter recapitulates the 'preface'.[13] In the second part, he made the points that Newton should have made, for the Newtonian understanding of the capacity of the elements of nature to raise themselves to order and perfection by the forces of attraction and repulsion is the finest demonstration of the existence of God, and by employing Newtonian physics Kant could eliminate appeal to the intervention of the deity where even the Newtonians had supposed it to be necessary. Appeal to divine intervention made no sense of such problems as the 'irregular' courses of some phenomena, (his conjecture that celestial bodies other than Saturn might exist was verified twenty-six years later by the discovery of Uranus with the aid of new telescopes); the density of the planets in inverse proportion to their distance from the sun; the distance of the planets from each other; and the fact that the axis of the earth was not perpendicular to the plane of its orbit. Kant's proposal was that one should think of the universe as having been constituted by the deity so that there would result a series of events in a matter-filled space.[14]

In the third main part of his essay he addressed himself to the question in the preface, as to how it could be said that the forces of nature, manifest as air, water and heat, 'things of such diverse nature' should serve the ends of man and living creatures generally.[15] This was the point at which he turned to 'finality' and found it coherent with 'mechanism'. To test the range of application of his proposals Kant chose also to embrace the question as to whether there were inhabitants on other planets. He appealed to the arrangement made by divine providence[16] to dispose matter for the benefit of living beings who may inhabit other planets. In this totality, the most despised insect[17] is as necessary as the highest class of thinking beings,[18] and there was no need to assume that human beings were members of a supposed highest class. In one of his rare, mildly humourous remarks,[19] Kant re-told the story of the lice in the beggar's hair, who had thought themselves to be the masterpieces of creation. One of them, a Fontenelle of his race, found that he had somehow transferred himself to the head of a nobleman, there to discover that there were other living beings, lice like himself. For the inhabitants of some planets, a Green-lander or Hottentot would seem by comparison to be a Newton, and for others, a Newton would be regarded the way men regard an ape.[20] Kant was following opinions voiced by Leibniz[21] when he suggested that as the density of the planets was inversely proportioned to their distance from the sun, the inhabitants of the planets have an appropriate physical constitution, this in turn affecting their mental capacities. However complex the arrangements, however immense the cosmos, the divine reason comprehended it, and had so constituted the elements of matter that the required dispositions of varying degrees of complication would come by themselves. Later in life Kant seems to have been rather embarrassed by these speculations of his, which served as an imaginative illustration of his general thesis. He could in fact dispense with this section and rely on part two, chapter seven, as a response to the question of his preface and as a statement of his theological convictions in 1755, which could be allowed to stand.

In chapter seven, 'Of the creation in the whole extent of its infinitude both in space and time', Kant expressed the pleasure he experienced at integrating speculative cosmogony and moral conviction.[22] Principles of explanation learned from Newton, yielding an event-filled cosmos, produced arrangements suitable for the existence of rational and moral beings.[23] Kant's overall perspective made explicable and tolerable the presence of what was apparently disorderly and absurd. The perfection of the universe moved the imagination with its immeasurable greatness, variety and beauty. Kant did not at this juncture quote Edmund Burke in this connection, but one may at this point notice the latter's *Philosophical enquiry into the origin of our ideas of the sublime and beautiful*.[24] Burke wrote that 'Hardly anything can strike the mind with its greatness, which does not make some sort of approach towards infinity; which nothing can do whilst we are able to perceive its bounds ... There is a passage in the book of Job amazingly sublime, and this sublimity is principally due to the terrible uncertainty of the thing described'. The sublime may be the 'concomitant of terror' as with Job's descriptions of the war horse, the wild ass, the unicorn, and above all, Leviathan. When one speaks of God, 'the scripture alone can supply ideas answerable to the majesty of this subject. In scripture, wherever God is represented as appearing or speaking, everything terrible in nature is called up to heighten the awe and solemnity of the divine presence. The psalms and the prophetical books are crowded with instances of this kind'.[25]

The 'approach to infinity' in Kant's case arises from his contemplation of space, 'that infinite receptable of the Divine Presence',[26] and the science of number furnishes another clue. There can be no greater number, and this realisation provides the mind with a notion of infinity. There is here[27] 'no end, but an abyss of a real immensity, in presence of which all the capability of a human conception sinks exhausted'. The divine creative activity is without limit: 'the field of the revelation of the Divine attributes is as infinite as these attributes themselves. Eternity is not sufficient to embrace the manifestations of the Supreme Being, if it is not combined with the infinitude of space'.[28] Infinity in terms of the future succession of time, 'by which eternity is unexhausted, will entirely animate the whole range of space to which God is present, and will gradually put it into that regular order which is conformable to the excellence of His plan'.[29]

Kant began from a theological position, and he employs a further point from his theology, passing beyond the 'probable reasoning'[30] culled from Newton and the astronomers of his day. He proposed on analogy with the solar system that the universe itself has a centre. In other words, he prescribed what the deity must have done to have made the best universe. The systematic connection[31] obtaining for the parts obtains for the whole, and the universe itself has a 'fulcrum'. There need be no suspicion that a universe which developed itself from its elements might dissolve back again to those elements. What he referred to as 'common dependence' of the elements on one another, promotes universal harmony. The connecting power of attraction and centrifugal force produces a universe exhibiting the character of 'that stability which is the mark of the choice of God. It is therefore much more in conformity with that choice to make the whole creation a single system which puts all the worlds and systems of worlds, that fill the whole of infinite space, into relation to a single centre'. Creation, 'or rather the development of nature',[32] begins at the centre, and from there extends itself. So Kant wrote:

> Let us dwell upon this idea for a moment with the silent satisfaction it brings. I find nothing which can raise the spirit of man to a nobler wonder, by opening to him a prospect into the infinite domain of omnipotence, than that part of my theory which concerns the successive realization of the creation.

In the context of considering this vast perspective, Kant turned to the problem of natural evil. His view was that nature brings forth animals and plants to make up for the loss of others, 'the victims of time',[33] and if, for example, portions of the earth are buried in the sea, 'nature repairs the loss and brings forth other regions which were hidden in the depths of being in order to spread over them the new wealth of her fertility'. By analogy, Kant proposed that it was in 'the same way worlds and systems perish and are swallowed up in the abyss of eternity; but at the same time creation is always busy constructing new formations in the heavens, and advantageously making up for the loss'. The world we inhabit has 'a certain stability in itself which according to our conceptions, approaches an endless duration'; but when the time comes for it to perish, Nature's prodigality more than makes up for its disappearance. Similarly, so far as disasters on the human scale are concerned, 'The injurious influences of infected air, earthquakes, and inundations sweep whole peoples from the earth; but it does not appear that nature has thereby suffered any damage'. Kant simply proposed that we should 'accustom our eye to these terrible catastrophes as being the common ways of providence, and regard them even with a sort of complacency',[34] since the 'Phoenix of nature, which burns itself only in order to revive again in restored youth from its ashes', will carry on the 'plan of the Divine revelation, in order to fill eternity, as well as all the regions of space, with her wonders'.[35]

It is by no means the case that such complacency in itself secures the interests of rational creatures. A further supposition was needed, were these disasters not to be regarded as unmitigated disasters. A familiar trait in the eighteenth century's evaluation of the Christian tradition,[36] was that human souls were destined to survive all the transformations of nature. 'This happiness, which Reason of herself could not be bold enough to aspire to, Revelation teaches us to hope for with full conviction'.[37] According to Kant's understanding of revelation, the immortal spirit will be freed from the fetters which have bound it to that which is transitory, and find happiness in fellowship with the deity, 'this primary source of all perfection', and 'the true attracting point of all excellence'.[38] This is the nearest Kant appears to have approximated to the view that the ultimate destination of man is the 'vision' of God, subordinating all employment of reason to that ultimate vision. Addison's hymn 'When all thy mercies O my God, my rising soul surveys', (translated by Brockes, together with 'The spacious firmament on high', as well as by Frau Gottsched) sounded the right note for Kant at this point. As Kant said,

> When we have filled our minds with such contemplations, the sight of a starry heaven in a serene night affords a sort of delight which only noble and pure souls can feel. In the general silence of nature and the calm of the senses, the hidden intuitive power of the immortal spirit speaks an ineffable language and presents us with undeveloped ideas which can be sensed but not described.[39]

Re-phrased and with an additional source of awe attached, this expression of piety was to reappear in a much quoted passage from the second of Kant's Critiques.[40] At this earlier stage, however, it recalls what Kant's biographers recount about his mother's piety, and the instruction she gave to her children, taking them out of Königsberg into the countryside, and to see the heavens on a clear evening.[41] It seems to be typical of the piety transformed by the new world-view,[42] whether we read about Frau Gottsched,[43] Maupertuis,[44] one of Kant's pupils and later colleagues the political philosopher C.J. Kraus,[45] or Burke, as before. The latter wrote that

> *magnificence* is likewise a source of the sublime. A great profusion of things which are splendid or valuable in themselves, is *magnificent*. The starry heaven, though it occurs so very frequently to our view, never fails to excite our idea of grandeur. This cannot be owing to anything in the stars themselves, separately considered. The number is certainly the cause. The apparent disorder augments the grandeur, for the appearance of care is highly contrary to our ideas of magnificence. Besides, the stars lie in such apparent confusion, as makes it impossible on ordinary occasions to reckon them. This gives them the advantage of a sort of infinity.[46]

For Kant, there is no ultimate conflict between what serves the glory of the deity and the interests of rational beings, if fellowship with the deity will enable the soul to enjoy a complete vision of the concordance of the universe.

Further comments expressing Kant's optimistic vision were to be found in his *New exposition of the first principles of metaphysical knowledge*,[47] which does not at first sight look as though it would contain a discussion of theodicy.[48] Of the same year as the *Universal natural history*, the style is different, since it was a formal Latin dissertation defended in public at the Albertina, produced to qualify Kant to teach philosophy. Kant made it clear that the actual determined what could be said of the possible,[49] and the determination of a particular thing depended upon its links with other actually existing things. So he gave priority to 'dependence' rather than 'pre-established agreement'. He agreed with Leibniz about the interdependence of things with one another, but interpreted it so as to be able to speak of the way in which 'all things take place in natural conjunction, connectedly and inseparably'.[50] He could still write of 'a whole sequence of interwoven grounds right back to the first condition of the world', a first state which 'directly exhibits God as creator'. From such a ground, things are derived in the course of time by the operation of physical laws. He used one image here which was exceptional for him,[51] that the first condition of the world was 'as it were a fountain and gushing spring from which all things take their course by an infallible necessity'. F.E. England commented that Kant was here using a figure from Plotinus to illustrate the emanation of the various orders of being from God. Thus:

> the spring, overflowing, produces what comes after it, and this in turn gives rise to the next stage and so forth. There is no actual dispersion of the higher into the lower forms, no diminution of the higher in giving rise to the lower. The order throughout is not a temporal, but a logical order of connection.[52]

To that we may add that in the middle ages, as in for example Guillaume de Machaut's *Lay de le fontaine*, the image of source, fountain and stream represented the trinity of Father, Son and Holy Spirit. It is not that either Plotinian or Trinitarian thinking is explicit in Kant, merely that he drew on a classical image to express his sense of the world's dependence on a divine source.

Kant's argument from the reciprocity of things to the divine being[53] served a useful purpose in eliminating Manicheism.[54] Had the Manicheans been correct, and the world governed by two equally primary principles, one would not be able to discern and demonstrate the interconnection of things.[55] The deity is the source of all thinkable reality, without himself being determined by it. The clean operation of divine reason without hindrance was expounded by way of the comment that 'there is no need on the part of an infinite intelligence, for the abstraction of universal notions and for a combining of such notions, nor for a colligation made for eliciting consequences'.[56] Conceiving of the deity's intuition of the whole, and indeed his intimate presence to each particular thing[57] Kant wrote that 'the same *schema* of the divine intellect which gives them existence has fixed their reciprocities by conceiving their existences as correlated', the schema of the divine intellect being 'an enduring act (generally called conservation)'. Had things been conceived in isolation from one another, it would not be possible for rational beings to think through the conception of things in terms of mutual interconnection in such a way as to approximate to the divine schema.

In the divine being, spontaneous action proceeds from internal principle,[58] and similarly with human spontaneity. So Kant thought he could deal conclusively with the problem of evil in the section 'refutation of doubts' between two oddly named characters, Caius and Titius. The latter affirms that 'in undertaking the primordial affairs of the universe, God started a series which includes, in a fixed nexus of reasons bound together intimately and interconnectedly, even moral evils, and corresponding to them physical evils'.[59] (Kant does not think there is necessarily an exact correspondence between a particular moral evil and a particular physical evil, only that in agreement with Leibniz, he supposed that every action has its consequences and that physical evil was an appropriate accompaniment to moral evil). Moral evil was the result of choice which was not for the good on the part of beings capable of determining themselves for the good. Rational beings who act irrationally frustrate themselves and their possibilities of satisfaction and happiness. The deity, who is then not the immediate author of their mistakes, in his infinite goodness[60] strives to overrule irrational choice, without destroying liberty, 'by advising, warning, encouraging, supplying the means'. And in his wisdon the deity elicits good even from the effects of human depravity, and this further enables 'the manifestation of the divine glory in its infinite variety'. Kant here gives expression to some wholly familiar features of the Christian tradition, as Leibniz for one had reminded him, such as the divine permission of evils, the interpretation of natural evil as in some respect punishment for moral evils, the divine providential rule for the ultimate good of creatures who sometimes are able to do otherwise than they do.

The opportunity to put optimism to the test albeit at a distance, was the appalling disaster of the Lisbon earthquake, the worst of a series of earthquakes which threatened civilised and optimistic Europeans and their way of looking at things. It will be recalled that Voltaire had been provoked by the disaster to write his poem about it, and its publication, and the accompanying poem on natural law, had elicited optimistic response from Rousseau. Kant utilised information provided by the natural philosophers to serve the purposes of his theology. A short preliminary discussion[61] announced a treatise of 1756,[62] on the history and natural description of the most remarkable features of the earthquake which shook a great part of the earth at the end of 1755. Having read the *Universal natural history*'s remarks that epidemics, earthquakes and floods sweep whole peoples from the earth without nature as such suffering any damage,[63] coupled with belief in the immortality of the soul, the opinions he expressed in 1756 are wholly to be expected. Kant as yet finds nothing morally offensive in theodicy, nor does he give us any sense that he is 'touched in his own skin' by it.[64] It is through the examination of nature that man is enabled to praise his creator,[65] and the recent earthquakes summon him to further reflection. There is a note of sheer obedience here, which arises and can only arise from fundamental trust in the divine being. Earthquakes happen as a result of laws implanted in nature by the deity, not by his intervention, and either man has no right, or has lost the right, to expect that the operation of those laws will be unfailingly opportune for him.

Not until he was writing his third *Critique* and the short theological essays of his latest years did he give greater weight to nature's indifference to man. In the 1750s he relied on the goodness of the deity almost with hesitation. By the 1790s divine goodness is the presupposition of divine justice, and it is divine justice on which he comes to rely in the first instance. His analysis of human morality takes precedence over rational satisfaction at the spectacle of the world with a corresponding shift in his concept of deity. However, in 1756, having philosophized about the phenomena of nature and the 'purposes' they might in themselves serve,[66] Kant picked up a point from his introduction - the supposition that things could have been better arranged for us had providence only consulted us. We are creatures born to die,[67] strangers without property, so to speak. We should bear without a sense of outrage the deaths of a comparatively small number of people, for they are being stripped by death of what they would lose in the natural course of things in any case. We should not exaggerate the devastation but take to heart that we have no ultimate happiness here on earth. We should enjoy the benefits of nature, and take steps to avoid calamity. The deity is to be adored for the very rationality of human beings, a rationality which can enable them to avoid further disaster and govern themselves justly.[68] Disaster should inspire us to philanthropy and the intelligent management of our affairs. One should neither be impatient with the ways of providence, nor try to guess at the ways in which the deity governs the world. Certainly one should not suppose that those who suffer such a disaster are necessarily more wicked than those who have been spared the experience. One might criticise what Kant has said here by citing Karl Jaspers, where he proposes a new appropriation from biblical religion at its frontier with philosophical meaning. Jaspers urged that we should allow extremes to work in our souls, and that forgetfulness is the danger.[69]

We must regard all suffering, including that which did not touch us, as something which ought to touch us, and from which we are saved without our deserving it. Indifference is all the more untrue in face of the terrible evil which can strike us all, and of which indeed men speak, but without its becoming a reality in their souls.

One does not feel that the reality of suffering has as yet bitten into Kant in the way it had into Jaspers.

In the year of the publication of *Candide*, the 1759 'Some reflections on optimism', is an unambiguous reaffirmation of Leibniz, and a contribution to the ongoing discussion of the Berlin Academy's award of the essay prize to Reinhard.[70] Kant seems by now to have chosen to rely entirely on Leibniz and largely to have abandoned allusions to Pope, perhaps because he was clear how any value Pope[71] might have depended in turn on the value of what Leibniz has to say, just as he saw how fundamental the ontological argument was to any style of argument for the existence of the deity. It appears that Mendelssohn,[72] whilst supporting the Leibnizian position never regarded Leibniz' arguments as virtually conclusive, as Kant did for a time. It is somewhat strange to find an affirmation of Leibniz functioning as an announcement of lectures not only on metaphysics and ethics, but on physical geography, mathematics and mechanics, (all part of the sub-faculty of philosophy) despite having encountered such amalgams in Kant's work. We may suppose that this short formal statement of his theological position was most important to him as a foundation for his work. Also, it was written in Russian-occupied Königsberg, as was the major essay of 1763, *The one possible basis for a demonstration of the existence of God*.[73] Even though it seems that Königsberg benefited from the presence of the Russian officers, the occupation must at least have served as a reminder of the utter horror and ruin the war was causing elsewhere. The lecture announcement functioned as an expression of Prussian confidence for the future, even though it is not explicitly addressed to the current political problem. Kant made it clear later on his life, that he held that war was the greatest evil men could inflict on one another, whilst applauding the courage of the soldier and the fortitude of a nation at war - provided, as he said, that war was 'conducted with order and a sacred respect for the rights of civilians'.[74]

Kant began his lecture announcement[75] by observing that an adequate concept of God includes the supposition that if God chooses, he chooses the best. The novelty of Leibniz' work lay in the way in which he employed his concept of deity. Kant agreed with Leibniz that the deity in his wisdom possesses knowledge of all possible worlds, one of which worlds is the best conceivable. The deity is the ground of all reality, and his wisdom comprehends all the perfections that are possible for created beings. Such perfections are somehow in accord with the divine perfections, their source.[76] Any particular thing is held to be perfect if it has the full complement of perfections that are proper to it, that in combination with one another fall under its 'rule'. The more perfections a particular thing has in combination gives the whole its place in the order of reality. The world itself contains innumerable grades of perfection which the eternal creation preserves.[77] It seems meaningful to think of the perfections of the world as a whole, although a rational being cannot comprehend the series, which in accordance with the law of continuity it is impossible to complete. Nor does thinking about a best world depend upon our being able to think of a greatest number, or the most rapid movement. So Kant argues for the existence of a reality which is all that created perfection can be in comparison with its creator, that reality superior to all other. One cannot, therefore, compare two worlds allegedly possessing the same perfections, and yet distinguishable, as nevertheless equal in their degrees of reality. If they are distinguishable, their perfections would be related to one another so as to make one possible world have a different degree of reality from any other world. One of these worlds has the most perfection possible, and so is the one worthy of being brought into existence. The limits of the best world are those that can be indicated only by negation - that is, what the world lacks as compared with the deity. Because this statement of optimism is not brought into relation with a particular disaster or suffering, Kant can write of 'privation' in this sense, but this is unusual for him. At least it can be said for him that he does not offend by describing particular natural evils, 'happenings' which arouse a sense of outrage, as 'privation'. On the other hand he displays no unease about what sense it makes to talk of the 'whole' in this way, let alone to attempt to relate the whole to an alleged deity. The deity, meantime, was held to be wholly independent and self-sufficient, being omnipresent and having creative power. There is a 'gap' between the deity and the ladder of being which has produced this particular 'shoot' of being, the actual experiencable world, the best world. One has to suppose that the deity chose what was most worth the choosing, and to choose thus, with a full assessment of the objective, is of the essence of free action.[78] The deity in his wisdom and goodness has chosen what serves the well-being of the world's citizens. However insignificant one is, one can appreciate being a member of the chosen scheme and do what one can to further one's comprehension of it. Kant believed that the deity takes pleasure in the existence of the rational beings in his scheme, that the whole was the best, and everything exists for its good.

Kant went on to explore optimism in relation to information prompted by natural philosophers and theologians. Whereas the *Universal natural history* had as it were focussed on the cosmic context of human experience, in the 1763 *The one possible basis for a demonstration of the existence of God* (which he had begun to write in 1761) Kant so to speak concentrated on the world of living creatures on the earth's surface, and related that in turn to the cosmic context, and both alike to the divine providence. Here another Hamburg writer, H.S. Reimarus[79] was of help to him, a Reimarus surprising to anyone who thinks of him solely as a critic of the biblical writings, able in rational theology to draw on his expertise as an orientalist as well as on his philosophical training.[80] Reimarus had produced two works of natural theology, extended prose versions of Brockes one might say, and principally concerned with 'ends' in nature. One of these works written for 1755 concerned itself with the origin of living creatures.[81] His sources included Hume's essay on the populousness of ancient nations, a work by Süssmilch (to which Kant in turn refers) the works of Bolingbroke,[82] Haller, Maupertuis and Buffon to name but a few, together with important citations from the *Theodicy* and the letter of Leibniz to which Koenig had appealed, all underpinned by Leibniz' concept of deity. The physical mechanical explanation of living things was simply insufficient[83] and like others, he appealed to Malebranche's 'seeing all things in God'[84] as the destiny for the human soul or spirit, with the recommendation to pursue virtue in this life.[85] Like Kant for some years to come, Reimarus subordinated the employment of reason to the expection of the 'vision' of God. His second work on instinct in animals[86] followed the same sort of plan as his former work, with elaborations from the 'physiologists'. One feature of this work is his judicious use of Luther and biblical quotation to support his case, and at least one may say that he was free from obsession with the book of Genesis.

If nothing else, these works may have helped Kant to formulate the characteristics of his own position. Leibniz' theology was closely associated in the minds of its readers with teleological explanation. The question was to be whether it need be so associated, and whether it could instead satisfactorily be associated with the mechanical, i.e. nonteleological explanation which Kant had begun to explore in his cosmology, and which he had thought to be an indispensable, primary route of explanation, though without necessarily excluding the relevance of teleological patterns. He was endeavouring to explain an impersonal and non-sentimental nature, with its own autonomous principles of explanation, autonomous in relation to some forms of religious apologetic, but nevertheless the proper context for human development, and transparent to deity. So apart from the ever-recurring problem of the status of the 'eternal verities' within Leibniz' theology, there was to be a further major problem. If Leibniz' theology could as it were be detached from one kind of explanation of nature and attached to another, questions had to be asked about its status as 'knowledge'. Could there be a knowledge of a transcendent deity as there could be knowledge of nature? In a few years time, his attempt to formulate the operational rules for the knowing and moral subject drove him to ask further questions about the status even of knowledge of nature, and of the worth of human action if it could not be held to be in its own way a representation of the divine ordering of living beings. Kant had to debate the merits of the pattern of explanation of nature in terms of 'fixity of forms' as against a 'history of nature', as well as discuss the question whether rational beings were not allowed to order their affairs as were things in the world free of divine interference. Kant came to experience to the full the conflict of reason against reason, which for him was an approximation to being 'touched in his own skin', with almost disastrous consequences for his faith in the deity. He would also have believed himself to be on the verge of destruction in his innermost self had he had to acknowledge in himself a thorough-going intention to lie, for example, and an intention systematically to set himself against the good of another person by so doing.

Kant was explicit about what he meant to do by writing the 1763 essay. It was to explain how one could ascend to the apprehension of the deity by means of natural philosophy rather than rely solely on doctrine from 'revelation'.[87] In the writing of his first *Critique* he had not merely to abandon but to destroy any route of ascent to the deity, showing that there could be no knowledge which applied beyond the reach of what we could make thinkable for ourselves. In 1763 he had reached the position that he did not suppose that the deity could be finally conceptualised, but simply proffered arguments which he hoped went some way towards supplying a measure of rational satisfaction, deploying a number of themes which he interwove with one another. He began by remarking on some features of his concept of deity[88] for his readers. He reminds us of remarks made in the 1755 *Universal natural history*, and the 1759 lecture announcement. To begin with, he does not attempt to do more than indicate the direction in which he will move, because to discuss the concept purely *a priori* does not do justice to the range of his problem. In the meantime, he affirms that God's *fiat* with regard to a possible world adds no new determination to it, but posits the whole series of things 'absolutely'. The proposal that the deity of the fiat exists means that to an existing being are proper such predicates as 'omnipotence'. Professor D.M. MacKinnon has recently recalled C.C.J. Webb's insight into the importance of the ontological argument. He held that it was the most overtly religious of all the rational theistic proofs. 'One of its deepest assumptions must be found in the suggestion that where the concept of God is concerned, we are enabled almost immediately to reject what is clearly inadequate'.[89]

It would appear here that Kant was relying on a form of *a priori* argument in this essay as a criterion for a more or less adequate concept of the deity. However, he is not offering his argument as a rigorous demonstration, and this is where he began to show further signs of difference from Leibniz.

The first part of what he had to say approximates very closely to a crucial set of paragraphs in his first *Critique*, paragraphs in which he provided an account of how it could have been supposed that the ontological argument was satisfactory as a proof of the existence of the deity. (Like Kant's argument in 1763, however, it may still serve as a criterion of concepts of deity.) In the 1763 essay he notes[90] only that when we use the verb 'to exist', we use it logically to relate a predicate to its subject, as in the example he has given, 'God is omnipotent'. When the verb is not being used as a copula, it directs us to the actual, without which there is nothing to think about. Kant allows himself to suppose that an absolutely necessary being exists, since its non-existence could be thought to annul the material of all that is conceivable.[91] The existence of the deity is proposed as the ground of the possibility of the concept of deity, a deity who is held to create the possibilities of nature, its immanent basic laws. Then every other thing or object of thought exists insofar as it is 'given' by him. The deity is one and simple[92] (so much for the Manicheans); the ground of all being is not itself divisible into many substances. Everything is comprehended by the deity, though he is unalterable and eternal. So Kant distinguished between determinations proper to the deity and realities which are 'consequences' of his being their ground. For instance, the inpenetrability of bodies, their extension and so on, are not properties of intellect and will as such, nor are 'positive' characteristics, such as the pain in the sensations of intelligent being. The world is not an 'accident'[93] of the deity, since as Kant mildly puts it, in the world one comes across shortcomings, variability in oneself and in all other beings - all contrary to the determinations of the deity. (It was in this connection that he later touches on the subject of 'natural evils', in terms of what may threaten the vitality of living things.) God is 'simple', all other reality is 'given' by him as 'ground', and the greatest reality which can be included in a being is included in him. However, it is important to notice that Kant explicitly emphasized his caution about treating his remarks as a finally satisfying 'proof' of transcendent deity, for he said that one could not have a logically perfect proof of a being in which intellect and will cohere together with the greatest possible reality. Intellect and will are of inestimable value to Kant as a 'spiritual being' for whom thought as well as action is a manifestation of freedom, and intellect and will are predicated of deity as spirit. He simply concedes the concept, whilst acknowledging that the subject matter of theology precludes final comprehension by us. As with Leibniz, Kant affirms[94] that the deity's will is in conformity with the deity's intellect in order to make some sense of relating his theology to the order, beauty and perfection discernible in the universe. It was not enough merely to say that God was the 'ground' of everything that was possible, or to speak of productive power without reference to intellect, or to order without cognition and resolution without the latter attributes. The deity would be a 'blind' ground, only marginally different from the 'fate' of the ancients by being conceived of as adequate, united and independent. So Kant's way of dealing with the problem of the 'eternal verities' in correcting Leibniz (following on from his correction of the Manicheans) was to stress that unity, harmony and order, the goodness and perfection of agreement, are of the essence of deity. The 'possibilities' of things are in agreement with their 'ground'. The divine will expresses the deity's eagerness for certain consequences, and the divine nature itself provides the concordance of possibilities which the divine will expresses. The deity (that than which nothing greater can be thought) produces the best world (that than which nothing better can be thought). However, in so far as theodicy depended upon the treatment of the ontological argument as a rigorous demonstration, Kant already realises that theodicy cannot be provided in this way.

In the second main part of his 1763 work Kant re-examined the question of whether there was in indispensable reference from order and harmony in the world of experience to the deity. In other words, he also explores the *a posteriori* routes[95] of Leibniz and his followers, and sees whether *a priori* and *a posteriori* can be made to coincide in their objective. In this second part he drew extensively on material familiar to readers of the *Universal natural history* papers on earthquakes and the *New exposition*. However, he had reached the point where he had two improvements to suggest. One is that he was not now concerned with external finality, things cohering together, but with 'internal' finality. It was now the unity and harmony in the internal being of things which impressed him, and which seemed so appropriate in relation to a deity who could comprehend the internal consistency of a developing universe. The reciprocation of determinations to form wholes suggested to him that he could presuppose a chief ground of the essences of things.[96] The maxim that nature does nothing in vain[97] and his further elaboration of the character of living organisms were later to be an important feature of part of his discussion in the third *Critique*. His appeal is that we should direct attention to the inner coherence of organisms, rather than to the kinds of finality more readily accessible to the human eye and to older apologetic. It is this 'internal' finality which raises the problem of the adequacy of explanation by 'mechanism' as it had for Reimarus. As compared with Leibniz, the difference is that Kant located the 'possibilities' of things not solely in the divine ground, but in actual things themselves, as in the *New exposition*. As on the macroscopic, cosmic scale, things were let to make themselves, this was so on every level down to the most microscopic. He turned to the actual realm of experience in order to explore the adequacy of his concept of deity rather than rely solely on speculation about the divine being. In this connection, he drew attention to Maupertuis' interpretation of the least action principle,[98] that even the most general laws are subjected to a governing principle, and that the greatest economy is observed in the operation of the laws of matter. The principle expressed a reference to propriety, beauty and consistency. He agreed with Maupertuis in making matter and its laws depend upon the will of God,[99] but this must be understood to mean a will acting upon a thorough grasp of the possibility of what was to be decided upon, though we may not appeal to the divine wisdom and will for our comprehension of natural processes. From this basis he reminded his readers of his earlier, cosmic perspective of the best of all possible worlds.[100]

There are many powers in nature, earthquakes and storms for example, which have the capacity to destroy individuals, whole states and even the whole of humanity, so there is a question as to how man, capable of investigating both microscopic and macroscopic nature, is to regard himself. (Kant was spared having to consider humanity's devising means to obliterate itself.) He could allow that the deity might have so disposed the original state of the creation that such disasters would come about at an appropriate time. At least, such a supposition was preferable to thinking of direct divine intervention in such matters, with all the superstitious terror such a thought reflects. Equally, he would not allow the pious to regard their 'blessings' as the result of direct intervention either. Like Leibniz, he found himself able to suppose that human wickedness could meet with a retribution which came about in connexion with the laws of cause and effect in nature, without wanting to apply such a supposition to a particular case. But it could be regarded as an instance of external finality, as much as the benefits and blessings of natural order. However, the main point he wants to make is that the course of nature is good insofar as what flows from it is good, and that the deity comprehended in his decree a world in which everything mostly fulfils the rule of the best by a natural coherence.[101] The deity chose the world because through natural coherence perfect ends could be most precisely attained. It is to the precise attainment of internal finality and perfection at the microscopic level that he must now deploy the fundamental laws of matter in motion, as in explanation of the infrastructure of animals and plants. He preferred to suppose that there was a first divine disposition of plants and beasts, a fitness not merely to 'unfold' but genuinely to procreate their like in consequence of natural law. He was well aware of the speculations of Maupertuis and Buffon as to how such procreation took place, but found the suggestions unintelligible and arbitrary.[102]

The notion of deity does not collapse into that of nature[103] - he reminds his readers repeatedly that he has to ascend from nature to an apprehension of deity. Nature was undeniably impressive, filling the soul with astonishment, humility and awe, moving it to immediate and unshakeable conviction of the wisdom, foresight and power of the deity, with consequences for moral endeavour. Kant's respect for this kind of argument remained for most of his life because he appreciated the close connection between it and the aspiration to order one's moral life, that which is at the disposition of human rational capacity and foresight. Eventually it seems that Kant could make sense only of that theology which sustains a disinterested morality. Theology which appears as a disinterested metaphysics, which represents only a purely intellectual ideal is subordinate to a moral ideal and only as so subordinate may it shape self-understanding. So far as theology was concerned, there was to be no toying with the intellectual in and for itself.

In the final paragraph of his *Universal natural history* Kant had expressed deep emotion at the sight of the star-filled heavens. In 1763 he turned to the microscopic to be rendered all but speechless:

> when I watch how in one drop of water so many animal races of a predatory kind, equipped with tools of destruction, are destroyed by even more powerful tyrants of this water-world; when I look at the intrigues, the scenes of revolt in one drop of water, and then from there lift my eyes upwards to see the immeasurable space teeming with worlds as if they were dust-particles -no human language can express the feeling stirred up by such a thought, and all subtle metaphysical dissection looks very foolish compared with the sublimity and dignity peculiar to such intuition.[104]

One point Kant was making here was that he did not want to launch forth into a kind of religious apologetic that could only too easily be discredited. For example, Süssmilch,[105] a distinguished Berlin cleric, had wanted to talk of 'providence' when trying to understand why it was that more boys were born than girls. He had established his reputation in 1741,[106] with a work intermingling questions of social and biological importance with an apologetic aim, displaying the providential ordering of things. However, later attention to population statistics had made him more circumspect in his attempts to relate theology to variations in the human species. Kant repeated his hesitation about too ready an appeal to 'moral' grounds, that is, to the will of the deity. He reaffirmed that 'revelation' had taught the dependence of the world on the deity but he saw no necessity to allow premature and dogmatic illustration of that dependence.[107] So, whereas ancient philosophers had proposed that the deity was the 'workmaster' who gave form to already existing matter (leading to another variant of Manicheism) Kant corrects them by grounding the inner coherence of individual 'wholes' in the deity, in whom the essences of things are in harmony as it were according to an admirable plan.[108] There is no competition within the godhead, and the deity is said to comprehend the ground of the inner possibilities of things, in harmony with his wisdom and his will and in this sense he is the author of matter and the 'groundstuff' of natural things. So he eliminated the appeal to external finality readily associated with Voltaire's witticisms,[109] such as the reason that we have noses is to put spectacles on them, or that nature places water horizontally so that it could be used as a looking glass. The argument is not from a known divine cause to its effects, but starts from the extraordinary things of nature (extraordinary as compared with things of human making). The question is about what may be said given that they are of such extraordinary complexity. If mechanism means employing the minimal number of explanatory principles to make nature explicable, it would seem that it can aid the mind's ascent to the divine author, bearing in mind the considerable risks of error, in this as in other routes taken by human reason. As Pope had said 'Go, teach Eternal wisdom how to rule - then drop into thyself and be a fool!'

Next Kant reconsiders the relation of this kind of explanation to the interests and benefits of rational beings, and for this he turns back again to 'cosmogony'[110] and to the summary of some of his earlier work. The crucial section here is the very last 'contemplation'[111] in which Kant attempted to expound what he meant by the divine all-sufficiency, mentioned in the preface[112] of his 1755 work, and which completes what he had begun to say about the deity in the first part of this essay of 1763. By thinking of the divine all-sufficiency he attempted to grapple with a concept which 'stayed' whatever could be thought by men of dust, who dared to 'reconnoitre' behind the curtain which hides from created eyes the secrets of the inscrutable. When he affirmed the deity's all-sufficiency, he was attempting to summarise the main theological proposal of the whole essay, that whatever there is, is what it is because it is 'given' through him. And human language may let the infinite deity say to himself: 'I am from eternity to eternity, without me there is nothing, but something exists insofar as it exists through me'. It is congruity without collision in the possibilities of things which wisdom chooses. Only thus is the origin of good surrendered without loss into the hands of a single being. Having said this, Kant turns to the physical structure of rational beings.[113]

The organic structure of the human body represents multiple

functions united in one whole. It has capacities to renew itself and to repair injuries done to it, and it is a matter for careful reflection that it endures so long despite its delicate texture in a context which provides so many grounds for its ruin. Kant's exposition of the capacities of the living organic structures of rational beings awaits further exploration in important shorter essays, produced during the decade of the Critiques. For the time being he refers to an all-sufficient deity in relation both to minimal principles of explanation and to his cluster of remarks on what actually is best in nature as man discovers it. The divine cognition as 'infinite' stands to any other cognition one could propose as in mathematics the 'infinite' stood to all possible numbers, which it surpasses.[114] Thinking of the deity's perfections as infinite fills the soul with wonder, but what Kant wants to affirm by 'all sufficient' is the unattenuated possession of all perfection. So Kant's conviction is that things in nature, whether inorganic or organic are made by the deity to be self-productive. In the case of organisms the reciprocation of intricate 'mechanisms' produces organisms which are integral wholes - nature does nothing in vain, an expression of the least action principle, applies on the microscopic as on the macroscopic scale, and it is from the consideration of the microscopic that one ascends to reflection on the deity, whose knowledge of all the delicate intricacies is complete. The infinite potential of creaturely activity in all its diversity is combined with the overall harmony of one being with another.

It has already been noticed that Kant had taken notice of Maupertuis' use of Hume, accepting that his argument to a divine 'cause' was not such as to defy the most audacious scepticism, since we can properly be said to judge the existence and character of the cause only as it were in proportion to its effects.[115] We may conjecture that there is only one author of an immense whole in which we notice 'unity and thorough combination', but we do not know all that is created, and may only suppose that what is unknown to us is conditioned in the same way. Kant reiterated the point that he could not offer a rigorous demonstration of the existence of the deity but only direct attention to what he proposed was the one source of reality. Similarly, he wrote about a best world, with the difference at this stage that he did not employ the 'escape' of the immortal spirit from the threats and disasters of the world as he had in 1755. He was approaching the turning point where 'theoria' as the ideal of reason will be subordinated to 'praxis' as the ideal of reason. This in turn raises questions about whether there can be any point in referring to the deity as 'the true attracting point of all excellence', for example, or whether this did not represent a 'Platonic' strain in Kant's thinking from which he was to do his best to emancipate himself.

In this connection it may be significant that he made certain remarks in another work of 1763, the *Attempt at introducing negative quantities into philosophy*,[116] in which Kant gave his attention to Maupertuis' *Essai de philosophie morale*.[117] The second chapter of this work was headed 'Que dans la vie ordinaire la somme des maux surpasse celle des biens', as part of Maupertuis' excursus into empirical psychology. This last for Kant meant 'the metaphysical science of man based on experience',[118] by which one could learn some facts useful for living. What seems to have caught Maupertuis' attention was the way in which 'evils' stand out against the background of experience and practice directed towards the 'good', and that is is far more difficult to give an account of the latter than of the former. Kant was busy fostering the study of anthropology, that is the study of man engaged in those relationships in which he develops moral freedom.[119] This is the subject matter of morality which has its own principles of organisation. Kant refused to agree with Maupertuis that it was appropriate to apply mathematical method to the analysis of physical sensation, and thereby to estimate the sum of human happiness. Human happiness occupied a place of high status in Kant's thinking, but he thought that this way of trying to estimate it was inappropriate. In any event, he rejected Maupertuis' 'negative' conclusion, if only because it was insignificant for the central problem or morality, which was moral worth, rather than intellectual calculation of happiness. On the subject of moral worth one can spot here what will in fact come to be a central feature of Kant's concept of deity, though not characteristic of his deity so far indicated: 'it is impossible to judge the virtue of others from their actions; that Judge, who looks into all hearts, has reserved that judgement for Himself'.[120] The divine presence to each particular thing which he thoroughly comprehends in its inner coherence as well as in its relationship to other existing things, is a feature of deity to be noted for rational and moral beings, which remains as a feature of the greatest importance in Kant's optimistic world-view. A theodicy which allows for the existence of particular evils for the sake of a greater long-term good is inescapably confronted with the question as to whether the price may not be too high to pay. Kant never quite despairs or believes that the price may be too high.

> Tell me frankly, I appeal to you - answer me: imagine that it is you yourself who are erecting the edifice of human destiny with the aim of making men happy in the end, of giving them peace and contentment at last, but that to do that it is absolutely necessary, and indeed quite inevitable, to torture to death only one tiny creature, the little girl who beat her breast with her little fist, and to found the edifice on her unavenged tears - would you consent to be the architect on those conditions?[121]

Kant comes to realise that it is human wickedness rather than human experience of 'natural evil' that is central for theodicy, as he turns from disinterested rationalism to reflection on disinterested morality. Then trust in divine justice becomes the crucial feature of his theodicy. Here that feature is barely indicated. It remains to be developed on the other side of his philosophical revolution. What survived the revolution was confidence in the divine providential overruling of all events for the sake of harmony without particular interpositions of divine action into nature in the form of 'grace' or 'miracle'.

The concept of the deity as the judge of the content and goals of moral striving comes to mean that each rational being is transparent to an omnipresent deity, who comprehends the most intricate interior workings of animate beings. Its importance lies in relation to Kant's view of the infinite possibilities of the activity of rational creatures. There is a danger that such activity could become an end in itself. The virtues of an heroic mode of life might lead to a view in which evils of one sort or another would be placed in the centre of attention, that evil would be enjoyed or even fostered in connection with the sheer exhilaration of destroying or overcoming it. This is also important for Kant's later assessment of political revolution, and the elements of political philosophy which relate his theodicy to this world of human experience. For example, H.R. Mackintosh wrote about the way in which there seems in Hegel's work to be no confrontation between the deity and the guilty creature:

> Evil is that which is on the way to good, raw material which is not yet Spirit. But this deduction of sin, however dialectically entertaining, is one more proof that moral evil forms the hard pebble-stone on which, sooner or later, a purely speculative system is obliged to break its teeth. What we start with as evil, our own and utterly damning, finally emerges from the process as good, with its own aesthetically justified place in the scheme of things. Logic is used like a conjuror's handkerchief, under cover of which, at a certain stage, there is substituted for one object another that is totally different in kind.[122]

A theodicy of creation which lets things make themselves is for Kant sufficient to account for physical evils, but for moral evils rational beings are to be held accountable to a divine scrutineer. There is to be no buying back of good in the embrace of evil.[123] This new emphasis in Kant's theology also appeared in his response[124] to a 1763 Berlin essay competition, where it became even clearer that the bare statements of a metaphysical theology were to be transposed into those of a moral theology. The competition question was whether metaphysical truths in general and in particular the first principles of natural theology and of morality were susceptible of the same clarity as mathematical truths. If they were not so susceptible, there was a question about the nature and degree of their certitude, and whether this degree was sufficient for conviction. The competition was won by Mendelssohn[125] on a casting vote from Sulzer, and Kant wrote to Formey expressing his pleasure at Mendelssohn's success. For the present purpose, Kant's *Enquiry concerning the clarity of the principles of natural theology and ethics* contains a summary of his philosophical theology at this time.[126] He wrote of the divine omnipresence:

> I apprehend easily that that being on which everything else is dependent, since it is itself independent, will, by its presence, indeed, determine the *place* of everything else in the world; but it cannot itself have a place among them, for then it would belong to the world. God is, therefore, not really in a place; he is present to all things in all *places* where *things* are.

In relation to the divine omnipresence he went on to write of the divine omniscience that:

> it can be apprehended that there is no difference at all between knowledge of the future, past or present, with respect to the activity of the divine understanding, but that he apprehends them all, as real things of the universe; and this foreseeing can be imagined much more definitely and much more clearly in God than in a thing, belonging to the totality of the world.

Kant can 'imagine' the divine apprehension and foresight, but this does not mean that he believes he can give a speculative account of them. He begins in fact to refer to what Karl Jaspers later wrote of as 'ciphers of transcendence'[127] and Kant himself as 'symbolic anthropomorphism', pointers to the transcendent not literally translatable. Hans Saner's remarks on Kant's rational concepts which transcend all possible experience are as applicable to Kant's symbolic anthropomorphism arising from his analysis of morality as to Jasper's 'ciphers of transcendence':

> What we say about them is always what we do not mean. Thought has found no words for them, so to speak. All statements about them are therefore laden with negations that take back what has been said, yet without stating it more validly in the reversal. An intentional theoretical approach to the substance of these concepts is impossible. Kant therefore seeks access to them via the ought. He asks what they mean to us, and what we ought to do to realise their substance in humanity.[128]

Kant indicates the source of his symbols when he went on to remark of the deity that

> judgment about his free actions, about his foresight, about the procedure of his justice and goodness, can only have a certainty in this branch of knowledge through approximation, or one which is moral; for here there is still much that is undeveloped even in the concept that we have of these determinations in ourselves.[129]

One further point may be made at this stage. There is a question about the place Kant allowed to 'emotion' in his theology. It is the case that he came to mistrust the 'messy warm empirical psyche'[130] but he certainly indicates profound emotion in his expressions of gratitude to the deity, his experience of astonishment and awe, and indeed humility in his reflections on himself as a rational being in the natural physical order, and called attention to his emotion several times. For example, he referred to a sort of delight which only noble and pure souls can feel at the sight of the star-strewn heavens, and to the sublimity and dignity of his feelings when comparing what one could see under a microscope of the teeming life in a drop of water as compared with the heavens. He certainly expects a moral being to understand benevolence when that is akin to compassion, and in particular there is sense in saying that Kant had a passion for truthfulness. Although Simone Weil's theology is very different from that of Kant, one of her remarks illumines his stance when she wrote of her experience of temptation: 'The temptation of the *inner life* (all emotions that are not absorbed *immediately* by methodical thought and effective action). Put aside all actions that do not attain the *object*'.[131] Her notes are also apt when she wrote: 'All I would require is to have a little less courage to cease believing that God is'.[132] She said that it was a mistake to suppose that such a belief would be less certain or of less value - rather the contrary. It is belief rather than certitude in the sense that the idea of God does not impose itself on the mind. There is not even 'an appearance of proof', only what she referred to as the 'incomparable accord' between the realm of mind and the realm of nature.

In the 1760's as we have seen, interest in Leibniz' work was regenerated by the publications of Dutens and Raspe. During the 1760s and 1770s Kant himself was approaching the point where he would bring himself to affirm his own Copernican revolution. Meantime, in 1770, and his appointment to a chair of logic and metaphysics he produced his professorial inaugural dissertation,[133] another formal Latin exposition, *On the forms and principles of the sensible and intelligible world*. He could still argue that

> the human mind is not affected by external things and the world is not open by inspection by it to infinity, except *in as much as the mind itself together with all other things is sustained by the same infinite force of one being*. Hence the mind only senses external things through the presence of the same common sustaining clause'.[134]

He could still refer to space as 'phenomenal omnipresence', the cause of the universe being present 'inwardly' to all things. He commented that Malebranche's view was least distant from his own, that is, Malebranche's view 'that we intuit all things in God' - without wanting to follow Malebranche in all his 'mystical investigations', any more than he wanted to follow Leibniz in his. This is the last stage at which

Kant proffers the goal of his intellectual fulfilment as an approximation to the divine vision and comprehension of things, and is still prepared to use principles of explanation associated with such a goal. In particular we may note three which he cited, which seem formally to summarise the main thrust of his thinking.[135] He affirmed that 'all things in the universe take place in accordance with the order of nature'; that 'principles are not to be multiplied beyond what is absolutely necessary'; and that 'No matter at all comes into being or passes away and all the vicissitudes of the world concern its form alone'. As one can see from this formulation, there is no indispensable reference to the deity implicit in these principles, but Kant juxtaposes them with what he had said about the sustaining of the human mind by the presence of the transcendent yet sustaining cause. He has said of the deity that 'since as the ideal of perfection he is the principle of cognising, he is at the same time, as existing really, the principle of the coming into being of all perfection whatsoever'.[136] And so in summary

> the UNITY *in the conjunction of substances in the universe is a consequence of the dependence of all from one*. Hence the form of the universe is witness to the cause of its matter, and only *the unique cause of all things taken together is the cause of its entirety*, nor is there any *architect* of the world who would not be at the same time its *creator*.[137]

However, the dissertation was also about the sensible world, and not merely the intelligible world. Kant refused to accept that the 'sensible' was obscured thought, but began to defend the view that it was to be known through 'intuition' rather than through 'pure reason'. There were forms and principles of the sensible world, and forms and principles of the intelligible world, and in the dissertation Kant attempted to explain how one interrelated with the other, in what areas such interrelation was legitimate and in what areas it was illegitimate. He is still experiencing what Professor MacKinnon indicates as the craving to jump out of his cognitive skin,[138] that is a craving which is illegitimate by the criteria he was shortly to explore in the writing of the first *Critique*.

Notes

1. KW 1, 185-191; ET W. Hastie, ed. M.K. Munitz, *Universal natural history and theory of the heavens*, Ann Arbor, 1969, *Space, time and creation*, Collier, 1957, pp.150-154.
2. KW 17, 3703-3705.

3. KW 1, 232-3; Hastie, pp.32-33.
4. F.A. Paneth, 'Thomas Wright and Immanuel Kant, pioneers in stellar astronomy', Royal Institute of Great Britain, Lecture of April 6th, 1951, pp.1-12.
5. KW 1, 222; Hastie, p.18. Cf. H. Heimsoeth, *Astronomisches und Theologisches in Kants Weltverständnis*, Steiner, 1963; P. Laberge, *La théologie Kantienne précritique*, Ottowa U.P. 1973.
6. KW 1, 58-59 and 62; ET Rabel, *Kant, pp.6-7*.
7. *KW 1, 222; Hastie, p.17*.
8. *KW 1, 230; Hastie, p.29*.
9. One should compare KW 5, 378, 400; Meredith, C.T.J., p.27, p.54.
10. *KW 1, 226; Hastie, p.23*.
11. *KW 17, 3704*.
12. *KW 1, 225; Hastie, p.23*.
13. *KW 1, 234; Hastie, p.34*.
14. *KW 1, 339*.
15. *KW 1, 225; Hastie, p.23*.
16. *KW 1, 363f*. The whole of the work, including part 3 not translated by Hastie, is now available with an excellent introduction and notes by Stanley L. Jaki, Scottish Academic Press, 1981. At this point, cf. Jaki pp.193-4.
17. *KW 1, 353; Jaki pp.184-5*.
18. *Cf. B. de Fontenelle, Entretiens sur la pluralité des mondes*, 1686; Herrn Bernhards von Fontenelle, *Gesprache von mehr als einer Welt*, trans. J.C. Gottsched, Breitkopf, 1730, pp.107f. Cf. *The Achievement of Bernard de Bovier de Fontenelle* ed., L.M. Marzak, Sources of Science 76, Johnson reprint 1970.
19. KW 5, 332-335; Meredith, C.A.J., 199-202 on laughter.
20. KW 1, 359-360; Jaki p.190.
21. Eg. *Theodicée*, p.331; Huggard, p.330.
22. Cf. KW 3, 535 and 5, 467-468.
23. KW 1, 333; Jaki p.169.
24. London, 1767, 5th ed. Cf. KW 5, 277; Meredith, C.A.J., p.130.
25. Burke. p.107-8, 121. Cf. J.C. Gottsched, *Ausgewälte Werke* 6, 2 ed. J. Birke and B. Birke, *Versuch einer Critischen Dichtkunst*, de Gruyter, 1973, pp.501-502, 'Von dogmatischen Gedichten' on the dramatic qualities of 'Job'. And Wesley, *Dissertationes in librum Jobi*, 1736, C. Rivington, etc. No. XLIII, 334, 'Poetica descriptio animalium', includes Behemoth, Leviathan and 'equus Jobi', and quotations from Dryden. No. XXXIX, 302, pp.73, 16-17 is on 'De origine mali', including section 4, 'Bailaei systema Manichoreum' and its refutation, though without mention of Leibniz. The 'refutation' draws only on scripture and some of the early fathers and is mostly concerned with human sin. Bayle is mentioned primarily because Manicheism is discussed.

26. KW 1, 306; Hastie, p.136.
27. KW 1, 256; Hastie, p.65. Cf. the 1764 *Observations on the feeling of the beautiful and sublime*, KW 2, 210; Goldthwait, pp.49-50: 'A long duration is sublime. If it is of time past, then it is noble. If it is projected into an incalculable future, then it has something of the fearsome in it. A building of the remotest antiquity is venerable. Haller's description of the coming eternity stimulates a wild horror, and of the past, transfixed wonder'.
28. KW 1, 309-310; Hastie, p.140.
29. KW 1, 314; Hastie, p.145. On p.146 Hastie translates the verse of Haller's which so impressed Kant, and to which he alludes several times in his writings:
Infinity! What measures thee? / Before thee worlds as days, and men as moments flee! / Mayhap the thousandth sun is rounding now; And thousands still remain behind! / Even as the clock its weight doth wind, / A sun by God's own power is driven; And when its work is done, again in heaven / Another shines. But thou remain'st! To thee all numbers bow.
Cf. Haller's statement of his theology, *Briefe über einige Einwürfe nochlebender Freygeister wieder die Offenbarung*, 1775-76, with a new edition 1778, the year of his death, Typographische Gesellschaft of Bern, especially 1, 22-23, 43-44, 60-61, 143-144 on his hope of eternal life for the soul, with special reference to Job 19, 26-27; and his immense enjoyment of life, p.239.
30. KW 1, 315; Hastie, p.147.
31. KW 1, 310; Hastie, pp.140-141.
32. KW 1, 312; Hastie, p.143.
33. KW 1, 317f; Hastie, p.149f. Cf. KW 5, 427-428; Meredith, C.T.J., pp.89-90.
34. KW 2, 319; Hastie, p.151.
35. KW 1, 321; Hastie, p.154.
36. J. Pieper, *Death and immortality*, trans. R. and C. Winston, Burns & Oates, 1969, p.104f.
37. KW 1, 321; Hastie, p.155. And Hastie translates another stanza of Haller's:
And when the World shall sink, and Nothing be once more, / When but its place remains and all else is consumed: / And many another heaven, by other stars illumed, Shall vanish when its course is o'er: / Yet thou shalt be as far as ever from thy death, / And as today thou then shalt breathe eternal breath.
38. KW 1, 330; Hastie, p.165.
39. KW 1, 367; Rabel, p.26.
40. KW 5, 162; Abbott, p.260.
41. R.B. Jachmann, *Immanuel Kant, geschildert in Briefen an einen*

Freund, Nicolovius, 1804, pp.99-100 and cf. pp.113-124 on religion.
42. Lichtenberg on *Nikolaus Kopernikus* ed. G. von Selle, Gräfe & Unzer, 1943 represents a later stage of 'enlightenment'. Whilst committed to the Copernican revolution he had moved from Lutheranism through Kant to an anthropological 'spirituality'. He came to regard established religion as he experienced it as a kind of Shamanism, and natural religion as a kind of 'sinking fund'. Cf. Schöffler, *Deutschen Geist*, pp.212f.
43. *Der Frau Luise Adelgunde Victoria Gottschedin, sämmtliche Kleinere Gedichte* ... *Ihr gestisteten Ehrenmaale, und hrem Leben*, Breitkopf, 1763. She especially loved the book of Job, the psalms, the works of Casper Neumann, and revered and delighted in the providence of the highest being revealed in nature, especially the phenomena of the heavens.
44. Maupertuis, *Oeuvres*, 1, p.51. Whilst it was not always possible to explain, one could always admire the spectacle of the heavens, not only the everyday appearances of sun and moon in balance with one another, but at the pole, the Aurora Borealis and days without night. This was in no way to disparage the tiniest creature, each in its own way as suitable as a subject of reflection as the planet Jupiter. Cf. p.79f, 'Discourse sur les différantes figures des astres, ou l'on essaye d'expliquer les principaux phenomenes du Ciel'.
45. C.J. Kraus, *Vermischte Schriften*, 8, p. 441, a comment from one of his friends, recorded in J. Voigt's *Das Leben des Professor Christian Jacob Kraus*, Königsberg U. Press, 1819, which makes up vol.8.
46. Burke, p.140.
47. ET F.E. England, *Kant's conception of God*, Humanities Press, 1968, pp.212-252.
48. The problem of theodicy appears at the outset, however KW 1, 392; England, p.220.
49. KW 1, 414; England, pp.250-1.
50. KW 1, 399; England, pp.229-30.
51. KW 1, 403; England, p.336.
52. England, pp.137-8.
53. KW 1, 414; England, p.250.
54. Cf. KW 18, 6214, 6219.
55. Cf. KW 4, 237-238.
56. KW 1, 405; England, p.238.
57. KW 1, 413; England, pp.248-9. Cf. I, 483 from the *Monadologia physica* of 1756.
58. KW 1, 402; England, p.233.
59. KW 1, 404; England, p.236.
60. KW 1, 405; England, p. 237.
61. KW 1, 419f.

62. KW 1, 431f.
63. KW 1, 318; Hastie, 150.
64. Eg. the story of the girl born without a nose: 'I sit and look at myself all day and cry. I have a big hole in the middle of my face that scares people even myself so I can't blame the boys for not wanting to take me out. My mother loves me, but she crys terrible when she looks at me. What did I do to deserve such a terrible bad fate? Even if I did do some bad things I didn't do any before I was a year old and I was born this way ...' Cited in W. Kaufmann, *The faith of a heretic*, Anchor, 1963, pp.157-158.
65. Cf. L. Chapplelow, *A commentary on the book of Job*, II: The paraphrase, Bentham, 1752, pp.410-11.
66. KW 1, 455.
67. KW 1, 456.
68. KW 1, 458.
69. K. Jaspers, *Vom Europäischen Geist* trans. R. Gregor Smith, *The European Spirit*, S.C.M., 1948, p.62. Jaspers was writing in the aftermath of European knowledge of what had been done in concentration and extermination camps. Cf. also K. Jaspers, *The origin and goal of history* trans. M. Bullock, Routledge & Kegan Paul, 1953, p.141f.
70. Polonoff, *op.cit.*, p.163 note on the minor controversy caused by Kant's reaffirmation of Leibniz.
71. KW 17, 3704.
72. Altmann, *Mendelssohn*, p.112 on the third 'Philosophical dialogue' in its 1771 version.
73. KW 2, 62f. Cf. KW 1, 239, the heading of chapter 8, part 2, of the *Universal natural history*, Hastie, p.42: 'The essential capacities in the natures of things to raise themselves to order and perfection, is the most beautiful Demonstration of the existence of God'.
74. KW 5, 262-263; Meredith, C.A.J., pp.112-113.
75. KW 2, 29f; Rabel, pp.40-42.
76. Eg. Thomas Aquinas, *Summa Theologiae*, 1, 2, a. 3 way 4; A. Kenny, *The five ways*, Routledge & Kegan Paul, 1969, p.70f.
77. KW 2, 32-33.
78. KW 2, 34-35.
79. KW 2, 161.
80. D.F. Strauss, *op.cit.* 5, 229f, 'Hermann Samuel Reimarus und seine Schutzschrift für die vernunftigen Verehrer Gottes' (1862).
81. H.S. Reimarus, *Die vornehmsten Wahrheiten der naturlichen Religion*, Bohn, 1755. Cf. *Hermann Samuel Reimarus 1694-1768 ein 'bekannter Unbekannter' der Aufklärung in Hamburg*. Vandenhock & Ruprecht, 1973.
82. Ibid., 3, 206.
83. Ibid., p.86f.

84. Ibid., p.649.
85. Ibid., p.724.
86. H.S. Reimarus, *Allegemeine Betrachtungen über die Triebe der Thiere, hauptsächlich über ihre Kunsttriebe: zum Erkenntnis des Zusammenhanges der Welt, des Schöpfers, und unser selbst.* 2nd ed., Bohn, 1762. And see p.376, including Job 35, 10-11, and 39, 17-20.
87. KW 2, 68, 117, 137; Cf. KW 2, 124. ET *The one possible basis for a demonstration of the existence of God* by G. Treash, Abaris Books, 1979, gives the translation on the page facing the reprinted German text. The earlier ET Treash refers to on p.32 as being by Willich was more likely by J. Richardson, who published a series of Kant translations.
88. KW 2, 74.
89. D.M. MacKinnon, *The problem of metaphysics*, C.U.P., 1974, p.71.
90. KW 2, 78f.
91. KW 2, 82.
92. KW 2, 84-85.
93. KW 2, 90. Cf. P. Fruchon, ' "Problèmes Kantiens" pour une théologie naturelle', *Archives de Philosophie*, 34, 1971, 117-206, p.203: 'Seul l'homme *imago Dei* peut penser Dieu par analogie avec lui-même. Seul l'homme qui, du'un point de vue pratique, pense Dieu créateur, lui-même et le monde comme création, peut se penser jusqu'au bout comme posant la question du sens de la totalité existente'.
94. KW 2, 88f. Cf. KW 15, 1448; 19, 7687.
95. KW 2, 93f.
96. KW 2, 95-97.
97. This maxim is an expression of the 'least action' principle with natural organisms as its objects. KW 5, 376; Meredith, C.T.J., pp.24-25.
98. KW 2, 98-9. Cf. Polonoff, *op.cit.*, p.165.
99. KW 2, 100-102. Cf. KW 4, 443; Abbott, p.62.
100. KW 2, 104f.
101. KW 2, 109.
102. KW 2, 115. Cf. C. Kiernan, vol. 59a of *Studies on Voltaire* on science and the enlightenment in eighteenth century France.
103. KW 2, 116f.
104. KW 2, note p.117; Rabel, p.56. Cf. Beattie, *Evidences*, 2, 152: 'Every new discovery in the visible universe ought to give elevation and a new impulse to the pious affections: and the further we see that the works of God extend, the more let us be overwhelmed with devout astonishment, in the contemplation of his infinite, eternal and universal Being'.
105. KW 2, 122. Cf. Harnack, 1 : i, 459-461.

106. J.P. Süssmilch, *Die Göttliche Ordnung in den Veränderung des menschlichen Geschlects*, Spener, 1741.
107. KW 2, 125. Cf. KW 17, 4134-4135.
108. KW 2, 123. And KW 2, 132.
109. KW 2, 131. Cf. Voltaire, *Philosophical dictionary*, pp.205-7 on 'End, final causes'.
110. KW 2, 136f. Cf. Jaki pp.197-208.
111. KW 2, 151.
112. KW 1, 223; Hastie, p.20.
113. KW 1, 152-153.
114. KW 1, 153.
115. KW 2, 160. Cf. KW 2, 203, 370, and G. Tonelli, 'Kant und die Antiken Skeptiker', in *Studien zu Kants Philosophischer Entwicklung*, Olms, 1967, pp.93-124.
116. KW 2, 179f (part 2).
117. Maupertuis, *Oeuvres*, 1, 171f.
118. KW 2, 309.
119. Cf. F.P. van de Pitte, *Kant as a philosophical anthropologist*, Nijhoff, 1971; E. Cassirer, *Rousseau, Kant, Goethe*, Princeton U.P., 1963.
120. KW 2, 200; ET Rabel, p.49.
121. F. Dostoyevsky, *The Brothers Karamazov*, trans. D. Magarshack, Penguin, 1958, 1, 287.
122. H.R. Mackintosh, *Types of modern theology*, Nisbet, 1937, p.116.
123. Cf. I. Murdoch, *The sovreignty of good*, Routledge & Kegan Paul, 1970, p.82.
124. KW 2, 273f; ET G.B. Kerferd and D.E. Walford, *Kant: Selected pre-critical writings and correspondence with Beck*, Manchester U.P., 1968.
125. Altmann, *Mendelssohn*, ,pp.112-130.
126. KW 2, 297; Kerferd/Walford, pp.30-31.
127. K. Jaspers, *Philosophy*, trans. E.B. Ashton, Chicago U.P., 1971, 3, p.119f.
128. H. Saner, *Kant's political thought*, trans. E.B. Ashton, Chicago U.P., 1967, pp.25-26.
129. KW 2, 2, 297; Kerferd/Walford, p.31.
130. I. Murdoch, *Sovereignty*, p.81.
131. S. Pétrement, *Simone Weil : A life*, trans. R. Rosenthal, Mowbrays, 1976, p.220.
132. *Ibid.*, p.68.
133. KW 2, 387f; Kerferd/Walford, p.47f.
134. KW 2, 409-410; Kerferd/Walford, p.79.The reference to Malebranche is to the 1691, Latin version of *De la Recherche de la Verité*, Book 3, part 2, chapter heading to 6. Werkmeister, *op.cit.*, p.44

translates KW 17, 4741: In physico theology the main rule is 'One must have recourse to God as an immediate cause, not indeed of any particular fact, but in general with regard to the ultimate substrate of the world except in the case of revelation'. And KW 17, 4754: The revelation of God through reason 'of his existence or of his will' - 'must procede every other; for it gives us the first correct concept of which every other can be tested', and both, his existence and his will, 'God can reveal to us only inwardly through works or words.' And 17, 4750: We have 'a feeling of God's omnipresence' but not of being absorbed by him.

135. KW 2, 418-419; Kerfered/Walford, pp.90-91.
136. KW 2, 396; Kerferd/Walford, p.60.
137. KW 2, 408; Kerferd/Walford, p.76. Cf. KW 2, 406; Kerferd/Walford, pp.74-75.
138. MacKinnon, *The Problem of Metaphysics*, p.55.

PART IV
AFTER 1781 : MORAL SENTIMENT AND AUTHENTIC THEODICY

Rousseau's Savoyard priest had pondered on 'the fate of mortals, adrift upon the sea of human opinions, without compass or rudder, and abandoned to their stormy passions with no guide but an inexperienced pilot who does not know whence he comes or whither he is going'.[1] Kant assessed Hume's response to this fate in terms of Hume's having 'put his ship aground, to bring it into safety, on the shore of scepticism where it may lie and rot'. Kant preferred a more adventurous project: 'what I want to do is to give it a pilot who will be able to sail the ship safely wherever he will, using sure principles of navigation drawn from knowledge of the globe, and equipped with a complete set of charts and a compass'.[2] Yet the success of the adventure depended upon willing acknowledgement of limitation as well as the invigorating prospect of possible achievement. The 'pilot' learns piecemeal, arguing inductively, relying on experiments, revising again and again his estimate of what is conceivable. His charts and compass - his ability to project lawfulness into nature - help him gradually to systematise the details of the knowledge he acquires into a satisfying construct. He himself constitutes, through his intellectual and experimental activity, the very world insofar as it can be the world for him. He learns that 'reason has insight only into that which it produces after a plan of its own', and constrains nature 'to give answer to questions of reason's own determining'. He approaches nature in order to be taught by it, but not 'in the character of a pupil who listens to everything that the teacher chooses to say, but of an appointed judge who compels the witnesses to answer questions which he has himself formulated'.[3]

The pilot must learn to distinguish between what he can and cannot be said to know, and is not to suppose that he is managing to approximate to that knowledge of his world that a deity, an 'intellectus archetypus' might be deemed to have of his creation. The pilot has to acknowledge that he may never find the answers to what appear to be significant questions. He may be inspired to continue his reach for comprehension by the ideal of an unimpeded vision of the whole, but deceives and so confuses himself if he thinks he can somehow step out of the time-bound sequential character of his mode of acquiring knowledge to secure a vantage point from which he could survey not merely the objects in his visual field (though this field may be both vast and detailed with the right technical equipment) but all possible visual fields. Neither calculation nor equipment however sophisticated will finally eliminate a certain opacity in his own reason and in nature which both entices and baffles him.[4] Only an 'archetypal intellect' could enjoy the kind of knowledge for which the pilot craves, that is, an intellect which created rather than constituted its own objects.[5]

The concept of such a creator, a deity, was to be understood as a device by means of which the pilot could remark on the stringencies imposed by his own proper abilities. And yet,

> who does not see the impossibility of stopping at the thoroughgoing contingency and dependency of everything that he can think and assume according to principles of experience alone, and does not feel himself compelled, despite all prohibitions not to lose himself in transcendent ideas, to seek peace and satisfaction, beyond all concepts which he can justify by experience, in the concept of a being of which the idea in itself is such that there can indeed be no insight into its possibility, although it also cannot be refuted, because it concerns a mere being of the understanding, but without this idea reason would have to remain for ever unsatisfied?[6]

Kant had long since arrived at his estimate of the value of the ontological argument, as he taught his auditors in his lectures on philosophical theology[7] and the readers of his *Critiques*, as Jaspers summarised: 'To state God's being in my thought of God says nothing, because the verb 'to be' covers whatever I think, and if this unique verb 'to be' makes me think that by itself it says something, I turn a matter of grammar into a matter of fact'.[8] In any case, the bearing of a being of such transcendent perfection as the argument intends upon the human predicament is not immediately evident.[9] Ready eagerness to believe in a deity may function at a level of relatively detached intellectual curiosity,[10] and continue to find support for belief in argument which relies upon purposive orderliness in nature,[11] seeming to be akin to the sober disposition of the affairs of life by a morally sensitive person. Quite apart from Kant's criticism that this manner of argument depends on the ontological argument in the end, preoccupation with theodicy now came to render it untenable. Kant had said that reason approaches nature in the character of an appointed judge. The mood of ready eagerness to believe is challenged by giving greater weight to experiences of grief and outrage at some features of the context in which he finds himself. To modulate the juridical metaphor, suppose there to be in court a prosecuting counsel[12] who demands to be told why those features should not count as testimony to the 'guilt' of the accused deity deemed to be responsible for them. It might be possible to distract the attention of the court from the matter, but not, perhaps, for long. The issue has somehow to be settled.

Kant himself was by no means indifferent to what seemed to be the need to provide release from the sheer strain[13] of coming to terms (from the human point of view) with the ambiguity of precisely that order which might otherwise be praised as providential. However, he now noted that 'it is more in keeping with the limitations of human reason to speak of *nature* and not of *providence*', since cause-effect relationships have to do only with 'the bounds of possible experience': '*Modesty* forbids us to speak of providence as something we can recognise, for this would mean donning the wings of Icarus and presuming to approach the mystery of its inscrutable intentions'.[14]

Kant's own search for 'peace and satisfaction' had led him to an argument for a deity which he now subjected to scrutiny afresh. He had thought of the deity as that which conditions 'the possibility of all things as their *ground*', as one, simple, all-sufficient, eternal etc.,[15] 'a therefore for every wherefore', a self-subsistent, original, creative reason.[16] He now supposed this concept to be no more than a notional point of reference,[17] lying outside the interconnections we may make between items of our knowledge, but useful to orientate it. 'It is as if a diagram were misread, because a point, which functioned only in its geometrical construction, was taken to represent something'.[18] The supreme being is a mere ideal, but a flawless one, completing and crowning knowledge.[19] Objects reflected in a mirror are seen as behind it, and the use of a mirror helps us to see not only the objects which lie before our eyes, but 'those which lie at a distance behind our back'.[20] Kant proposes theology 'as if', as Hartnack explains: it is not the 'as if' of the assertion, 'He acts as if he were a millionaire' - which he is not. Rather, it is the 'as if' of possibility, that is to say, 'He acts as if he were a millionaire' - which he may perhaps be.[21]

Human reason requires 'unconditioned necessity' as the 'last bearer of all things', but to attempt to think it pushes reason to the edge of a 'veritable abyss'.[22] Thus Kant re-wrote part of the concluding 'contemplation' of his 1763 essay on the one possible basis for a demonstration of the existence of God. There he had allowed his deity to say to himself: 'I am from eternity to eternity, without me there is nothing, but something exists insofar as it exists through me'. In his first *Critique* he had his deity put to himself what Jaspers called a dizzying, fictitious and unanswerable question.[23] 'We cannot put aside, and yet cannot endure the thought, that a being, which we represent to ourselves as supreme amongst all possible beings, should, as it were, say to itself: 'I am from eternity to eternity, and outside me there is nothing save what is through my will, *but whence then am I*?"[24] Kant as it were balances on the edge of the abyss by his theology 'as if'. On the one hand he insists that we are wholly ignorant of the manner of the deity's action, and of his ideas, 'in which the principles of the possibility of the natural beings are supposed to be contained', and so cannot explain nature by moving from the deity downwards.[25] On the other hand, he proposed that 'as universal laws of nature have their ground in our understanding, which prescribes them to nature', so particular empirical laws must be regarded (in respect of that which is left undetermined in them by more universal laws), according to a unity 'such as they would have if an understanding (though it be not ours) had supplied them for the benefit of our cognitive faculties', but this is not to be taken as implying that such an understanding must actually be assumed.[26] We may 'look upon all connections in the world *as if* it originated from an all sufficient necessary cause'.[27] In this theology, the least action principle is thought to be a principle that enables thought to go ahead, rather than an expression of the discernible rationality of nature in its dependence upon an all-sufficient deity. It was an example of a maxim of reason, having to do with the possible perfection of knowledge of an object.[28] Just as modesty forbids us to speak of 'providence', (itself an indirect way of referring to the deity) likewise it forbids us to speak of the deity where we may more intelligibly refer to 'nature': 'everything in the world is good for something or other, nothing in it is in vain'.[29] More precisely, we may say that 'an organized natural product is one in which every part is reciprocally both end and means'.[30] He had written of the divine intellect as having conceived of the existence of particular things as correlated, but he now views the 'reciprocal causality of substances in respect of their accidents' not in terms of that enduring act of the divine intellect, but as having to do with the operation of human cognition within the bounds of possible experience.[31]

Outside the dispassionate study of the natural order, it might be argued that no more than the deity of the ontological argument was the 'all sufficient necessary cause' relevant to the human predicament. If those principles of explanation which had been thought to indicate the mode of his relation to his creation were so readily translatable into 'nature', Kant like the Humean sceptic might have made all reference to the deity redundant at a further stage of his thought. That he did not do so was because, as Farrer later put it, there were attachments of some kind between the theistic thesis Kant preferred and issues arising in the field of action, though Farrer himself did not suppose that the kind of 'contextual encouragement' Kant offered would take the weight of religious belief.[32] Hume had remarked that moral philosophy was in the same condition as natural philosophy before the time of Copernicus,[33] and Kant's programme included providing a pilot for the human 'ship' adrift in the sea of 'stormy passions' as well as the sea of opinion about the natural order. It was by attention to this central area of his work that he found himself provoked to keep on resisting the total elimination of theological language from his writing. Admittedly, such language, wherever it was to be found, was to be understood as following the route of the *via negativa*. Even here, there was an important difference in Kant's use of this 'way' as compared with its use in fostering those styles of speculative and mystical theology Kant did want to eliminate.[34] There can be no 'schematism' in theology, that is, no procedure linking images or representations with concepts and perceptions in time. On the one hand, as he pointed out, we do not expect to dispense with the schematism of analogy as a means of explanation. For instance: 'I can *make comprehensible* to myself the cause of a plant (or of any organic creature, or indeed of the whole purposive world) only by attributing intelligence to it, on the analogy of an artificer in his relation to his work (say a watch)'. Yet it would be a mistake to conclude that 'the cause (of the plant and of the world in general) must itself *possess* intelligence'.[35] To take another example, beavers and men alike engage in constructive work. Instinct in beavers and reason in men stand in like relations to their respective constructions, but this does not justify an inference that 'because man employs *reason* for what he constructs, beavers must possess reason also', though we may correctly infer that such animals are not machines, as Descartes mistakenly contended, and that 'despite their specific difference, they are living beings and as such generally kindred to man'.[36] Again, he could use the 'law of the equality of action and reaction in the mutual attraction and repulsion of bodies' to picture to himself 'the social relations of the members of a commonwealth regulated by civil laws', but he would not ascribe the notions of physical attraction and repulsion to the citizens of the state.[37] Analogy helps to explain relationships between things and persons within the spatio-temporal context, analogy clearly understood to be the similarity of two relations between quite dissimilar things, but of which we have knowledge. On the other hand, analogy in theological language is the attempt to relate the world of the senses to the unknown, merely to know it 'for what it is for me, namely in respect of the world of which I am a part'.[38] For instance, 'as promotion of the happiness of children ~ a is related to parental love ~ b, so the well-being of the human species ~ c is related to the unknown in God ~ x, which we call love'. Such love has no similarity with any human inclination, but 'we can posit its relation to the world as similar to that which things in the world have among themselves'.[39]

Hume's objections to anthropomorphism in theology were strong, but crude anthropomorphism is not inevitable if Kant's 'negative way' is followed. Kant wanted to attribute certain properties to the relation the deity may have to the world, and so argued for '*symbolic*' anthropomorphism, which concerns language and not the object.[40] He does not claim knowledge of the deity, but merely a 'mode of representation', an *indirect* presentation, where no direct presentation is possible.[41] However indirect the presentation, something positive has to be said if anything is to be said at all, and Kant used the 'via eminentiae', the application of such terms to the deity as can admit of a supreme degree, or some supremely perfect version of them.[42] He had to choose appropriate terms. As D.M. Emmet commented on 'mirror images', the question is whether the study of man's own image in the glass indicates 'a reference to something beyond itself', and expresses 'the character of some actual *relation*, which is controlling the appropriateness of the symbols used'. Then the question arises as to whether the symbol seems to be an inevitable way of expressing the relation in which we stand 'to something of whose intrinsic nature we have no direct apprehension'.[43] Were 'love' the inevitable central symbol, Kant might have continued to argue that the product of the divine will must be the greatest whole of everything possible, the most perfect world. 'The divine purpose regarding the human race (the creation and guidance of man) cannot be conceived except as an end of love, i.e., God's aim is the happiness of mankind'. Kant added that one might say (in human terms) that the deity 'created rational beings as if it were from a need to have someone beside himself whom he could love, or by whom he could be loved'.[44] Scripture went further in order to make men comprehend the divine love for the human race, in ascribing sacrifice to the deity, 'a sacrifice performed in order that even those who are unworthy may be made happy', though Kant commented that we cannot rationally conceive how the all sufficient being could sacrifice what belongs to his bliss or possession.[45] Kant made a number of tentative observations on what the divine love for man might mean, notably such as making good human deficiency,[46] and so including the divine moral approbation of men, resulting in a verdict of 'Him who judges from love', love based upon wisdom.[47] He used the word 'fortunate' to mean everything worthy of being wished for, which can neither be foreseen nor brought about by us, 'for which, therefore, if we wish to name its source, we can offer none other than a gracious Providence',[48] that providence which may be justified in the history of the world, given that moral principle is never extinguished and reason is implemented in law.[49] Divine love could be expressed also as having to do with 'rewards in the world to come', paraphrased as 'a soul-elevating representation of the consummation of the divine benevolence and wisdom in the guidance of the human race';[50] and with grace, the finding in someone of 'a kind of prior responsiveness to the divine perfection and transformation of his or her action',[51] to use D.M.

MacKinnon's paraphrase. Yet Kant wanted all reference to the divine love to be pushed into background of one's attention so far as possible. Rational beings, as Hume had shrewdly commented at the end of his essay 'of miracles' in the *Enquiry*, tend to respond to talk of miracle with irrationality, the subversion of all principles of understanding. In picking up Hume's point, Kant observed that reference to the divine love in general, and to grace in particular, tended to foster indolence, a leisurely awaiting from above what should be sought from within man,[52] for 'anything, even the most sublime, dwindles under the hands of men when they turn the idea of it to their own use'.[53] Kant knew how respect for the moral law could be distorted by coercion, and how a courageous and joyous obedience could become a fear-ridden and dejected hatred of law,[54] yet love too had its distortions, such as the unwillingness to acknowledge things to be as they are, to value happiness above moral worth, to be reluctant to reckon with the cost of such worth to a particular individual, given that human beings are characterised not only by respect for moral worth but by inexplicable, radical evil.

The famous passage of the second *Critique* recalled the ending of the 1755 *Universal natural history*. His vision of the heavens began from the place he occupied in the world of sense, though enlarged his understanding of his place in it 'to an unbounded extent with worlds upon worlds and systems of systems, and moreover into limitless times of their periodic motion, its beginning and continuance'. This view also annihilates his importance as an animal creature, provided briefly with 'vital power', which has to render back its matter to the planet it inhabits, a mere speck in the universe.[55] The righteous man of the third *Critique* may be subjected to all the evils of want, disease, and untimely death, just as are all other animals, until one wide grave engulfs them all, 'and hurls them back into the abyss of the aimless chaos of matter from which they were taken'.[56] In the 1791 essay on theodicies Kant recalled that Job is 'honoured' by being enabled to see the harmful and terrible things that there are in the natural order, things which do not seem to agree with the idea of a plan established with wisdom and goodness. Even if the whole does have an 'order', the connection between that order and the moral order remains unclear.[57] Awe at the natural order will in itself provide no guide, though Kant continued to express it, whether at 'the profound wisdom of the divine creation in the smallest things' or of its majesty in the great'. He described it as a 'soul elevating' power, such that words, even those of 'the royal supplicant David' pass away as empty sound, because 'the emotion arising from such a vision of the hand of God is inexpressible'.[58] Certainly Kant placed such weight on the importance of human happiness and fulfilment that he experimented with argument for the deity's existence, as a 'necessary supposition' to bring about such fulfilment making the connection between the natural and the moral clear, at least as an *ideal* state of affairs.[59] Yet this mode of argument itself seemed to make it difficult to focus attention where it needed to be focussed, on moral worth and human dignity no matter what the apparent cost.

Kant thought there was nothing profoundly puzzling about such worth and dignity. Even quite young children could experience the elevation of soul, the inspiration of the wish to be able to act in a like manner to the person who could act with entire honesty, without any view to advantage 'of any kind in this world or another', under the greatest temptations of apparent necessity, or of allurement.[60] He had many examples of the kinds of pressures to which people could be subjected - the threat of death, of disinheritance, persecution, loss of freedom, destitution for oneself and one's family at one extreme, and more commonly perhaps, the inoffensive lie to extricate oneself from an unpleasant business, or to obtain some advantage for a loved and well-deserving friend.[61] There were also pressures of temperament, whether of the person who is emotionally rather 'cold', indifferent to others, though patient and enduring in trouble - as Kant says, not the meanest product of nature even if not framed to be a philanthropist - to problems of temperament brought about by circumstance such as the self-absorption resulting from hopeless sorrow.[62] He was not trying to describe moral heroism, though circumstances might sometimes require such adherence to what moral obligation requires as to demand 'the sacrifice of all that can have any value for the dearest inclinations'.[63] At such a point, instancing the fate of 'the Holy one of the Gospels', Kant would not speak of the 'highest good', the union of happiness and desert in some allegedly blessed future[64] but only of there being an 'asylum', that is an ultimate sanctuary for morality,[65] despite all earthly appearances to the contrary.

Despite the formalism of some of his writing, it has become clear through the writing of Mary Midgley, for instance, that Kant was not trying to suffocate feeling for the sake of an impossibly austere and ascetic morality. He was concerned to stabilise emotion, and to combat sentimentalism, 'floods of tears, storms of passion, love at first sight, scenes and embraces, spasms of self-pity, and finally, if possible, shooting oneself in despair', with its familiar slogan, '*Then* they'll be sorry ...'[66] He did not develop in great detail his exploration of the possibility that imagination and feeling may educate thought,[67] or move a person to the clarity of thought which knows why a particular obligation must be shouldered. On the other hand he argued that one could learn to love what was at first merely highly esteemed, and that the practice of beneficence to the neighbour could produce a readier inclination to beneficence to a wider circle, even including those initially cateogrised as one's enemies.[68] This process is akin to that by which the observer of nature 'takes liking at last to objects that at first offended his senses' when he comes to appreciate the adaptation of their organization to its context. 'So Leibnitz spared an insect that he had carefully examined with the microscope, and replaced it on its leaf, because he had found himself instructed by the view of it, and had as it were received a benefit from it'.[69]

The focus of his attention was on what had to be done to cleanse oneself from the confusions of self-interest, a cleansing inescapable in the effort to respect others and show to them the impartiality their human dignity and well-being demands. Like the analyst who adds alkali to a solution of lime in hydrochloric acid, precipitating the lime,[70] Kant wanted to identify the essential elements in personal interaction which elicited an appropriate, awe-filled, but rational response which could be articulated. 'What is that in you which may have to do battle against all the forces of nature within you and round about you, and to conquer them when they come into conflict with your moral principles?'[71] He found persons to be capable of careful and critical discrimination, capable of owning themselves and their activities, without making themselves exceptions to whatever guidelines for those activities they formulated, and to be capable of self-appraisal. For each other, they represent sources of allegiance which may thwart their own individual self-loves.[72] John Benson has recently commented on the 'autonomous man' that 'if autonomy calls for a supple mind it also calls for a stiff neck', and that the balance between stiffness and suppleness is hard to strike and may not be right for all circumstances.[73] Central to Kant's understanding of personality is having the courage to go on struggling to find that balance, to approximate to a self-discerned paradigm of purity of intention, the 'perfect accordance of the will with the moral law' which would be holiness.[74]

Just as Kant did not find it impossible to contrast the human intellect with the divine archetypal intellect (without arguing that he could know that there was such a divine intellect) so he contrasted the struggle for purity with divine 'holiness in substance'[75] the ideal of a being who infallibly acted for the good of the other and could not act otherwise. Instances of approximation to the ideal were not impossible to find by any means, such as in the humble plain man, 'in whom I perceive uprightness of character in a higher degree than I am conscious of in myself'. It is his example that 'exhibits to me a law that humbles my self-conceit when I compare it with my conduct: a law, the *practicability* of obedience to which I see proved by fact before my eyes'.[76] Certainly, as D.M. MacKinnon has put it, 'the good will, the treatment of ourselves and our fellows as ends and not as means, these things are not butterflies which we can capture and pin like so many moral prizes in a glass case',[77] but it is possible to recognise in others evidence of the human capacity for perfection. The supreme instance of such perfection, so far as human eye can see, would be of a person whose words and actions were evidence of inner ease as well as of ready willingness to serve the interests of others, and who, though tempted 'by the greatest allurements' would take upon himself whatever afflictions came his way, even a hideous and shameful death, for the good even of his enemies.[78] Reason authoritatively furnishes the conception of morality, but such an example, 'the Holy one of the Gospels' for instance, puts beyond doubt the feasibility of what the law commands.[79]

Hume had complained of the niggardliness of nature,[80] but Kant makes of nature's strict parsimony the 'as if', the supposition that nature had willed that whatever man achieved in culture, institutions, and supremely in his moral life, he would have made himself, through his own actions, 'worthy of life and of well-being'.[81] We only first learn to know our powers 'by making trial of them'.[82] If it is the case, as he had suggested, that everything is good for something or other, nothing in it is in vain, (even poisons have their use)[83] and that every part of an harmonious natural product exhibits the reciprocation of means and ends, then human dignity requires attention to the prompting of reason to attend to the well-being of others (they are ends in themselves, not means to another's ends) as well as to one's own perfection. Like an organism in which everything was reciprocally means and ends, someone who exhibited the spontaneity, coherence and serenity of 'a heart which is happy in the *performance* of its duty (not merely complacent in the *recognition* thereof)'[84] would have come to recognise the adequacy of reason for its selfdiscriminated tasks. Kant found a further clue to its adequacy and to the way reason can have practical effect in an harmonious way by thinking further about the 'aesthetic character' of virtue, seen in her true form, without trinkets,[85] but even with her own graces. (Analogously, the sovereign who personifies the law, is not subject to coercion, can rightly be entitled 'gracious lord').[86] He admitted the insight of the artist as giving him a clue to the making of something whose purpose was intrinsic to itself. Nature is capable of being regarded 'in such a way that in it the conformity to law of its form it at least harmonises with the possibility of the ends to be effectuated in it according to the laws of freedom'.[87] Admittedly, within the limits of the artist's material, with which his reason in all its faculties, speculative, unifying, supplying meaning has to come to terms, he can experience the harmonious interplay of nature and moral reasoning:

> We frequently apply to beautiful objects of nature or of art names that seem to rely upon the basis of a moral estimate. We call buildings or trees majestic and stately, or plains laughing and gay; even colours

are called innocent, modest, soft, because they excite sensations containing something analogous to the consciousness of the state of mind produced by moral judgements.[88]

Furthermore, one can say that the interest taken in the taste of others helps to foster communicability, not only about taste, but about morality, and could help to develop a highly critical attitude to 'the dear self which is always prominent'.[89]

The 'dear self' is also (unfortunately) the source of a graceless lack of integrity. It is because the human agent does recognise his obligations to himself and others and yet finds himself free also to act in ways contrary to fulfilling his obligations that he comes to be at odds with himself, knowing that he should not treat others as grist to his own mill, but doing it all the same. This is despite the realisation that he appears to have all he needs to glorify the deity by obedience to self-imposed principles of action in the service of the neighbour and in the quest for his own holiness.[90] His moral ideal rules out the attribution to the deity of such attributes as the desire of glory and dominion, 'combined with the awful conceptions of might and vengeance',[91] and in any case the limitations of the human intellect are such that *'God and eternity* with their *awful majesty'* do *not* 'stand unceasingly *before our eyes'*.[92] The limitations on knowledge rule out the idea that we should assess the present state of the human world as the most perfect whole possible, since we should know all possible worlds in order to compare them with this one - be omniscient, in other words.[93] In any case, it is human understanding that cannot avoid 'the necessity of drawing a distinction between the possibility and actuality of things' - even if something does not yet exist, 'we may yet always give it a place in our thoughts, or if there is something of which we have no conception we may nevertheless imagine it given'. An understanding into whose modes of cognition this distinction did not enter (he means the divine intellect) would express itself by saying, 'All objects that I know *are*, that is, exist',[94] - as Cassirer commented, a last, indirect criticism of the Leibnizian theodicy.[95] Theological conviction need neither threaten nor overwhelm him.

Nor are moral beings as it were killed with kindness, as though the deity were to be conceived by analogy with a paternal government which treats its subjects as immature children, 'who cannot distinguish what is truly useful or harmful to themselves', and who would therefore be obliged 'to behave purely passively and to rely on the judgement of the head of state as to how they *ought* to be happy, and upon his kindness in willing their happiness at all.[96] For Kant, such a government would be the greatest conceivable despotism, suspending the entire freedom of its subjects, making puppets or automata of them,[97] - only the freedom of a turnspit, which when once wound up, moves of itself.[98] There is room for 'true moral disposition', for a rational creature can find his own way of sharing in the satisfactions that correspond to the worth of his person. Pope had written in the *Essay on Man*,[99] 'Who finds not Providence all good and wise. Alike in what it gives, and what denies?' Kant recalled these lines by affirming that this may well be true, that is, 'that the unsearchable wisdom by which we exist is not less worthy of admiration in what it has denied than in what it has granted'.[100]

Kant allowed the thought to occur to him of what sort of world he would create into which he would place himself as a member. He would will the kind of world in which it was possible for him to meet the demands 'reason lays down as conditioning happiness', even though in this world he saw himself paying a heavy price in happiness.[101] Yet he finds himself not only freely affirming this world, but in the very rationality by which he affirms it screening a dangerous, invisible foe,[102] responsible for moral evil differing from moral goodness not as earth differs from heaven but as hell differs from heaven, to use the Christian representation of the immeasurable gulf that separates the two.[103] It has been argued by Emil Fackenheim for one that Kant's shift to radical evil is made for a strictly philosophical reason, that is, the need to give a full and adequate justification of moral freedom.[104] It did not make sense to describe a villain as weak-willed, that is, willing the good insofar as he willed at all, and insofar as he follows evil the will-less victim of powerful inclinations. The crucial new assessment is that man is 'conscious of the moral law but has nevertheless adopted into his maxim the (occasional) deviation therefrom',[105] which is to say that the life all human beings live presupposes a decision for evil. The only remedy is a whole-hearted and thorough reversal of the decision for evil, the transformation of cast of mind and grounding of character for the good.[106] There is thus an answer to the question he poses, 'How indeed can one expect something perfectly straight to be framed out of such crooked wood?'[107] The answer has to do with the experience of being able to choose the good, despite the fragility, impurity and perversion of that ability instanced in evil choices. A moral being will thus willingly suffer the pain of remorse as an effectual means of eradicating its cause. Put another way, the pain would arise as a result of experiencing humility, 'taking the form of an uncompromising judgement upon his shortcomings'.[108] Even when hs is experiencing self-contentment, ('analogous to the self-sufficiency which we can ascribe only to the Supreme Being')[109] he can never be absolutely sure that his motives, ultimately inscrutable to him, were absolutely pure of self-interest. Even 'the Holy One of the Gospels' turns to the one addressing him with the ascription of goodness to ask, 'Why call ye Me (whom you see) good; none is good (the model of good) but God only (whom ye do not see)?'[110]

Having avoided the evil of smugness Kant had to avoid self-commendation for being so self-critical, so distrustful. He had further to extricate himself from what Hans Jonas called the 'labyrinthine structure of subjectivity *per se*, the agent relishing itself and all its possibilities', for what it thinks, it also endows with reality. Those evil possibilities 'discovered, i.e. invented, i.e. created by itself, obtain with such discovery already a share in the realization of the will and thus as it were get their money's worth out of it'.[111] The very attempt at holiness of will may condemn itself to be an unholy will (perhaps Leibniz' deity has such a will in Kant's view). Certainly, truthfulness about oneself is central to self-assessment: 'truthfulness, if adopted as a basic principle, delivers us from the anxiety of making our lies agree with one another and of not being entangled by their serpent coils'.[112] Much criticised for his totally uncompromising stance on truthfulness, more that one commentator has seen the connection between this stance and his religious convictions. Kant is not alone in taking the issue seriously. Edmund Leach has recently suggested that our ability to tell lies is perhaps our most striking human characteristic, deriving from our possession of language, which allows us to plan and engage in wilful deception on a massive scale.[113] For Kant, this is the death not only of the very possibility of self-knowledge but of the free and open communication he rightly prized. 'Lying is the throwing away, and as it were the obliteration of one's dignity as a human being'.[114] Yet further, it is important to recognise the centrality of truthfulness to what Kant meant by saying that he was morally certain that there was a God.[115] Here, as Jaspers rephrased Kant, one has to do with the very ethos of Biblical religion, which demands veracity at all costs,[116] not only because it is essential to human dignity, but because it remains the only possible mode of conceiving a relation to transcendent deity. He does not need the talents of a poet[117] to express this relation, only the ability to think and speak as truthfully as any honest man does, and to deliberate about how things ought to be.

Moral certainty rests on what Kant called subjective grounds of the moral sentiment.[118] When he wrote in the first and third *Critiques* about moral certainty, moral belief, and moral faith, in both cases he connected what he had to say with the distinction between opinion, fact and conviction.[119] As has already been suggested it may be that he was thus deliberately alluding to Butler's difficult paragraph on probability as the guide of life in his *Analogy*.[120] It will be recalled that Butler had distinguished between matters of speculation, matters of practice and questions of great consequence, in which belief and action outstrip the balance of probable reasoning. In both *Critiques* Kant cites as an example of opinion (Butler's matter of speculation) one of his own early proposals, that there are rational inhabitants on other planets, supposing that whilst experience could in principle settle the question, man would never be so near the planets as to be able to find out. What Butler had referred to as a matter of practice Kant referred to as a matter of fact, for instance, something capable of being verified by experience, and in the third *Critique* explicitly instancing the experience of the exercise of freedom. In the first *Critique* freedom is perhaps alluded to in Kant's remark about 'the magnificent equipment of our human nature, and the shortness of life so ill-suited to the full exercise of our powers'.[121] It is Butler's question of great consequence which Kant treats in terms of subjective grounds of the moral sentiment, that is, being free of doubt, but inescapably the result of personal conviction. 'Though it does indeed sound dangerous, it is in no way reprehensible to say that every man *creates a God* for himself, nay, must make himself such a God according to moral concepts',[122] or put otherwise, 'I must not even say, '*It is* morally certain that there is a God, etc.', but '*I am* morally certain, etc."[123] It is a matter of great consequence in that it is connected with uncompromising commitment to human dignity, the search for purity of intention and impartial action in the service of others no matter what the pressures are to weaken that wholehearted commitment. Kant is prepared to use the word 'faith', explicitly picked up as he says from Christianity, to mean 'the moral attitude of reason in its assurance of the truth of what is beyond the reach of theoretical knowledge', and '*freely* approved by reason'.[124] As he asks, 'who, indeed, is now the unbeliever? Is it he who trusts, without knowing how that for which he hopes will come to pass; or he who absolutely insists on knowing the way in which man is released from evil and, if he cannot know this, gives up all hope of this release?'[125]

Kant experimented with the meaning of the deity as a postulate, a necessary supposition in his search for ways of expressing his personal conviction, which he meant to be not a conviction private to him but 'authentic' and universally valid.[126] For instance, describing a deity possessed of the highest perfection, one must say that he is omniscient, meaning that he knows 'my conduct up to the inmost root of my mental state in all possible cases and into all future time'.[127] *not* that he can 'see into the ends of nature in their entire context, and in addition ... conceive all other possible schemes, as compared with which the present would have to be estimated on reasonable grounds to be the best'.[128] One must say that he is omnipotent, to allot to virtue its fitting consequences; all good and just, 'since these two attributes, which unite to form *wisdom*, constitute the conditions under which a supreme cause of the world can be the source of the greatest good under moral laws'.[129] He must be eternal, so that the ultimate harmony of nature and freedom never fail, and omnipresent, 'that He may be immediately at hand for the satisfying of every need which the highest good demands'.[130] In a note in the *Religion* Kant carefully drew attention to the point that he was offering an interpretation of a notion he had earlier employed, following Newton, that is, the law of gravity represented as similar to divine omnipresence in the world of appearance. Kant then commented: 'This is not an attempt to explain it (for the existence of God in space involves a contradiction), but a sublime analogy which has regard solely to the union of corporeal beings with a world-whole, an incorporeal cause being here attributed to this union'.[131] Thus he endeavoured to represent his all-sufficient deity, having 'a single intellectual intuition of the whole existence of rational beings', since the deity 'to whom the condition of time is nothing', sees in this to us endless succession a whole of accordance with the moral law.[132] He never omits reminders of his procedure whenever he can conveniently include them. Suppose that he seeks as he does to *conceive* the deity as intelligence, 'while this is not alone allowable but unavoidable if I am to exercise certain functions of my reason, I have no right whatever to flatter myself that I am in a position to ascribe intelligence to that being and therefore to *cognize* it by one of its attributes', for in that case, he must omit all the conditions under which he knows an intelligence.[133]

Although these attributes are to do with a deity who is no more than a 'necessary supposition', allowable by the moral man without such a deity being essential for the practice of morality as Kant understands the matter, his deity is certainly necessary as an expression of Kant's sense that he cannot flourish in a vacuum: 'the introspection in which a part of our human dignity is rooted is parasitic upon response to an irreversible exterior order'.[134] Yet there are other attributes of deity which are interwoven with his moral sentiment which he advanced to express his profound emotional response to his discrimination of morality, and which identified for him the deity integral to his moral conviction in a way to which the deity of necessary supposition only approximates. Kant had identified as the 'final end' of creation,[135] that in relation to which 'the contemplation of the world may itself possess a worth'. This is a purpose which man alone can give to himself and which consists in what he achieves, in other words, his good will.[136] This Kant supposed to be the deity's ultimate end in creating the world and which coincides with the deity's restrictive conditions of harmony with the holiness of His will'.[137]

Given this identification, there were for Kant three moral attributes which included everything by which the deity was the object of religion, that is, holy lawgiver and creator; good governor and preserver; and just judge, and Kant used these three attributes as criteria for the meaning of the metaphysical perfections of the deity. The moral attributes were derived from his analysis of some of the elements of human dignity, such as the choice of self-legislation, the possibility of contentment with self as a result of obedience to self-discerned moral principle, and the necessity of austere self-appraisal. The elements of human dignity are associated by him with moral sentiments, such as gratitude and veneration towards the unknown cause of beautiful natural surroundings, when someone enjoys a sense of calm and serene enjoyment of existence; the need of feeling that in submitting to a voluntary sacrifice he is carrying out the command of a supreme lord; the sense of submission to a deserved chastisement when he has thoughtlessly diverged from the path of duty.[138] It was when he identified these sentiments in himself that he found himself able to identify the deity of whom he could be morally certain.

With this deity he avoided *self*-commendation for his distrust and found the 'asylum' for morality he needed. Certainly, as he said, looked at from the point of view of his inner self, he was a contemptible object.[139] It was this realisation that made him hear words of self-reproach addressed to him, the 'voice of a judge to whom he has to render account'. A mind inclined to 'give expansion to its moral sentiment', however fleetingly, voluntarily imagines 'an object that is not in the world, in order, if possible, to prove its dutifulness in the eyes of such an object also.[140] Admitting blameworthiness and thus no ground for benevolence in the judgement passed upon him,[141] and yet affirming the necessity of steadfastness in moral progress[142] he cannot refrain from the question 'what is to result from this right conduct of ours?'[143] It does sometimes happen that an unjust man, especially one with unusual powers for evil, does not die unpunished, and then the impartial observer sighs with relief and is reconciled with heaven.[144] Even when this was not the case, Kant found what he thought was an inevitable judgement forcing itself upon anyone who reflected upon right and wrong. As well as the voice of self-reproach, he heard another voice say 'that it must make a difference': 'It could never be that the issue is all alike, whether a man has acted fairly or falsely, with envy or with violence, albeit to his life's end, as far at least as human eye can see, his virtues have brought him no reward, his transgressions no punishment'.[145] Self-contentment itself could only be an analogue of what should make the difference to the virtuous rather than the false man. Moral sentiment prompts not only trust in the deity Kant had delineated, but the conviction that there was some meaning in speaking of a future life, another world, the prospect of a blessed future.[146] And yet he insisted:

> We know nothing of the future, and we ought not to seek to know more than what is rationally bound up with the incentives of morality and their end. Here belongs the belief that there are no good actions which will not, in the next world, have their good consequences for him who performs them; that, therefore, however reprehensible a

man may find himself at the end of his life, he must not on that account refrain from doing at least *one* more good deed which is in his power ... [147]

This hope is held to in the teeth of his awareness of the precariousness of morality, yet allowed to animate moral action. It is based upon a way of understanding human experience, a way which depends upon pledging himself to certain ideals, no matter what the apparent threat to those ideals, hoping for their realisation, even if that realisation is in a context beyond all but the barest possibility of imagination. So, 'when we consider the possibility that the end of this earthly life is not perhaps the end of all life, this in no way amounts to a *justification* of providence; it is rather a sovereign sentence passed by rational moral faith which can advise patience to then doubter but does not give him satisfaction'.[148]

****

Having finally assessed the pleas made by so-called advocates of the deity, Kant offered his 'authentic theodicy' to put a stop, once and for all, to activities of that kind. He reminded his readers of 'the necessary limits of our reflections on the subjects which are beyond our reach'.[149] Theodicy, as he had come to understand our situation, requires uprightness of the heart, sincere and undisguised confession of one's doubts and the avoidance of feigned convictions which one does not feel.[150] It is only the Job-like character who will be preferred in the eyes of the divine judge, even if initially it is the Job-like character who has the courage to voice his perplexities. He had insisted in the *Religion* that human freedom was absolutely required in all moral matters, in which he included the adoption of a religion, and on no account would he have it crushed underfoot. He wanted a place for the good will which says, 'Lord, I believe, help thou my unbelief!' This was (apart from a note) the concluding quotation of his section 'Concerning the guide of the conscience in matters of faith'. The note appended to the section was a comment on that quotation, and was concerned with sincerity, 'that *all that one says* be said with truthfulness', a sought-for quality of mind exposed to temptations, entailing many a sacrifice, to be guarded and cultivated earlier than any other virtue.[151]

His authentic theodicy was to be fostered by a particularly uncomfortable form of self-appraisal, so uncomfortable that it was experienced as though it were a thoroughly unwelcome encounter with another. It depended upon having developed the habit of attention to past action and present desires, and making them the object of self-scrutiny and self-sanction. Sincerity he held to be 'the main requirement in matters of faith and the disposition to falseness and deception as the main vice found in human nature'.[152] It was the inclination to lie, 'the falsity which has no intention to harm' which completely ruins a man's character. He insisted especially on 'this duplicity which lies hidden in the depths of the heart, because man manages to falsify his innermost sentiments before his conscience'.[153] Subject to 'the One who searches the heart', the 'all-seeing eye of a Judge of the world',[154] pretence will be dissolved without possibility of mistake.

This conviction, derived through the language which had served to make his moral experience clearer to himself, seems after all to rest on a further conviction that one might dare to give meaning to the 'love' of God. It was in his 1794 essay on eschatology that he reminded his readers that Christianity aims to promote love for the observance of duty and elicits it. It requires neither servitude nor anarchy, but wins to itself 'the hearts of men whose understanding is already illumined by the conception of the law of their duty. The feeling of freedom in the choice of their ultimate purpose is what makes the legislation worthy of their love'.[155] This love on *man's* part he had already interpreted as 'the disposition to obedience from one's own *free choice* and from approval of the law (the duty of a son)'.[156] So a *deity* who allowed that freedom might also make good human deficiency, whatever this might be, completing a man's well-intentioned endeavours,[157] and bringing about 'that highest good which is aimed at by morality but which transcends our powers'.[158] He seems, at one point at least, to have addressed himself, however tortuously, to the Christology found in the 'Causa Dei' of Leibniz, in his own effort to elucidate the article of faith that 'God is love'. He allowed himself to suggest that we could revere the Father, the loving one whose love is that of 'moral *approbation* of men so far as they measure up to His holy law'. We could revere his Son, 'the archetype of humanity reared and beloved by Him'. And we could revere the Holy Ghost, so far as the deity made his approbation 'dependent upon men's agreement with the condition of that approving love, and so reveals love as based upon wisdom'. We should not, however, invoke the deity in terms of this 'multiform personality', since He is ever but single: 'but we call upon Him in the name of that object loved of Him, which He Himself esteems above all else, with which to enter into moral union is our desire and also our duty'.[159] These words from the *Religion* refer directly to what he says in the preface to that work: that man seeks something he can love; and, though the law which rouses his respect does not acknowledge this object of love as a necessity, it extends itself on behalf of that object 'by including the moral goal of reason among its determining grounds', that goal being the union of happiness with moral worth.[160] That 'service of the heart', in spirit and in truth as he put it in the borrowed Scriptural phrase, was set in its ultimate dimension by Kant's authentic theodicy.[161]

Notes

1. Rousseau, *Emile*, trans. Foxley p.229. Cf. S. Zac, 'Religion naturelle et religions révelées selon Kant', p.125 of *Revue de Métaphysique et de Morale* 73:1, 1968, 105-126.
2. KW 4, 262; Lucas p.11.
3. CPR Bxiii. Cf. R.F. Atkinson, *Kant's first Critique*, Exeter U. P., 1981, on the distinction between content and structure which Kant did not make, and the recognition that conceptual structures have histories. And N. Rescher, 'The problem of noumenal causality in the philosophy of Kant', ch. 4 of *The primacy of practice: essays towards a pragmatically Kantian theory of empirical knowledge*, Blackwell, 1973, p.76: 'For *knowledge* of objects would not be knowledge of *objects* if the "objects" at issue did not have an ontological foothold outside the knowledge situation'. Rescher is arguing for another aspect of Kant's Copernican revolution, with the principle of sufficient reason in its regulative guise providing the warrant for 'this necessary postulation of an extra-experiential something that underlies experience', p.84.
4. Y. Yovel, 'Systematic philosophy: ambitions and critique', pp.667-674 of D. Henrich and K. Cramer (eds.) *Ist Systematische Philosophie möglich?* Grundmann, 1977.
5. KW 4, 355; Lucas pp.122-3. Cf. CPR B72 and B139. KW 5, 405-410; Meredith C.T.J. pp.60-67. And W.H. Walsh, 'Philosophy and Psychology in Kant's Critique', *Kant-Studien*, 59, 1966, 186-198.
6. KW 4, 352; Lucas pp.118-119. Cf. KW 8, 37-8. KW 5, 401-403; Meredith C.T.J. pp.56-57. And F.L. Peccorini, 'Transcendental apperception and genesis of Kant's theological conviction', *Giornale di Metafisica*, 1:27, 1972, 43-65; Allen W. Wood, 'Kant's Dialectic', *Canadian journal of philosophy*, 5:4, 1975, 595-614.
7. I. Kant, *Lectures on philosophical theology*, trans. Allen W. Wood and J.M. Clark, Cornell U.P., 1978, from *Gesammelte Schriften*, 28:2.
8. K. Jaspers, *Philosophical faith and revelation*, trans. E.B. Ashton, Collins, 1967, p.167.
9. P. Masterson, 'Experience and the affirmation of God', *Neue Zeitschrift für Systematische Theologie und Religionsphilosophie*, 2:1, 1980, 17-32, p.23.
10. D.M. MacKinnon, *Explorations in theology 5*, S.C.M., 1979, p.120.
11. KW 5, 475-478; Meredith C.T.J. pp.151-154. And R.C.S. Walker, *Kant*, Routledge & Kegan Paul, 1978, pp.165-177.
12. MacKinnon, *Explorations*, p.120.
13. J. Baillie, *Natural science and the spiritual life*, O.U.P. 1951, pp.33-34.
14. KW 28:2, ii, 1111-12; Wood, pp.153-4. And KW 8, 362; Reiss, *Kant's political writings*, p.109.

15. CPR B607-8; Cf. P. Festugiere's introduction to E. Kant, *La Théodicée et la Religion*, Vrin, 1931, pp.1-1v; and J. Moreau, *Le Dieu des Philosophes*, Vrin, 1969, pp.80-85.
16. CPR B613. Cf. P.F. Strawson, *The bounds of sense: an essay on Kant's Critique of Pure Reason*, Methuen, 1966, p.231 on 'fatigue of reason'.
17. D. Pears, *Wittgenstein*, Fontana, 1974, p.29.
18. Pears, p.29.
19. CPR B669.
20. CPR B673.
21. J. Hartnack, *Kant's theory of Knowledge*, trans. M.H. Hartshorne, Macmillan, 1968, p.140.
22. CPR B641; B650; B657.
23. Jaspers, *Philosophical faith*, p.272.
24. CPR B641.
25. K W5, 410; Meredith C.T.J. p.67.
26. KW 5, 180; Meredith, 'Introduction' p.19.
27. CPR B647.
28. CPR B694. Cf. CPR B425.
29. KW 5, 379; Meredith, C.T.J. p.28; CPR B727.
30. KW 5, 376; Meredith, C.T.J. p.24. Cf. S.C. Brown, 'The 'Principle' of Natural Order', pp.56-76 of S.C. Brown ed., *Philosophy of the Enlightenment*, Harvester, 1979; and J. Hintikka and H. Kannisto, 'Kant on "the great chain of being" or the eventual realization of all possibilities: a comparative study', pp.287-308 of Knuuttila, ed. *Reforging*.
31. B184.
32. A. Farrer, *Faith and speculation*, A. & C. Black, 1967, p.73f.
33. D. Hume, *Treatise*, 2:1, Section 3.
34. D. Cupitt, 'Kant and the negative theology', pp.55-67 of B. Hebblethwaite and S. Sutherland, *The philosophical frontiers of Christian theology*, p.64.
35. KW 6, 64-5; Greene/Hudson p.59, note
36. KW 5, 464; Meredith, C.T.J. p.136.
37. KW 5, 465; Meredith, C.T.J. p.137. Cf. KW 6, 449.
38. KW 4, 357; Lucas, p.124.
39. KW 4, 358; Lucas, p.125.
40. KW 4, 356-7; Lucas, pp. 123-4.
41. KW 5, 352-3; Meredith C.A.J. p.223. Cf. KW 6, 64-5; Greene/Hudson p.59, note. And F. Marty, 'Symbole et discours théologique chez Kant: Le travail d'une pensée', pp.55-92 of S. Breton etc., *Le mythe et le symbole: de la connaissance figurative de Dieu*, Beauchesne, 1977.
42. A.W. Wood, *Kant's rational theology*, Cornell U.P., 1978, p.91.

Cf. H.A. Wolfson, '*St. Thomas on divine attributes*', pp.673-700 of *Mélanges offerts à Etienne Gilson*, Pontifical Institute of Medieval Studies, 1959, esp. pp.682-685.
43. D.M. Emmet, *The nature of metaphysical thinking*, Macmillan, 1949, p.114: Professor Emmet was not there discussing Kant, but St. Paul, and K.E. Kirk's *The vision of God*.
44. KW 6, 488; Ellington, p.159.
45. KW 6, 65; Greene/Hudson, p.58, note. Cf. D.M. MacKinnon, 'Some epistemological reflections on mystical experience', pp.132-140 of S.T. Katz, ed., *Mysticism and philosophical analysis*, Sheldon, 1978.
46. KW 6, 120; Greene/Hudson, p.110.
47. KW 6, 145-6; Greene/Hudson, pp.136-137.
48. KW 6, 107; Greene/Hudson, p.98. note.
49. KW 7, 380; *On History*, p.128.
50. KW 6, 162; Greene/Hudson, p.150; Cf. KW 8, 339; *On History*, pp.83-4. And K.E. Kirk, *The vision of God*, Harper, 1966, Lecture 3:4.
51. D.M. MacKinnon, 'Kant's philosophy of religion', *Philosophy*, 50, 1975, 131-144, p.136. Cf. Kant's 1775 letter to Lavater, Zweig, *Correspondence*, pp.79-82, and Despland, *Kant on history and religion*, 228-236.
52. KW 6, 191; Greene/Hudson, p.180; and Cf. KW 6, 89; Green/Hudson, p.84.
53. KW 6, 8; Greene/Hudson, p.7.
54. KW 6, 24; Greene/Hudson, p.19, note.
55. KW 5, 161-2; Abbott, p.260.
56. KW 5, 452; Meredith, C.T.J. pp.120-121.
57. KW 8, 266; Despland, pp.292-3. Cf. in Rabel, *Kant*, p.vii, from Wasianski's memoirs of Kant. 'When Kant had discovered that in a bad summer swallows threw some of their own young out of the nest in order to keep the others alive, he said: 'My intelligence stood still. There was nothing to do but to fall on one's knees and worship".
58. KW 6, 197; Greene/Hudson pp.185-6. Cf. KW 5, 170; Meredith C.A.J. pp.121-2, on the sublimity of the starry heavens.
59. Cf. R.L. Sturch, 'The ethico-theology of Immanuel Kant', *Journal of Theological Studies*, NS, 26:2, 1975, 342-360; and G.J. Warnock, 'The primacy of practical reason', pp.179-191 of *Morality and Language*, Blackwell, 1983. On the importance of such fulfilment, see Rescher, p.129f. on 'The extra-pragmatic dimension of human purpose' in his *The primacy of practice*; and K. Ward, *The development of Kant's view of ethics*, Blackwell, 1972, p.121.
60. KW 4; Abbott p.28, note.
61. Some of the examples in the second *Critique*.
62. KW 4, 398; Abbott, p.14.

63. KW 5, 158; Abbott, p.256.
64. KW 5, 123; Abbott, p.220, note. Cf. Y. Yovel, *Kant and the philosophy of history*, Princeton W.P., 1980, Part 1, expounding the argument p.121 that the given world is the highest good *in potentia*, and that *human* proxis can make it so actually.
65. KW 6, 83; Greene/Hudson p.77.
66. p.159 of M. Midgley, 'The objection to systematic humbug', *Philosophy*, 1978, 53, 147-169; reprinted in her *Heart and Mind*, Harvester, 1981. And cf. her *Beast and man*, Harvester, 1978. On sentimentalism see KW 5, 272-3; Meredith, C.A.J., pp.125-6.
67. Cf. P. Gardiner, 'Freedom as an aesthetic idea', pp.27-39 of A. Ryan, ed., *The idea of freedom: essays in honour of Isaiah Berlin*, O.U.P., 1979; L.A. Blum on *Friendship, altruism and morality*, Routledge & Kegan Paul, 1980, pp.1-66. H. Arendt, *The life of the mind, 2 : Willing*, Secker & Warburg, 1978, pp.255-272 writes on Kant's interest in the 'enlargement of the mind', to train the imagination to go visiting, essential to impartiality, establishing the proper distance for evaluation, yet with the 'object'internalized so that the thinker can be affected by it. Thinking for oneself, putting oneself in the place of each and every other, and being consistent are maxims central to being a person in a communicable, shared context. Cf. H. Arendt, *Between past and future*, Meridian, 1963, p.219f.
68. KW 6, 402; Ellington, p.61. A Hofstadter, 'Kant's aesthetic revolution', *Journal of religious ethics*, 3:2, 1975, 171-191.
69. KW 5, 160; Abbott, p.258.
70. KW 5, 92; Abbott, p.186.
71. KW 6, 483; Ellington, p.152.
72. KW 4, 401; Abbott, p.17, note, Cf. A. Broadie and E.M. Pybus, 'Kant's concept of "respect" ', *Kant-Studien* 66, 1975, 58-64; A. Lazaroff, 'The Kantian sublime : aesthetic judgement and religious feeling', *Kant-Studien* 71, 1980, 202-220.
73. J. Benson, 'Who is the autonomous man?', *Philosophy*, 58, 1983, 5-17, p.16.
74. KW 5, 122; Abbott, p.218. Cf. B. Harrison's comment on 'the whole notion, which permeates Kant's moral philosophy, that morality can only ultimately be understood in terms of a set of ideal relationships that entirely transcend all considerations of common-sense mutual accommodation or rational self-interest: transcend all such considerations so radically, in fact, as to point mutely towards the possibility of a life after death', pp.226-7 of his essay 'Kant and the sincere fanatic, in S.C. Brown ed., *Philosophies of the Enlightenment*.
75. KW 5, 41; Abbott, p.130. And KW 5, 158; Abbott, p.256. f.KW 6, 66f., Greene/Hudson, p.60f.
76. KW 5, 77; Abbott, p.169. Cf. KW 6, 48-9; Greene/Hudson, p.44.

77. D.M. MacKinnon, 'Kant's agnosticism', *Blackfriars*, 28, 1947, 256-263, p.261. Cf. KW 5, 274; Meredith C.A.J., p.127-8: 'The fear that, if we divest this representation of everything that can commend it to the senses, it will thereupon be attended only with a cold and lifeless approbation and not with any moving force or emotion, is wholly unwarranted. The reverse is the truth. For when nothing any longer meets the eye of sense, and the unmistakeable and ineffaceable idea of morality is left in possession of the field, there would be need rather of tempering the ardour of an unbounded imagination to prevent it rising to enthusiasm, than of seeking to lend these ideas the aid of images and childish devices for fear of their being wanting in potency'.
78. KW 6, 61; Greene/Hudson, p.55. Cf. on the importance of the visibility in bodily manifestation of certain moral qualities, KW 5, 235-6; Meredith C.A.J. pp.79-80.
79. KW 4, 408-9; Abbott p.25.
80. Wollheim, *Hume*, pp.181-4.
81. KW 8, 20; *On history*, C.T.J., p.97.
82. KW 5, 178; Meredith, p.17, note from the introduction.
83. B771.
84. KW 6, 24; Greene/Hudson, p.19, note.
85. KW 4, 426; Abbott, p.44.
86. KW 8, 294; Reiss, p.77, note. And see B840f. on The 'regnum gratiae'.
87. KW 5, 176; Meredith, C.A.J., p.14, from the introduction. Cf. B854, 'Purposive unity is, however, so important a condition of the application of reason to nature that I cannot ignore it, especially as experience supplies one so richly with examples of it'.
88. KW 5, 354; Meredith, C.A.J., p.225. Cf.E. Cassirer, *Kant's life and thought*, trans. J. Haden, Yale U.P., 1981, pp.271-360 on the third *Critique*.
89. KW 4, 407; Abott, p.24. Cf. P. Guyer, *Kant and the claims of taste*, Harvard U.P., 1979, p.387. On the incommensurability of aesthetical and moral values, cf. A. Kolnai's essay, 'Aesthetic and moral experience', pp.187-210 of his *Ethics, value and reality*, Athlone, 1977.
90. KW 5, 83; Abbott, p.176.
91. KW 4, 62; Abbott, p.62.
92. KW 5, 147; Abbott, p.245.
93. KW 5, 138-9; Abbott, p.236.
94. KW 5, 402-3; Meredith, C.T.J., pp.56-7.
95. Cassirer, *Kant's life*, pp.353-4.
96. KW 8, 291; Reiss, p.74.
97. KW 5, 101; Abbott, p.195.
98. KW 5, 97; Abbott, p.191.
99. The end of section 6 of part 1.

100. KW 5, 148; Abbott, p.246.
101. KW 6, 5; Greene/Hudson, p.5.
102. KW 6, 57; Greene/Hudson, p.50.
103. KW 6, 60; Greene/Hudson, p.53. Cf. H. Arendt, *The life of the mind*: 2, pp.63-73 on 'The apostle Paul and the impotence of the Will'.
104. E.L. Fackenheim, 'Kant and radical evil', *University of Toronto Quarterly*, 23, 1954, 339-53.
105. KW 6, 32; Greene/Hudson, p.27.
106. KW 6, 48; Greene/Hudson, p.43.
107. KW 6, 100; Greene/Hudson, p.92. Cf. KW 8, 23; *On history*, pp.17-18. Cf. H. Arendt, *The human condition*, Doubleday, 1958, p.219, on 'the darkness of the human heart'; and A. Kolnai, 'The thematic primacy of moral evil', *Philosophical Quarterly*, 6, 1956, 27-42.
108. KW 5, 264; Meredith, C.A.J., p.114.
109. KW 5, 215; Abbott, p.215.
110. KW 4, 408; Abbott, p.25.
111. H. Jonas, 'The abyss of the will: philosophical meditation on the seventh chapter of Paul's Epistle to the Romans', pp.335-348 of *Philosophical essays: from ancient creed to technological man*, Prentice-Hall, 1974.
112. KW 6, 37; Greene/Hudson, p.32. Cf. H.J. Paton, 'An alleged right to lie. A problem in Kantian ethics', *Kant-Studien*, 45, 1954,190-203, and G.E.M. Anscombe, 'Modern moral philosophy', pp.26-42 of *Ethics, religion and politics: Collected philosophical papers* 3, Blackwell, 1981, p.27 on the point that it apparently never occurred to him that a lie could be relevantly described as anything but just a lie, e.g. a lie in such and such circumstances.
113. E.R. Leach, 'Men, bishops and apes', pp.19-21 of *Nature*, 293, 1981.
114. KW 6, 429; Ellington, pp.90-91.
115. B 857.
116. K. Jaspers, *The origin and goal of history*, trans. M. Bullock, Routledge & Kegan Paul, 1953, p.91, and his *Philosophy*, trans. F.B. Ashton, Chicago U.P., 1971, 3,66. Cf. E. Gilson, *The spirit of mediaeval philosophy*, trans. A.H.C. Downes, Sheed & Ward, 1950, pp.344-345; and S. Bok, *Lying*, Quartet, 1980, pp.42-46.
117. KW 5, 314; Meredith, C.A.J., 176. Cf. M. Warnock, *Imagination*, Faber & Faber, 1976, pp.35-71, and her address, 'Imagination - aesthetic and religious', *Theology*, 83, 1980, 403-409.
118. B 857. Cf. Allen W. Wood, *Kant's moral religion*, Cornell U.P., 1970, pp.10-37.
119. B 850-855, and KW 5, 467-473; Meredith, C.T.J., 140-144.
120. Cf. note 60 of I:ii.

121. B 855. Cf. D.M. MacKinnon, *The problem of metaphysics*, C.U.P., 1974, p.58f.
122. KW 6, 168-9; Greene/Hudson, p.157, note.
123. B 857.
124. KW 5, 471; Meredith, C.T.J., p.145.
125. KW 6, 172; Greene/Hudson, pp.159-160.
126. KW 6, 114; Greene/Hudson, p.105.
127. KW 5, 140; Abbott, p.238; B 843; and KW 5, 444; Meredith, C.T.J., p.111.
128. KW 5; 441; Meredith, C.T.J., p.107.
129. KW 5, 444, Meredith, C.T.J., p.111.
130. B 843.
131. KW 6, 138; Greene/Hudson, p.130, note.
132. KW 5, 123; Abbott, p.219.
133. KW 5, 484; Meredith, C.T.J., p.162.
134. D.M. MacKinnon, 'Some reflexions on time and space', of *Archivio di Filosofia*, 1980, 369-375, p.371.
135. KW 5, 434; Meredith, C.T.J., p.98.
136. KW 5, 442; Meredith, C.T.J., pp.108-9.
137. KW 5, 131; Abbott, p.228.
138. KW 5, 482; Meredith, C.T.J., p.159, note; and KW 5, 447-8; Meredith, C.T.J., pp.112-13.
139. KW 5, 443; Meredith, C.T.J., p.109.
140. KW 5, 447-8; Meredith, C.T.J., p.112-13.
141. KW 6, 140; Greene/Hudson, p.131, note.
142. KW 5, 123; Abbott, p.220, note.
143. KW 6, 5; Greene/Hudson, p.4.
144. KW 8, 260; Despland, p.288, note. Cf. KW 5, 449; Meredith, p.177, note.
145. KW 5, 458; Meredith, p.129.
146. KW 5, 123; Abbott, p.220, note - B857-8. Cf. E. Wolff, 'Kant et l'immortalité de l'âme', *Archives de Philosophie*, 34, 1971, 451-471; and D.M. MacKinnon, 'Power politics and religious faith: the fifth Martin Wight Memorial Lecture', *British journal of international studies*, 6, 1980, 1-15.
147. KW 6, 161-2; Greene/Hudson, p.150, note. Cf. S.W. Sykes, 'Life after death: the Christian doctrine of heaven', pp.250-271 of *Christ, creation and culture*, ed. R.W. McKinney; T.&.T. Clark, 1976.
148. KW 8, 262; Despland, p.289.
149. KW 8, 264-4; Despland, p.290-91.
150. KW 8, 266-7; Despland, p.293.
151. KW 6, 190; Greene/Hudson, p.178, note.
152. KW 8, 267; Despland, p.294.
153. KW 8, 270; Despland, p.296.

154. KW 8, 268-9; Despland, p.295, and KW 8, 330; *On history*, p.72. Cf. J. Wisdom, *Paradox and discovery*, Blackwell, 1965, pp.23-33; and D.Z. Phillips, *Religion without explanation*, Blackwell, 1976. pp.143-150.
155. KW 8, 338; *On history*, pp.82-3.
156. KW 6, 182; Greene/Hudson, p.170.
157. KW 6, 120,101; Greene/Hudson, p.110, p.92.
158. KW 6, 182; Greene/Hudson, p.170.
159. KW 6, 145-6; Greene/Hudson, pp.137-8.
160. KW 6, 7; Greene/Hudson, pp.6-7.
161. KW 6, 192- ; Greene/Hudson, p.180.

BIBLIOGRAPHY

M.B. Ahern, *The problem of evil*, Routledge & Kegan Paul, 1971
H.G. Alexander, ed., *The Leibniz-Clarke correspondence*, M.U.P., 1956
Allegemeine Literatur-Zeitung 3-4, 1785, reviewing J. Schultz, *Erlaüterungen über des Herrn Professor Kants Critik der reinen Vernunft*, 1784
D. Allen, 'Leibniz' relevance for today's Christianity', *Princeton seminary bulletin*, 1:1, 1977, 13-20
D. Allen, 'The theological relevance of Leibniz' Theodicy', *Akten des II. Internationalen Leibniz-Kongresses*, 3, Steiner, 1975, 83-90
D. Allen, 'Leibniz' two questions in 'De rerum originatione radicali', *Theoria cum praxi*, 3, 1980, Steiner
J. Allerhand, *Das Judentum in der Aufklärung*, Fromann-Holzboog, 1980
H.E. Allison, *Lessing and the enlightenment*, Ann Arbor, 1966
A. Altmann, *Moses Mendelssohn*, Routledge & Kegan Paul, 1973
A. Altmann, *Studies in religious philosophy and mysticism*, Routledge & Kegan Paul, 1969
Anon, *Pope, ein Metaphysiker!* Schuster, 1755
G.E.M. Anscombe, *Ethics, religion and politics : Collected philosophical papers 3*, Blackwell, 1981
H. Arendt, *Between past and future*, Meridian, 1963
H. Arendt, *The human condition*, Doubleday, 1958
H. Arendt, *The life of the mind*, Seeker & Warburg, 1978
R. Aris, *History of political thought in Germany from 1789-1915*, Allen & Unwin, 1965
R.F. Atkinson, *Kant's first Critique*, Exeter U.P., 1981
S. Atlas, *From critical to speculative idealism: the philosophy of Salomon Maimon*, Nijhoff, 1964
S. Axinn, 'Kant, authority and the French revolution', *Journal of the history of ideas*, 32, 1971, 423-432
D. Baker ed., *Reform and reformation: England and the continent*, Blackwell, 1979
J. Baillie, *Natural science and the spiritual life*, O.U.P., 1951
W.H. Barber, *Leibniz in France*, O.U.P., 1955

T.M. Barker ed., *Frederick the Great and the making of Prussia*, Holt, Rinehart & Winston, 1972
K. Barth, *Church Dogmatics:3*, trans. J.W. Edwards, T. & T. Clark, 1958
K. Barth, *Protestant theology in the nineteenth century*, trans. B. Cozens and J. Bowden, S.C.M., 1972
S.J. Baumgarten, *Geschichte der Religionsparteien*, ed. J.S. Semler, Halle, 1766/Olms 1966
J. Beattie, *An essay on the nature and immutability of truth*, Kincaid & Bell, 1770
J. Beattie, *Evidences of the Christian religion briefly and plainly stated*, Strahan, 1786
L.W. Beck, *Essays on Kant and Hume*, Yale U.P., 1978
L.W. Beck, *Early German philosophy*, Harvard U.P., 1969
E.A. Beller & M. du P. Lee, trans. and ed., *Selections from Bayle's Dictionary*, Princeton U.P., 1952
J. Benson, 'Who is the autonomous man?', *Philosophy*, 58, 1983, 5-17
P. Berger, *The social reality of religion*, Penguin, 1967
I. Berlin, ed. H. Hardy, *Against the current: essays in the history of ideas*, Hogarth, 1979
I. Berlin, 'Herder and the enlightenment' *Encounter*, 25, 1965, 29-48, 42-51
J.A. Bernstein, 'Ethics, theology and the original state of man: an historical sketch', *Anglican theological review*, 61:2, 1979, 162-181
E. Beyreuther, 'Halle und die Herrnhuter in den Rezensionen der Göttingischen Zeitungen von gelehrten Sachen...', *Jahrbuch der Gesellschaft für Niedersächsisches Kirchengeschichte*, 73, 1975, 109-134
E.A. Blackall, *The emergence of German as a literary language, 1700-1775*, Cornell U.P., 1978
L.A. Blum, *Friendship, altruism and morality*, Routledge & Kegan Paul, 1980
H. Blumenberg, *Die Genesis der Kopernikanischen Welt*, Suhrkamp, 1975
C. Bonnet, *La contemplation de la nature*, Rey, 1764; E.T. Longman, 1766
C. Bonnet, *La Palingénesie philosophique*, Bruyset, 1770
L.E. Borowski, *Darstellung des Lebens und Charakters Immanuel Kants*, Nicolovius, 1804
W.F. Bottiglia, 'Voltaire's Candide: analysis of a classic', *Studies on Voltaire*, 7, 1959
N. Boyle, 'Kantian and other elements in Goethe's "Vermächtnis" ', *Modern Language Review*, 73, 1978, 532-549
S. Breton etc., *Le mythe et le symbole*, Beauchesne, 1977

C. Brinitzer, *A reasonable rebel: Georg Christoph Lichtenberg*, trans. B. Smith, Allen & Unwin, 1960
A. Broadie and E. Pybus, 'Kant's concept of "respect" ', *Kant-Studien*, 66, 1975, 58-64
B.H. Brockes, *Auszug vornehmnsten Gedichte aus dem Irdischen Vergnügen in Gott*, Metzlersche Verlagsbuchhandlung, 1965
B.H. Brockes, *Versuch vom Menschen vom Alexander Pope*, Herold, 1740
S.C. Brown, ed., *Philosophers of the enlightenment*, Harvester, 1979
S.C. Brown, ed., *The philosophy of the enlightenment*, Harvester, 1979
T. Bruns, *Kant et l'Europe*, Saarlandes Universität, 1973
H. Brunschwig, *Enlightenment and romanticism in eighteenth century Prussia*, trans. F. Jellinek, Chicago U.P., 1974
Craig B. Brush, *Montaigne and Bayle: variations on the theme of scepticism*, Nijhoff, 1966
A. Buchholtz, *Die Geschichte der Familie Lessing*, Holten, 1909
P. Burg, *Kant und die Französische Revolution*, Dunker & Humbolt, 1974
E. Burke, *A philosophical enquiry into the origin of our ideas of the sublime and beautiful*, Dodsley, 1767
G. Burnet, *Some letters*, second edition, Acher, 1687
O. Büsch and W. Neugebauer, eds., *Moderne Preussische Geschichte*, de Gruyter, 1981
G. Calixt, ed. I. Mager, *Einleitung in die Theologie*, Vandenhoeck & Ruprecht, 1970
E. Callot, *Maupertuis: le savant et le philosophe*, M. Rivière et Cie, 1964
Cambridge History of Poland to 1696, C.U.P., 1950
F.L. Carsten, *The origins of Prussia*, Clarendon, 1954
J. Carswell, *The prospector: being the life and times of Rudolf Erich Raspe (1737-1794)*, Cresset, 1950
E. Cassirer, *Kant's life and thought* trans. J. Haden, Yale U.P., 1981
E. Cassirer, *Rousseau, Kant, Goethe*, trans. J. Gutman, P.C. Kristeller, J.H. Randall, Princeton U.P., 1963
O. Chadwick, *Lessing's theological writings*, A. & C. Black, 1956
L. Chappelow, *A Commentary on the book of Job*, Bentham, 1752
M.-D. Chenu, *Nature, Man and Society in the twelfth century*, trans. J. Taylor and L.K. Little, Chicago U.P., 1968
S. Clarke, *The works of Samuel Clarke D.D.*, Knapton, 1738
J.L. Clifford, ed., *Eighteenth century English literature*, O.U.P., 1959
A. Close ed., *Reality and creative vision in German lyric poetry*, Butterworth, 1963
H.J. Cohn ed., *Government in reformation Europe 1520-1560*, Macmillan, 1971

L.P. Courtines, 'Bayle, Hulme and Berkeley', *Revue de Littérature Comparée*, 1947, 416-428
L. Couturat, *La Logique de Leibniz d'après des documents inédits*, Alcan, 1901
K.H. Crumbach, *Theologie in Kritischer Öffentilichkeit: Die Frage Kants an das kirchliche Christentum*, Kaiser, 1977
R. Cudworth, *Systema Intellectuale huius universi*, trans. J.L. Mosheim, Meyer, 1733
Th.W. Danzel, *Gottsched und seine Zeit*, Dyk'sche, 1848
V. Delbos, *La philosophie pratique de Kant*, Presses Universitaires de France, 1969
J. Delvolvé, *Religion, critique et philosophie positive chez Pierre Bayle*, Alcan, 1906
P. Des Maiseaux, *Recueil de diverses pieces*, Du Sauzet, 1720
P. Dibon ed., *Pierre Bayle, le philosophe de Rotterdam: études et documents*, Elsevier, 1959
Dictionnaire de spiritualité 9, Beauchesne, 1976
D. Diderot, *Selected philosophical writings*, ed. J. Lough, C.U.P., 1953
W. Dilthey, *Selected writings*, trans. H.P. Rickman, C.U.P., 1976
W. Dilthey, *Gesammelte Schriften*, Teubner, 1927
H. Dippel, *Germany and the American revolution, 1770-1800*, trans. B.A. Uhlendorf, North Carolina U.P., 1977
W. Dobbek, *Johann Gottfried Herders Jungendzeit in Mohrungen und Königsberg 1744-1764*, Holzner, 1961
J.A. Dörner, *History of Protestant theology particularly in Germany*, trans. G. Robson and S. Taylor, T. & T. Clark, 1871
F. Dostoyevsky, *The Brothers Karamazov* trans. D. Magarshack, Penguin, 1958
A.M. Duncan trans., *Copernicus: On the revolutions of the heavenly spheres*, David & Charles, 1976
E.H. Dunkley, *The reformation in Denmark*, S.P.C.K., 1948
L. Dutens, *Memoirs of a traveller now in retirement*, Phillips & Dulan, 1806
P. Earle, *The world of Defoe*, Weidenfeld & Nicolson, 1976
J.A. Emery, *Esprit de Leibnitz*, Bruyset, 1772
D. Emmet, 'Theoria and the way of life', *Journal of Theological Studies*, NS, 17:1, 1966, 38-52
D.M. Emmet, *The nature of metaphysical thinking*, Macmillan, 1949
Encyclopaedia Britannica, J. Donaldson, 1773
F.E. England, *Kant's conception of God*, Humanities, 1968
B. Erdmann, *Martin Knutzen und seine Zeit*, Voss, 1876
J.E. Erdmann, *History of philosophy* trans. W.S. Hough, Sonnenschein, 1891
B. Fabian, ed., *Festschrift für Rainer Gruenter*, Winter, 1978

B. Fabian, W. Schmidt-Biggemann and R. Vierhaus eds., *Studien zum achzehnten Jahrhundert*, Band 2/3 Kraus, 1980
A. Farrer, *Faith and speculation*, A.E.C. Black, 1967
E.J. Feuchtwanger, *Prussia: myth and reality*, Wolff, 1974
J.P. Fleckenstein, *Gottfried Wilhelm Leibnitz: Barock und Universalismus*, Ott, 1958
C. Fleischauer, 'L'Akakia de Voltaire' *Studies on Voltaire*, 30, 1964, 7-146
G. Florey, *Geschichte der Salzburger Protestanten und ihrer Emigration, 1731-1732*, Bohlaus, 1977
B. Le Bovier de Fontenelle, *Oeuvres de Monsieur de Fontenelle*, Changuion, 1764
Herrn Bernhards von Fontenelle, *Gesprache von mehr als einer Welt*, trans. J.C. Gottsched, Breitkopf, 1730
A. Foucher de Careil, *Oeuvres de Leibniz*, Firman Didot Frères, 1859
A. Foulet, 'Zadig and Job', *Modern language notes*, 75, 1960, 421-423
E. Franck, *Philosophical understanding and religious truth*, O.U.P., 1963
G. Franz ed., *Beamtentum und Pfarrerstand, 1400-1800*, Starke, 1972
P. Fruchon "Problèmes Kantiens' pour une théologie naturelle', *Archives de Philosophie* 34, 1971, 117-206
F. Gause, *Die Geschichte der Stadt Königsberg in Preussen: 11*, Bohlau, 1968
Geheimen Staatsarchivs Preussischer Kulturbesitz, *Immanuel Kant: Leben, Umwelt, Werk*, WestKreuz-Druckerie, Berlin, 1974
S. Gilley, 'Christianity and enlightenment: an historical survey', *History of European ideas* 1;2 1981, 103-121
E. Gilson, *Being and some philosophers*, Pontifical Institute of Medieval Studies, 1949
E.Gilson, *The spirit of mediaeval philosophy*, trans. A.H.C. Downes, Sheed & Ward, 1950
J.C. Gottsched, *Ausgewählte Werke*, ed. J. Birke and P.M. Mitchell, de Gruyter, 1955-
J.C. Gottsched, *Grund-Riss einer Lehr-Arth*, Haude, 1740
L.A.V. Gottschedin, *Sämmtliche Kleinere Gedichte*, Breitkopf, 1763
S. Green, *Shaftesbury's philosophy of religion and ethics*, Ohio U.P., 1967
J.Y.T. Greig, ed., *The letters of David Hume*, O.U.P., 1932
M. Greschat, ed., *Zur Neueren Pietismus-Forschung*, Wissenschaftliche Buchgesellschaft, 1977
R. Grimsley, *Rousseau and the religious quest*, Clarendon, 1968
R. Grimsley, *The philosophy of Rousseau*, O.U.P., 1973
S. Grua, *Jurisprudence universelle et théodicée selon Leibniz*, Presses Universitaires de France, 1953

K.S. Guthke, *Literarisches Leben im Achtzehnten Jahrhundert in Deutschland und in der Schweiz*, Francke, 1975
P. Guyer, *Kant and the claims of taste*, Harvard U.P., 1979
S. Hafner, *The rise and fall of Prussia*, trans. E. Osers, Weidenfeld & Nicolson, 1980
W.W. Hagen, *Germans, Poles and Jews*, Chicago U.P., 1980
A. von Haller, *Brief über einige Einwürfe nochlebender Freygeister wieder die Offenbarung*, Typographische Gesellschaft, Bern 1778
J. A. von Haller, *A short account of His Majesty's late journey to Goettingen*, Schmidt, 1748
J. G. Hamann, *Werke*, Herder, 1951
A. Harnack, *Geschichte der Königlich preussischen Akademie der Wissenschaften zu Berlin*, Reichsdruckerei, 1900
J. Hartnack, *Kant's Theory of Knowledge*, trans. M.H. Hartshorne, Macmillan, 1968
P. Hazard, *European thought in the eighteenth century*, trans. J.L. May, Penguin, 1965
P. Hazard, *The European mind*, trans. J.L. May, Penguin, 1964
P. Hazard, 'Le problème du mal dans la conscience européenne du dix-huitième siècle', *The Romanic review*, 32, 1941, 147-170
H. Heimsoeth, *Astronomisches und Theologisches in Kants Weltverständnis*, Steiner, 1963
F.H. Heinemann, 'Toland and Leibniz', *The philosophical review*, 54, 1945, 437-457
M. Heinrichs, *Emanuel Swedenborg in Deutschland*, Lang, 1979
W. Heizmann, *Kants Kritik spekulativer Theologie und Begriff moralischen Vernunftglaubens im Katholischen Denken der später Aufklärung*, Vandenhoeck & Ruprecht, 1976
D. Henrich and K. Cramer, eds., *Ist Systematische Philosophie möglich?* Grundmann, 1977
J.G. Herder, *Sämtliche Werke*, ed. B. Suphan, Olms, 1967
K. Heussi, *Johann Lorenz Mosheim*, Mohr, 1906
J. Hick, *Evil and the God of love*, Macmillan, 1966
E.B. Hill, 'The role of 'le Monstre' in Diderot's thought' *Studies on Voltaire*, 97, 1972, 147-258
C. Hinrichs, *Preussentum und Pietismus* Vandenhoeck & Ruprecht, 1971
N. Hinske ed., *Was ist Aufklärung? Beiträge aus der Berlinischen Monatsschrift*, Wissenschaftliche Buchgessellschaft, 1973
F. Hipler ed., *Spicilegium Copernicanum*, Peter, 1873
A. Hofstadter, 'Kant's aesthetic revolution', *Journal of religious ethics*, 3:2, 1975, 171-191
H.S. Holland, 'The optimism of Butler's 'Analogy'', *Romanes Lecture*, Clarendon, 1908

J. Hostler, *Leibniz' moral philosophy*, Duckworth, 1975
J.M. Hostler, 'Some remarks on "Omne possibile exiget/existere"', *Studia Leibnitiana*, 5, 1973, 281-185
W. Hubatsch, *Frederick the Great: absolutism and administration*, trans. P. Doran, Thames & Hudson, 1975
W. Hubatsch et al., *Deutsche Universitäten und Hochschulen im Osten*, West Deutscher Verlag, 1964
W. Hubatsch, *Geschichte der evangelischen Kirche Ostpreussens*, Vandenhoeck & Ruprecht, 1968
H. Huber, 'Die Gottesidee bei Immanuel Kant', *Theologie und Philosophie*, 55, 1980, 1:1-43; 2:230-249
D. Hume, *A Treatise of human nature*, ed. E.C. Mossner, Penguin, 1969
Hume on religion, ed. R. Wollheim, Collins, 1966
D. Hume, *Enquiry concerning human understanding*, ed. L.A. Selby-Bigge, Clarendon, 1975
R.B. Jachmann, *Immanuel Kant, geschildert in Briefen en einen Freund*, Nicolovius, 1804
D.G. James, *The life of reason*, Longmans, 1949
K. Jaspers, *The origin and goal of history*, trans. M. Bullock, Routledge & Kegan Paul, 1953
K. Jaspers, *Philosphy*, trans. E.B. Ashton, Chicago U.P., 1971, 3
K. Jaspers, *Über die Bedingungen und Möglichkeiten eines neuen Humanismus*, Drei Vortrage, 1962
K. Jaspers, *Philosophical faith and revelation*, trans. E.B. Ashton, Collins, 1967
K. Jaspers, *The origin and goal of history*, trans. M. Bullock, Routledge & Kegan Paul, 1953
K. Jaspers, *The European spirit*, trans. R. Gregor Smith, S.C.M., 1948
K. Jaspers, *Philosophy*, trans. E.B. Ashton, Chicago U.P., 1971
Joachim-Jungius Gessellschaft, *Hermann Samuel Reimarus*, Vandenhoeck & Ruprecht, 1973
H. Jonas, *Philosophical essays*, Prentice-Hall, 1974
H. Jonas, *Philosophical essays*, Chicago U.P., 1980
K.G. Jones, 'The observational basis for Kant's cosmogony' *Journal of the history of astronomy*, 2, 1971, 29-34
H.W.B. Joseph, *Lectures on the philosophy of Leibniz*, O.U.P., 1949
L.M. Kahl, *Vergleichung der Leibnitzischen und Newtonischen Metaphysik*, Vandenhoeck, 1741
P. Kalweit, *Kants Stellung zur Kirche* Beyers, Thomas & Oppermann, 1904
G.S. Kane, 'The concept of divine goodness and the problem of evil', *Religious Studies*, 11:1, 1975, 49-71
E. Kant, *La Théodicée et la Religion*, Vrin, 1931, ed. P. Festugière

I. Kant, *Anthropology from a pragmatic point of view*, trans. M.J. Gregor, Nijhoff, 1974
I. Kant, *Critique of practical reason*, etc., trans. T.K. Abbott, Longmans, 1967
I. Kant, *Critique of pure reason*, trans. N. Kemp Smith, Macmillan, 1964
I. Kant, *Dreams of a Spirit-Seer*, trans. E.F. Goerwitz, Sonnenschein, 1900
I. Kant, *Lectures on philosophical theology*, trans. A.W. Wood and G.M. Clark, Cornell U.P., 1978
I. Kant, *On history*, L.W. Beck, R.E. Anchor, E.L. Fackenheim trans., Bobbs-Merrill, 1979
I. Kant, *Observations on the feeling of the beautiful and sublime*, trans. J.T. Goldthwait, California U.P., 1965
I. Kant, *Prolegomena to any future metaphysics that will be able to present itself as a science*, trans. P.G. Lucas, M.U.P., 1966
I. Kant, *Religion within the limits of reason alone*, trans. T.M. Greene and H.H. Hudson, Harper, 1960
I. Kant, *Selected pre-critical writings and correspondence with Beck*, trans. G.B. Kerferd and D.E. Walford, Manchester U.P., 1968
I. Kant, *The critique of judgement*, trans. J.C. Meredith, O.U.P., 1969
I. Kant, *The metaphysical principles of virtue*, trans. J. Ellington, Bobbs-Merrill, 1964
I. Kant, *The one possible basis for a demonstration of the existence of God*, trans. G. Treash, Abaris books, 1979
I. Kant, *Universal natural history and theory of the heavens*, trans. W. Hastie, ed. M.K. Munitz, Ann Arbor, 1969
I. Kant, *Universal natural history*, trans. and ed. S. Jaki, Scottish Academic Press, 1981
H.H. Kaplan, *Russia and the outbreak of the Seven Years War*, California U.P., 1968
H.H. Kaplan, *The first partition of Poland*, Columbia U.P., 1962
S.T. Katz, ed., *Mysticism and philosophical analysis*, Sheldon, 1978
W. Kaufmann, *The faith of a heretic*, Anchor, 1963
F. Kaulbach und U.W. Bargenda eds., *Nicolaus Copernicus zum 500 Geburtstag*, Bohlau, 1973
T.D. Kendrick, *The Lisbon earthquakes*, Methuen, 1956
A. Kenny, *The five ways*, Routledge & Kegan Paul, 1969
C. Kiernan, *The enlightenment and science in eighteenth century France: Studies on Voltaire*, 1973
C.S. King, *A great archbishop of Dublin, William King, D.D.*, Longman, Green, 1906
W. King, *An essay on the origin of evil*, trans. and ed. E. Law, 1731
K.E. Kirk, *The vision of God*, Harper, 1966

R. Klibansky and E.C. Mossner eds., *New letters of David Hume*, Clarendon, 1954
D. Knowles, *The evolution of medieval thought*, Longmans, 1962
S. Knuuttila ed., *Reforging the great chain of being*, Reidel, 1981
H.W. Koch, *A history of Prussia*, Longman, 1978
A. Kolnai, *Ethics, value and reality*, Athlone Press, 1977
A. Kolnai, 'The thematic primacy of moral evil', *Philosophical Quarterly*, 6, 1956, 27-42
F. Kopitzsch ed., *Aufklärung, Absolutismus und Burgertum in Deutschland*, Nymphenburger, 1976
Ed. G. Korff, text by W. Ranke, *Preussen: Versuch einer Bilanz*, Ausstellung Berlin, 1981, 1, Rowohlt
P.J. Korshin ed., *The widening circle*, Pennsylvania U.P., 1976
C. Kortholt, *Vir illustris G.G. Leibnittii*, Breitkopf, 1734-5
A. Koutsouvilis, 'Kant and the Christian command', *Heythrop Journal*, 14, 1973, 190-194
A. Koyré, *The astronomical revolution*, trans. R.E.W. Maddison, Methuen, 1973
C.J. Kraus, *Vermischte Schriften*, Königsberg U.P., 1819
P. Laberge, *La théologie Kantienne précritique*, Ottawa U.P., 1973
E. Labrousse, Pierre Bayle: 2, *Hétérodoxie et Rigorisme*, Nijhoff, 1964
J. Laird, *Philosophical incursions into English literature*, C.U.P., 1946
J.L. Larson, 'Kant's Swedenborg', *Scandinavia: an international journal of Scandinavian studies*, 14:1, 1975, 45-51
R.W. Last ed., *Affinities: essays in German and English literature*, Oswald, 1971
A. Lazaroff, 'The Kantian sublime: aesthetic judgement and religious feeling', *Kant-Studien*, 71, 1980, 203-220
E.R. Leach, 'Men, bishops and apes', *Nature*, 293, 1981, 19-21
I. Leclerc, *The philosophy of Leibniz and the modern world*, Vanderbilt U.P., 1973
G.W. Leibniz, *The Monadology and other philosophical writings*, trans. R. Latta, O.U.P., 1971
G.W. Leibniz, *New essays on human understanding*, trans. and ed. P. Remnant and J. Bennet, C.U.P., 1981
G.W. Leibnitz, ed. C.I. Gerhardt and J. Jalabert, *Essais de Théodicée*, Aubier 1962
G.W. Leibnitz, *Theodicy*, trans. E.M. Huggard, ed. A.M. Farrer, Routledge & Kegan Paul, 1951
G.W. Leibnitz, *Oeuvres philosophiques*, Schreuder, 1765
R.A. Leigh, 'Rousseau's letter to Voltaire on optimism, 18th August, 1756', *Studies on Voltaire*, 29, 1964, 247-309
R.A. Leigh ed., *Rousseau after two hundred years*, C.U.P., 1982
O. Lempp, *Das Problem der Theodicee in der Philosophie und Literatur*

des 18. Jahrhunderts bis auf Kant und Schiller, Olms, 1976
G.C. Lichtenberg, *Nikolaus Kopernikus* ed. G. von Selle, Grafe & Unzer, 1943
D.R. Lipton, *Ernst Cassirer: the dilemma of a liberal intellectual in Germany, 1914-1933*, Toronto, U.P., 1978
D.W. Livingston and J.T. King eds., *Hume: a re-evaluation*, Fordham U.P., 1976
L.E. Loemker trans. and ed., G.W. *Leibniz: philosophical papers and letters*, Reidel, 1956
F. Lötzsch, *Vernunft und Religion im Denken Kants: Lutherisches Erbe bei Immanuel Kant*, Böhlau, 1976
A.O. Lovejoy, *The great chain of being*, Harper, 1960
D.-J. Löwisch, *Immanuel Kant und David Hume's Dialogues concerning natural religion*, Rheinische Friederich Wilhelms Universität, 1964
J.R. Lucas, *A treatise on time and space*, Methuen, 1973
J.R. Lucas, *Butler's philosophy of religion vindicated*, Durham Cathedral lectures, 1978
M. Mack, ed., *Alexander Pope: An Essay on Man*, Methuen, 1958
D.M. MacKinnon, *A study in ethical theory*, A. & C. Black, 1957
D.M. MacKinnon, *Explorations in Theology*, 5, S.C.M., 1979
D.M. MacKinnon, 'Kant's philosophy of religion', *Philosophy*, 50, 1975, 131-144
D.M. MacKinnon, 'Power, politics and religious faith', *British journal of international studies*, 6, 1980, 1-15
D.M. MacKinnon, 'Some reflections on time and space' *Archivio di Filosofia*, 1980, 369-75
D.M. MacKinnon, *The problem of metaphysics*, C.U.P., 1974
H.R. Mackintosh, *Types of modern theology*, Nisbet, 1937
C.P. Magill, B.A. Rowley, C.J. Smith eds., *Tradition and creation: essays in honour of Elizabeth Mary Wilkinson*, Maney, 1978
L.M. Marsak ed., *The achievement of Bernard de Bovier de Fontenelle*, Johnson, 1970
W.H. Marshall, *The world of the Victorian novel*, Yoseloff, 1967
H. Mason, 'Voltaire and war', *The British Journal for eighteenth-century studies*, 4:2, 1981, 125-138
H.T. Mason, *Pierre Bayle and Voltaire*, O.U.P., 1963
P. Masterson, 'Experience and the affirmation of God', *Neue Zeitschrift für systematische Theologie und Religionsphilosophie*, 2:1, 1980, 17-32
P.L.M. de Maupertuis, *Oeuvres de Maupertuis*, Bruyset, 1768
W. Maurer, *Aufklärung, Idealismus und Restauration: Studien zur Kirchen und Geistesgeschichte in besonder Beziehung auf Kurhessen, 1780-1850*, Topelmann, 1930

F.H. Mautner, 'Lichtenberg as an interpreter of Hogarth', *Modern Language Quarterly*, 13, 1952, 64-80
J.A. May, *Kant's concept of geography*, Toronto U.P., 1970
C.E. McClelland, *State, society and university in Germany*, C.U.P., 1980
R.W.A. McKinney ed., *Christ, creation and culture*, T. & T. Clark, 1976
J. McManners, 'Paul Hazard and the 'Crisis of the European Conscience'', *Arts: the proceedings of the Sydney university arts association*, 2, 1962 73-68
A. Menhennet, *Order and freedom: literature and society in Germany from 1720-1805*, Weidenfeld & Nicolson, 1973
W.H. Mehl, *Germany in western civilization*, Alabama U.P., 1979
G. Meinhardt, *Die Universität Göttingen*, Vandenhoeck & Ruprecht, 1977
Mélanges offerts à Etienne Gilson, Pontifical Institute of Medieval Studies, 1959
J.D. Michaelis, *Compendium Theologiae Dogmaticae*, Vandenhoeck, 1760
M. Midgley, *Beast and Man*, Harvester, 1978
M. Midgley, *Heart and Mind*, Harvester, 1981
M. Midgley, 'The objection to systematic humbug', *Philosophy*, 53, 1978, 147-169
W.J. Milch, 'Georg Christoph Lichtenberg: On the occasion of the two hundredth anniversary of his birth', *Modern Language Review*, 37, 1942, 335-355
C. de S. Montesquieu, *Oeuvres Complètes*, Nagel, 1950
The Monthly Review, 32, 1765
J. Moreau, *Le Dieu des Philosophes*, Vrin, 1969
F. Morrelle 'Les idées religieuses de Kant en 1755-1760', *Revue Néo-Scholastique de Philosophie*, 30, 1928, 273-315
M. Morris, trans., *Leibniz: philosophical writings* Dent, 1968
H. Mortensen, 'Kants väterliche Ahnen und ihre Umwelt', *Jahrbuch der Albertus-Universität zu Königsberg*, 3, 1953
J.L. Mosheim, *Institutiones Historicae Ecclesiasticae*, Weygard 1755; trans. A. Maclaine, Cadell, 1826
J.L. Mosheim, *De odio Theologica*, Vandenhoeck, 1747
E.C. Mossner, 'Hume's early memoranda: the complete text', *Journal of the history of ideas*, 9, 1948, 492-518
H. Motekat, *Ostpreussische Literaturgeschichte mit Danzig und Westpreussen*, Schild, 1977
G. Müller and W. Zeller, eds., *Glaube, Geist, Geschichte*, Brill, 1967
M.K. Munitz, *Space, time and creation*, Collier, 1957
I. Murdoch, *The sovareignty of good*, Routledge & Kegan Paul, 1970

J.H. Newman, *University Sermons*, S.P.C.K., 1970
D. Norton, 'Leibniz and Bayle: Manicheism and dialectic', *Journal of the history of philosophy*, 2, 1964, 23-26
K. Oehler and R. Schaeffler eds., *Einsichten Gerhard Kruger zum 60 Geburtstag*, Klostermann, 1962
A. Osiander D.A., *Gesamtausgabe*, ed. G. Müller and G. Seebass, Mohn, 1975
F.A. Paneth 'Thomas Wright and Immanuel Kant, pioneers in stellar atronomy', *Royal Institute of Great Britain*, 6.4.1951
J. Papas ed., *Essays on Diderot and the enlightenment in honor of Otis C. Fellows*, Droz, 1974
P. Paret, *Clausewitz and the state*, Clarendon, 1976
J. Passmore, *The perfectibility of man*, Duckworth, 1970
H.J. Paton, 'An alleged right to lie. A problem in Kantian ethics', *Kant-Studien*, 46, 1954, 190-203
D.F. Pears, *Wittgenstein*, Fontana, 1974
F.L. Peccorini, 'Transcendental apperception and genesis of Kant's theological conviction', *Giornale di Metafisica*, 1:27, 1972, 43-65
S. Pétrement, *Simone Weil: a life*, trans. R. Rosenthal, Mowbrays 1976
D.Z. Phillips, *Religion without explanation*, Blackwell, 1976
J. Pieper, *Leisure the basis of culture*, trans. A. Dru, Fontana, 1965
J. Pieper, *Death and immortality*, trans. R. and C. Winston, Burns & Oates, 1969
F.P. van de Pitte, *Kant as a philosophical anthropologist*, Nijhoff, 1971
J. Piveteau, *Oeuvres philosophiques de Buffon*, Presses Universitaires de France, 1964
I. Polonoff, *Force, cosmos, monads and other themes of Kant's early thought*, Bouvier, 1973
R.H. Popkin, *Pierre Bayle: Historical and Critical Dictionary: selections*, with Craig B. Brush ed. and trans., Bobbs-Merrill, 1965
R.H. Popkin, 'Scepticism in the enlightenment', *Studies on Voltaire*, 25, 1963, 1321-1345
H. Preuschoff, 'Hohenzollern auf dem ermländischen Bischofsthron', *Kauskal* 88, 1955, 27-51
L.M. Price, 'Albrecht von Haller and English theology', *Publications of the Modern Language Association*, 41, 1926, 942-954
G. Rabel, *Kant*, O.U.P., 1963
O. Reboul, *Kant et le problème du mal*, Montréal U.P., 1971
R. Rees, *A theory of my time*, Secker & Warburg, 1963
J. Reeves, *The reputation and writings of A. Pope*, Heinemann, 1976
P.H. Reill, *The German enlightenment and the rise of historicism*, California U.P., 1975
H.S. Reimarus, *Allegemeine Betrachtungen über die Triebe der Thiere*, Bohn, 1762

H.S. Reimarus, *Die vornehmsten Wahrheiten der naturlichen Religion*, Bohn 1755
N. Rescher, *The primacy of practice*, Blackwell, 1973
W. Rex, *Essays on Pierre Bayle and religious controversy*, Nijhoff, 1965
W. Rieck, *Johann Christoph Gottsched*, Akademie Verlag, 1972
P. Riley, *The political writings of Leibniz*, C.U.P., 1972
A. Robinet, *Malebranche et Leibniz*, Vrin, 1955
R. Rouse and S.C. Neill eds., *A history of the ecumenical movement 1517-1948*, S.P.C.K., 1954
J.-J. Rousseau, *Collection complètes des oeuvres*, De la société Typographique de Geneve, 1782
J.-J. Rousseau, *Emile*, trans. B. Foxley, Everyman's, 1969
B. Russell, *A critical exposition of the philosophy of Leibniz*, Allen & Unwin, 1900
A. Ryan, ed., *The idea of freedom: essays in honour of Isaiah Berlin*, O.U.P., 1979
E. Sagarra, *A social history of Germany, 1648-1914*, Holmes & Meier, 1977
K.C. Sandberg, trans. and ed., *The great contest of faith and reason: selections from the writings of Pierre Bayle*, Ungar, 1968
K.C. Sandberg, 'Pierre Bayle's sincerity in his views on faith and reason', *Studies in philosophy*, 61, 1964, 74-84
H. Saner, *Kant's political thought*, trans. E.B. Ashton, Chicago U.P., 1967
R.L. Saw, *Leibniz*, Penguin, 1954
D.B. Schlegel, *Shaftesbury and the French deists*, N. Carolina U.P., 1956
M. Schlenke, *England und das Friderizianische Preussen 1740-1763*, Alber, 1963
G. Schmalenberg, *Pietismus-Schule-Religionsunterricht*, Lang, 1974
H.A. Schmidt, ed., *Hebdomada Sancta*, Herder, 1957
W. Schmidt-Biggeman ed., *Hermann Samuel Reimarus: Handschriften verzeichnis und Bibliographie*, Vandenhoeck & Ruprecht, 1979
H.-J. Schoeps, 'Christian Wolff-dreihundert Jahre alt', *Zeitschrift für Religions und Geistesgeschichte*, 31:2, 1979, 208-210
H. Schöffler ed. G. von Selle, *Deutscher Geist im 18. Jahrhundert*, Vandenhoeck & Ruprecht, 1956
H. Schöffler ed. G. von Selle, *Lichtenberg: Studien zu seinem Wesen und Geist*, Vandenhoeck & Ruprecht, 1956
J. Schollmeier, *Johann Joachim Spalding: ein Beitrag zur Theologie der Aufklärung*, Mohn, 1967
W. Schrader, *Geschichte der Friedrichs-Universität zu Halle*, Dummlers, 1894

P. Schrecker, 'Leibniz and the Timaeus', *The review of metaphysics*, 4:4, 1951, 495-505
P. and A.M. Schrecker, trans., *Leibniz: Monadology and other philosophical essays*, Bobbs-Merrill, 1965
H. Schüssler, *Georg Calixt: Theologie und Kirchenpolitik*, Steiner, 1961
R.B. Schwartz, *Samuel Johnson and the problem of evil*, Wisconsin U.P., 1975
G. von Selle, *Geschichte der Albertus-Universität zu Königsberg in Preussen*, Hölzner - Verlag, 1956
G. von Selle, *German thought in East Prussia*, Elwert Gräfe & Unzer, 1948
R.P. Sertillanges, *Le problème du mal: l'histoire*, Aubier, 1948
A. Seth, *Scottish philosophy: a comparison of the Scottish and German answers to Hume*, Blackwood, 1907
P. Siwek, 'Optimism in philosophy', *New Scholasticism*, 22:4, 1948, 417-439
F. Sontag, *Divine perfection*, S.C.M., 1962
O. Sonntag, 'Albrecht von Haller on Academies and the advancement of science', *Annals of science*, 32, 1975, 379-391
P.J. Spener, *Pia Desideria*, trans. T.G. Tappert, Fortress, 1977
G. Stanhope, *A mystic on the Prussian throne: Frederick William II*, Mills & Boon, 1912
L. Stephen, *History of English thought in the eighteenth century*, Smith, Elder, 1876
G. Stieler, *Leibniz und Malebranche und das Theodiceeproblem*, Reichl, 1930
D.F. Strauss, *Gesammelte Schriften*, Strauss, 1876
D.F. Strauss, *The life of Jesus critically examined*, trans. G. Eliot, ed. P.C. Hodgson, S.C.M., 1973
P.F. Strawson, *The bounds of sense*, Methuen, 1966
M. Stupperich, *Osiander in Preussen, 1549-1552*, de Gruyter, 1973
R.L. Sturch, 'The ethico-theology of Immanuel Kant', *Journal of theological studies*, NS, 26:2, 1975, 342-360
J.P. Süssmilch *Die göttliche Ordnung in den Veränderung des menschlichen Geschlects*, Spener, 1741
C.W. Swain, 'Hamann and the philosophy of David Hume', *Journal of the history of philosophy*, 5, 1967, 343-351
L.M. Teeter, 'Albrecht von Haller and Samuel Clarke', *Journal of English and German philology*, 27:4, 1928, 52-523
R. von Thadden, *Die Brandenburgisch-Preussischen Hofprediger im 17 und 18 Jahrhundert*, de Gruyter, 1951
S.B. Thomas, 'Jesus and Kant: a problem in reconciling two different points of view' *Mind*, 79, 1970, 188-199

R. Toellner, *Albrecht von Haller*, Steiner, 1971
G. Tonelli, 'Kant und die Antiken Skeptiker' pp.93-124 in *Studien zu Kants Philosophischer Entwicklung*, Olms, 1967
G. Tonelli, 'The law of continuity in the eighteenth century', *Studies on Voltaire*, 27, 1963, 1619-1638
G. Tonelli, 'Leibniz on innate ideas and early reactions to the publication of the Nouveaux Essais (1765)', *Journal of the history of philosophy*, 12, 1974, 437-454
F. Valjavec, 'Das Woellnersche Religionsedikt und seine geschichtliche Bedeutung', *Historisches Jahrbuch der Görres-Gesellschaft*, 72, 1953, 386-400
J.A. Vann and S.W. Rowan, *The old Reich: essays on German political institutions 1495-1806. Studies presented to the International Commission for the history of representative and parliamentary institutions*, 48, 1, 1974
C.E. Vaughan ed., *The political writings of Jean-Jacques Rousseau*, C.U.P., 1915
P.Vignaux, *Philosophy in the middle ages*, trans. E.C. Hall, Meridian, 1959
H.-J. de Vleeschauer, *The development of Kantian thought*, trans. A.R.C. Duncan, Nelson, 1962
F-M.A. de Voltaire, *Candide, Zadig and selected stories*, trans. D.M. Frame, Signet, 1961
F-M.A. de Voltaire's *Correspondence*, ed. T. Bestermann, Institut et Musée Voltaire, 1957
F-M.A. de Voltaire, *Philosophical Dictionary* trans. and ed. T. Besterman, Penguin, 1971
F-M.A. de Voltaire, *Oeuvres Complètes*, Garnier, 1877
I.O. Wade, *The intellectual origins of the French enlightenment*, Princeton U.P., 1971
I.O. Wade, *Voltaire and Candide*, Princeton U.P., 1959
R.C.S. Walker, *Kant*, Routledge & Kegan Paul, 1978
J. Wallmann, 'Zwischen Reformation und Humanismus. Eigenart und Wirkung Helmstedter Theologie unter besonderer Berucksichtigung Georg Calixts,' *Zeitscrift für Theologie und Kirche*, 74, 1977, 344-370
W.H. Walsh, *Kant's moral theology*, O.U.P., 1963
W.H. Walsh, 'Philosophy and psychology in Kant's Critique', *Kant-Studien*, 59, 1966, 186-198
W. Warburton, *Commentary on Pope's works*, Knapton, 1752
K. Ward, *The development of Kant's view of ethics*, Blackwell, 1972
G.J. Warnock, *Morality and Language*, Blackwell, 1983
M.C. Washburn, 'Dogmatism, scepticism, criticism: the dialectic of Kant's "silent decade" ', *Journal of the history of philosophy*, 13, 1975, 167-176

R. Wegener, *Das Problem der Theodicee in der Philosophie und Literatur des XVIII Jahrhunderts*, Niemeyer, 1909
W. Wendland, *Ludwig Ernst von Borowski*, Thomas & Oppermann, 1910
W.H. Werkmeister, *Kant's silent decade: a decade of philosophical development*, Florida U.P., 1979
J. Wesley, *Dissertationes in librum Jobi*, Rivington etc. 1736
J. Wesley, *A survey of the wisdom of God in the creation*, Fry, 1777
L.P. Wessell, G.E. *Lessing's theology: a reinterpretation*, Mouton, 1977
R.S. Westman ed., *The Copernican achievement*, California U.P., 1975
P. Wiener ed., *Dictionary of the history of ideas*, Scribners, 1973, 4
P. Wiener ed., *Leibniz: selections*, Scribners, 1951
J. Wisdom, *Paradox and discovery*, Blackwell, 1965
E. Wolff, 'Kant et l'immortalité de l'âme', *Archives de philosophie*, 34, 1971, 451-471
H.M. Wolff, 'Brockes' religion', *Publications of the modern language association of America*, 62, 1947, 1124-1152
K.H. Wolff and Barrington Moore, eds., *The critical spirit: essays in honor of Herbert Marcuse*, Beacon, 1967
A.W. Wood, *Kant's moral religion* Cornell U.P., 1970
A.W. Wood, *Kant's rational theology*, Cornell U.P., 1978
A.W. Wood, 'Kant's Dialectic', *Canadian journal of philosophy*, 5:4, 1975, 595-614
N.W. Wraxall, *Memoirs of the courts of Berlin* second ed., Cadell & Davies, 1800
K.E. Yandell, *Basic issues in the philosophy of religion*, Allyn & Bacon, 1971
Y. Yovel, *Kant and the philosophy of history*, Princeton U P., 1980
S. Zac, 'Religion naturelle et religions révélées selon Kant', *Revue de Métaphysique et de Morale*, 73:1, 1968, 105-126
C.D. Zangger, *Welt und Konservation. Die theol. Begründung der Mission bei G.W. Leibniz*, Theologischer Verlag, 1973
A. Zweig ed., *Kant: Philosophical correspondence 1759-99* Chicago U.P., 1967
G. Zippel, *Geschichte des Königlichen Friedrichs-Kollegium zu Königsberg*, Hartungsche Buchdruckerei, 1898